Teaching

one 1 Pagers

2 VOLUME

Evidence-informed summaries for busy educational professionals

Jamie Clark

hachette LEARNING

Together we unlock every learner's unique potential

At Hachette Learning (formerly Hodder Education), there's one thing we're certain about. No two students learn the same way. That's why our approach to teaching begins by recognising the needs of individuals first.

Our mission is to allow every learner to fulfil their unique potential by empowering those who teach them. From our expert teaching and learning resources to our digital educational tools that make learning easier and more accessible for all, we provide solutions designed to maximise the impact of learning for every teacher, parent and student.

Aligned to our parent company, Hachette Livre, founded in 1826, we pride ourselves on being a learning solutions provider with a global footprint.

www.hachettelearning.com

To order, please visit www.HachetteLearning.com or contact Customer Service at education@hachette.co.uk / +44 (0)1235 827827.

ISBN: 978 1 0360 1405 6

First published in 2025 by
Hachette Learning,
An Hachette UK Company
Carmelite House
50 Victoria Embankment
London EC4Y 0DZ
www.HachetteLearning.com

The authorised representative in the EEA is Hachette Ireland, 8 Castlecourt Centre, Dublin 15, D15 XTP3, Ireland (email: info@hbgi.ie)

Impression 10 9 8 7 6 5 4 3 2 1
Year 2029 2028 2027 2026 2025

A catalogue record for this title is available from the British Library

Front cover designed by Jamie Clark
Typeset by Hachette Learning

TESTIMONIALS

PAUL A. KIRSCHNER

Emeritus Professor of Educational Psychology

If you're reading this, you've decided to make the jump from being an experienced teacher to becoming an expert one. You've chosen to make your teaching and your students' learning more effective, efficient, and fulfilling. Clark's *Teaching One-Pagers Volume 2* is the perfect roadmap for this journey. It's a practical, accessible guide through the sometimes dark and murky enchanted rainforest that is teaching and learning, helping you find your way and avoid the bears and big bad wolves that undoubtedly will cross your path. Buckle up; this is just the beginning.

PAMELA SNOW

Professor of Cognitive Psychology and Co-Director of SOLAR

It's rare that I open a book about classroom teaching and am certain within minutes, that it will be a winner with teachers, but this one will be. In *Teaching One-Pagers Volume 2*, Clark has achieved the seemingly impossible – an accessible, attractively presented, strongly evidence-informed and hard-hitting volume that teachers can take knowledge and practical skills from, right now. Teachers who peruse this text in their lunch break will have new knowledge and skills to make their afternoon classes more successful than their morning ones: knowledge translation in action.

SIMON BREAKSPEAR

Author, senior lecturer and Founder of Strategic Schools

Teaching One-Pagers is an indispensable resource for overloaded educators seeking evidence-informed insights. This new collection distils complex educational ideas into rigorous, accessible, and actionable summaries, perfect for improving professional dialogue and classroom practice. By presenting research about learning culture and teaching in digestible chunks, it empowers educators to engage meaningfully with evidence and explore areas of relevance and interest more deeply. This practical guide is essential for enhancing teaching and fostering professional growth.

MARK DOWLEY

Author, teacher and Associate Head of Staff Development

This book will accelerate your progress to becoming an evidence-informed and high-performing school. *Teaching One-Pagers Volume 2* is perfect for increasing access to educational research, allowing for more informed and productive conversations between colleagues. My school uses one-pagers as pre-reading for our teams when discussing complex topics, and they have vastly increased the knowledge of our staff and positively impacted the outcomes for our students. Next time you have a meeting, make sure you have a one-pager!

HAILI HUGHES

Director of Education at IRIS Connect and IQTS Mentor Lead

Teaching One-Pagers Volume 2 is another essential resource for educators, full of practical, research-informed strategies to enhance teaching. Jamie Clark combines his deep understanding of pedagogy with relatable examples, empowering teachers to implement evidence-based practices in their classrooms. Whether you're refining your craft or exploring new approaches, this book is a treasure trove of wisdom and inspiration for fostering effective, impactful learning environments.

ZACH GROSHELL

Director of Steplab USA, educational consultant and author

In *Teaching One-Pagers Volume 2* Jamie Clark has meticulously curated the most effective theories and techniques, sifting through the academic maze and translating the jargon into teacher-speak. Each page delivers the goods fast – just like in his first book – but this time with even more insights that are sure to empower teachers. Clark's style is for you to spend less time deciphering and more time delivering lessons that work for kids. This book truly is indispensable!

JOSH GOODRICH

Teacher, Co-Founder and CEO of Steplab

Teaching One-Pagers Volume 2 offers a mind-blowing collection of some of the best insights available on student learning and how to make it happen. Jamie is a master of capturing and condensing the very best information so that teachers can access what they need, when they need it. To top if all off, volume 2 has a new and welcome focus on implementation: the stories from school leaders about using one-pagers to build great PD are both practical and inspirational. An invaluable addition to any school CPD library.

LEKHA SHARMA

Author, teacher and School Improvement Advisor

Teaching One-Pagers Volume 2 is a powerful compendium of distilled educational wisdom. Drawing on evidence-informed practice, Jamie pulls out key conceptual ideas and presents them in an easily accessible and concise manner. Perfect for teachers and leaders who are short on time but want to go BIG on evidence-informed thinking. An incredibly helpful book for PD and knowledge generation that will no doubt shape and support school improvement at all levels.

DAVID GOODWIN

Author and Trust Wide Teaching and Learning Lead

Tom Sherrington's *The Learning Rainforest* has long been my favourite educational book, blending the art and science of teaching. Clark's *Teaching One-Pagers Volume 2* serves as the ideal companion to Sherrington's work, offering over 60 concise, beautifully illustrated summaries that bring the rainforest metaphor to life. By distilling key ideas like Mode A and Mode B teaching, Clark provides busy educators with practical tools to strike a balance, fostering a more holistic approach to teaching and learning.

ROBERT COE

Professor and Director of Research and Development

Jamie Clark has done it again! Another volume of concise, practical, visual, evidence-rich summaries, designed to give time-poor teachers an introductory overview of key ideas. If you like your professional learning to be bitesize yet comprehensive, attractive yet authoritative, practical yet theoretically grounded, then this is the book for you. It contains a digest of the ideas from literally hundreds of robust studies, books and papers, concentrated into clear visual summaries. Such a great resource!

CARL HENDRICK

Author and Professor of Applied Sciences

A central challenge that every classroom teacher faces is translating the vast ocean of research into practice. *Teaching One-Pagers Volume 2* answers this challenge and equips educators with concise guides to evidence-based strategies like retrieval practice, effective questioning, and cognitive load management, all presented in economic, visually engaging formats. A truly indispensable resource for improving both teaching precision and student outcomes.

NATHANIEL SWAIN

Teacher, instructional coach, director and senior lecturer

As teachers, we are constantly navigating the dual challenge of building students' foundational knowledge while supporting them to break free from the basics and unlock the full potential of their cognitive effort. Clark's *Teaching One-Pagers Volume 2* serves as a quick-reference guide that offers research-informed techniques to support the development of core skills and knowledge, as well as open-ended applications of learning. A must-read for educators, this book offers solutions for classroom teaching and helps students thrive.

MUM AND DAD

For teaching me the value of hard work, humility, and perseverance – this book is for you.

JAMIE CLARK is the Head of Professional Growth at Mercedes College in Perth, Western Australia. Originally from Huddersfield, West Yorkshire, Jamie taught English in the UK for six years before relocating to Australia in 2015.

A specialist in teacher professional development, Jamie has presented at education conferences across Australia. He is passionate about teaching and learning, focusing on driving effective practice through instructional coaching and improving student outcomes with research-based, high-impact strategies.

Jamie's first book, *Teaching One-Pagers*, is an international bestseller, widely used in schools for professional development, helping busy teachers reflect on their practice, deepen their knowledge, and explore further reading.

You can follow Jamie on social media or visit his website for free, high-quality downloadable content, including a range of new one-pagers and educational posters.

X: @XpatEducator
LinkedIn: jamieleeclark85
Website: www.jamieleeclark.com

ACKNOWLEDGMENTS

Creating *Teaching One-Pagers Volume 2* has been a deeply rewarding journey, and I owe a great deal of gratitude to those who have supported me along the way.

First and foremost, I'd like to thank my wife, Lucy, and my children, Finley and Evie, for their patience, understanding and unwavering support throughout this process. Your love and encouragement have been my anchor, even when I disappeared into the depths of writing and illustrating! Let's be honest, producing two books in one year is probably not what any of us signed up for, so thank you for tolerating my endless muttering about this project!

A special thanks to my friend Noel Patterson for keeping me fuelled with coffee and generously offering me the use of his office – a much-needed sanctuary to chip away at this book. To my friend and critical ally, Lou Cimetta, thank you for witnessing the evolution of my work over the years and offering thoughtful feedback that has pushed these pages to be their best. To my former colleague Johnny Ho, thank you for your willingness to listen to my reflections on this project – your thoughts and suggestions have been invaluable.

A massive thanks to Tom Sherrington, whose ideas and insights have not only shaped this book but continue to inspire educators around the world. Without your inspiring work, this volume would not have come to life.

Lastly, I extend my gratitude to the educators, readers and followers who have downloaded, shared and promoted my posters and one-pagers. Your enthusiasm for this format has been the driving force behind this volume and I hope you find these pages both practical and inspiring.

Thank you all for your support and ongoing dedication to great teaching.

FOREWORD

BY TOM SHERRINGTON

My experience working in the sphere of teacher development has convinced me of the power of a set of shared ideas across a group of teachers. Once you have established shared understanding of concepts and practices between colleagues, their capacity to develop their craft and engage in meaningful feedback conversations accelerates significantly. My work with schools has also taught me a great deal about the many barriers impeding ideas from research or from other schools, from travelling across space and time to reach into the corners of the system where most busy, hard-working teachers reside. There's a long road from an idea being presented in a research paper, book, blog or training day to a group of teachers changing their practice.

Sometimes, it takes a punchy, crisp summary of a research paper or a full-blown teaching tome to penetrate, which is why Jamie Clark has found such great success with his one-pagers. Effective summaries need to balance brevity with integrity, maintaining the essence of the ideas in just enough detail to allow quick dissemination and meaningful discussion to follow. It helps hugely if their visual design supports quick navigation. Jamie is an absolute master of the genre and this second volume is a superb continuation of the first. Each one-pager can serve as the stimulus for immediate discussion; they inspire action and fire enthusiasm as well as always pointing in the direction of further reading and the wider research that lies beyond.

I'm absolutely delighted that Jamie has opted to borrow from my book, *The Learning Rainforest*, using the metaphor as a framework for shaping this collection of ideas. Much as I did when writing my book, Jamie has encountered the challenge of curating a balanced collection of ideas that support instructional teaching as well as popular and productive learning modes where students are the drivers, without presenting them, artificially, as opposing poles or alternatives to each other.

In order to convey the need for an optimal balance for any given context, I coined the notion of Mode A and Mode B teaching, referenced by Jamie across this book. Mode A teaching is the instructional teaching practice central to ensuring all learners develop secure foundational knowledge – the

THE LEARNING RAINFOREST LEADS TO THREE AREAS OF ACTIVITY:

ESTABLISHING THE CONDITIONS
Creating classrooms rich in challenge where students also feel safe, supported and motivated.

BUILDING THE KNOWLEDGE STRUCTURE
Ensuring students develop secure schemas for the key concepts in subject disciplines, weaving together knowledge in all its forms: factual, procedural, experiential.

EXPLORING THE POSSIBILITIES
Supporting students to develop agency as learners with confidence to pursue meaningful inquiry, express their ideas orally, work creatively and collaboratively, pursuing excellence in whatever form that might take.

'all' being the key to creating truly inclusive classrooms. But, to deliver the rich curriculum experience that all children are entitled to, over time, a healthy dose of Mode B teaching is essential – it is not an optional extra. Here students are given space to explore their own ideas, to choose specifics of how they communicate ideas or which examples to study within a topic.

Surely every student should, at some point in their school career, have the opportunity to give an oral presentation or a speech that means something to them, to pursue an inquiry into an area of study that's particularly fascinating to them, or to assemble a research project where they communicate what they find out in a form they have chosen, rather than it always being mandated by the curriculum. I used to find giving roughly 20% of my teaching time to Mode B activity hugely beneficial, leading to deeper understanding and greater student confidence and enjoyment than if I'd only done Mode A teaching. But that's not a formula – it was just my sense of my A:B balance. Others will find their own.

Importantly, the one-page form is the vehicle – it's the content that matters and, without question, *One-Pagers* represents an incredible feast of ideas. Crucially, what Jamie has assembled in this book is a selection of ideas all expressed very much from his own perspective as a teacher. It's fascinating to read his take on each of these areas and I'm convinced that teachers and schools that share this book around will benefit hugely from the ensuing conversations.

Tom Sherrington

Author, consultant and *Teaching WalkThrus* Co-Founder

CONTENTS

Volume 2 is organised into three collections:

COLLECTION 1: SCHOOL CULTURE
COLLECTION 2: MODE A TEACHING
COLLECTION 3: MODE B TEACHING

Teaching one Pagers | 2 VOLUME

INTRODUCTION

Teaching One-Pagers Volume 2 is crafted with a holistic view of both the art and science of teaching in mind. This volume offers over 65 one-page summaries that cover key topics such as school culture, evidence-based instruction, and ways to foster a lifelong joy for learning. Like before, I have designed this book as a practical tool to support professional development and serve as an antidote for time-poor teachers who are often overwhelmed and bogged down in the messy day-to-day reality of schools. Throughout these pages, you will discover a wealth of research and ideas from inspirational educational voices and expert teachers who have made it their life work to drive improvement in the profession.

One such influential figure is Tom Sherrington, whose work I have followed for years on X (formerly Twitter). I've always admired Tom's work because he has the rare knack of translating the complexities of teaching into simple terms and actionable insights through his blog and publications. His book, *The Learning Rainforest* (2017), forms the framework for *Teaching One-Pagers Volume 2* because it resonates deeply with my own vision and values of what constitutes effective teaching and great schools. Sherrington's work masterfully bridges the art and science of teaching, using the metaphor of a rainforest to reflect the nuances of school environments. His central metaphor is clever and encourages educators to reflect on whether their schools operate more like controlled *plantations* or dynamic *rainforests*.

Sherrington explains that in a plantation-style system, teachers are often constrained by rigid structures that prioritise compliance, uniformity and accountability. These environments are characterised by a strong emphasis on control. For instance, teachers may be required to use prescriptive frameworks, such as mandating that learning objectives must always be written on the board (waste of time!). Schools with the plantation mindset are conventionally driven by standards, data and short-term gains such as exam results and (dreaded) graded-lesson observations. I have worked in a school like this before and found it to be not only excessively demanding but unnaturally restricting. As a newly qualified teacher (NQT) in 2009, I was required to plan and teach using a rigid 'six-part lesson' structure, which included introducing the learning objective, a starter activity, delivery of new information, demonstration of new learning, student practice, and a review – all in 55 minutes! While this structure initially provided my novice teacher-brain with a clear and helpful framework, it left little wiggle room for much needed flexibility and professional agency. Author and thinker Daniel Pink (2009) in his book *Drive* explains that giving people autonomy doesn't mean abandoning accountability. It means fostering a culture where people feel empowered to make decisions and take ownership of their outcomes. He explains, 'The best leaders recognise that for people to thrive, they must feel they have control over their tasks, their time, their techniques, and their teams.'

Sherrington's rainforest system represents a more organic, flexible environment where teachers and students are given autonomy to explore, innovate and thrive within a high-challenge, high-trust culture. Here, learning is viewed as complex and schools aim to cultivate diverse talents and encourage experimentation with a variety of evidence-informed teaching methods. In this rainforest model, as Sherrington (2017) explains, 'teachers thrive where there is a high level of autonomy', and creative, maverick approaches are celebrated as long as they deliver results. This mindset nurtures a culture where learning is viewed as an evolving process, rich in variety, and students are encouraged to engage with learning in their own ways. Schools with a rainforest mentality recognise the importance of building knowledge through excellent teaching, while also appreciating that much of what truly matters in education is intangible and not easily measurable. They place value on fostering a joy for learning, rather than relying solely on rigid, data-driven approaches.

This is why I value Tom's book so much. It serves as a reminder that, as educators, our role is not only to accept that there will always be some level of plantation thinking in our schools, but also to work towards

JAMIE CLARK

Volume 2 is crafted with a holistic view of both the art and science of teaching in mind, offering over 65 one-page summaries designed to support professional development and serve as an antidote for time-poor teachers navigating the messy realities of schools.

TOM SHERRINGTON

The rainforest metaphor stems from the idea that 'plantation thinking', which assumes uniformity in teaching and learning, can be restrictive. In contrast, rainforest thinking embraces diverse forms of excellence. (2020)

TOM SHERRINGTON'S TREE METAPHOR USED AS THE FRAMEWORK FOR THIS BOOK

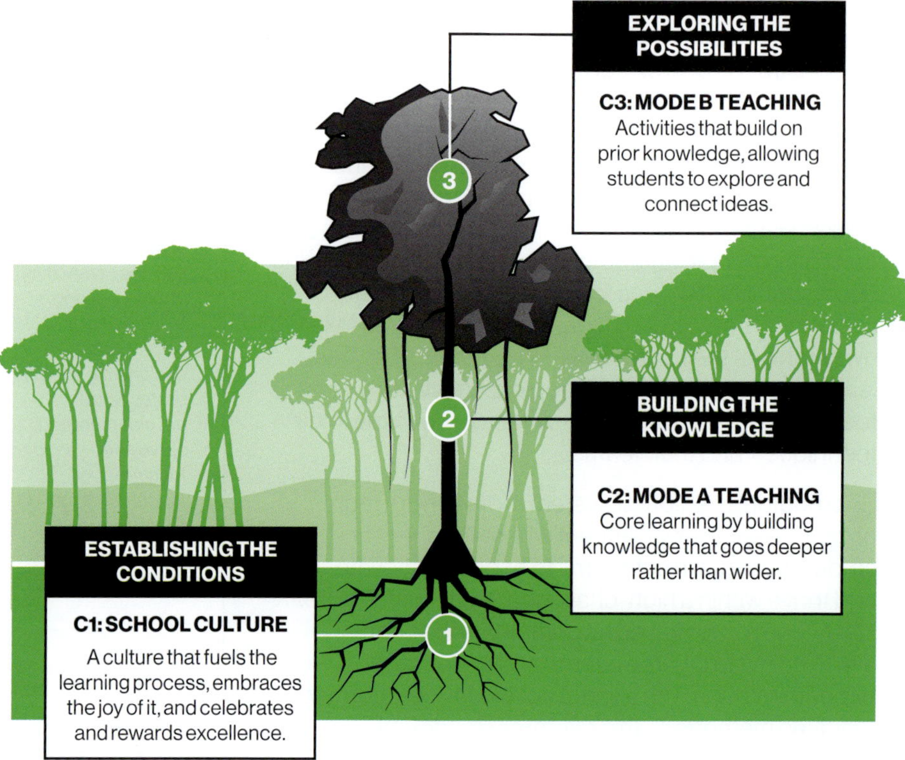

shaping a thriving rainforest environment where students and teachers alike can flourish. Sherrington's vision is ambitious and challenging, but achievable with the right approach. He explains that the following structure is required to achieve a thriving rainforest environment: *Establishing the Conditions for Growth, Building the Knowledge* and *Exploring the Possibilities*. These core elements are visualised in the diagram above and form the main structure of this book. Despite the influence of Sherrington's work, it's worth emphasising that the topics in this volume reflect my own schemas as an experienced teacher, shaped by years of practice and grounded in my personal experiences and perspectives.

So, let's begin exploring the structure of this handy volume in more detail. In **Collection 1: School Culture**, we start by addressing how school culture is fundamental in establishing rich and fertile ground to stimulate growth.

A VISUAL OVERVIEW OF MODE A AND MODE B TEACHING

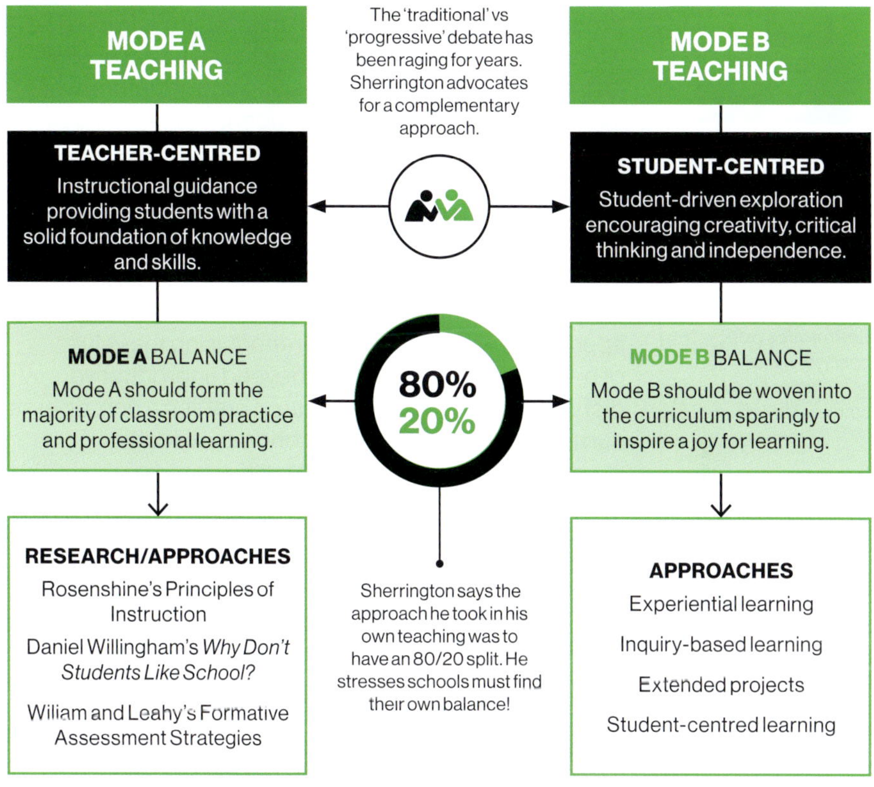

Summaries in this collection are divided into principles (the overarching ideas) and practices (the practical classroom strategies). These one-pagers specifically focus on whole-school behaviours and attitudes that promote a culture of high expectations and excellence in teaching and learning.

Collections 2 and 3 focus on what Sherrington calls Mode A and Mode B teaching. The diagram above highlights my interpretation of Sherrington's Mode A and Mode B model. Though seemingly opposites, both are essential ingredients for providing a well-rounded and balanced educational diet for teachers and students. Notably, Sherrington (2020) emphasises that there is not a strictly set balance for Mode A and Mode B approaches: 'The split between Mode A and Mode B depends on the learners, the curriculum, and the context. It's about finding your own blend.'

TOM SHERRINGTON

Learning requires discipline in building knowledge and also space for creativity and exploration. Both modes work best when they complement each other.

ROBERT COE

Great teaching must be defined by its impact: a great teacher is one whose students learn more. It cannot be defined by compliance to a particular set of practices, however soundly based, nor by the demonstration of specific skills.

The Mode A and Mode B framework also offers a fresh perspective on the long-standing traditional vs progressive debate. Too often this debate is framed as a binary choice, with 'trads' focusing solely on explicit instruction, knowledge acquisition and structure, while 'progs' emphasise creativity, student-led exploration and flexibility. However, as Sherrington (2018a) suggests, effective teaching is not about choosing sides but finding the right balance: 'It's a bit like the ingredients in a balanced diet. Some things only need to be present in very small doses to keep us fit and healthy – but they are still absolutely essential. We'd be much weaker specimens without them.' By recognising the value of both modes, we can move beyond unproductive dichotomies and instead focus on crafting a rich, diverse curriculum that builds and extends knowledge.

Collection 2: Mode A Teaching builds on the first *Teaching One-Pagers* and delves deeper into building knowledge through instructional practices. The one-pagers in this collection are firmly rooted in research that highlights the importance of cognitive architecture: the limitations of working memory and the importance of building, retrieving and strengthening schemas in long-term memory. If learning happens when there is a change in long-term memory (Kirschner et al, 2006), it makes sense that Collection 2 includes a tonne of strategies designed to optimise memory retention, secure focus, reduce cognitive load and promote the transfer of knowledge.

Finally, in **Collection 3: Mode B Teaching**, I have included a series of summaries that are values-driven. While educational research plays a role in supporting these one-pagers, the main purpose for their inclusion is to show what is possible once the core knowledge structure is firmly rooted. These one-pagers focus on providing students with empowering opportunities that allow them to take the reins and express their learning creatively through collaborative talk and independent projects. A curriculum enriched with these Mode B experiences transforms the learning environment into a thriving, diverse space. Unlike the rigid uniformity of

THE EDUCATION ENDOWMENT FOUNDATION'S MECHANISMS APPLIED TO ONE-PAGERS

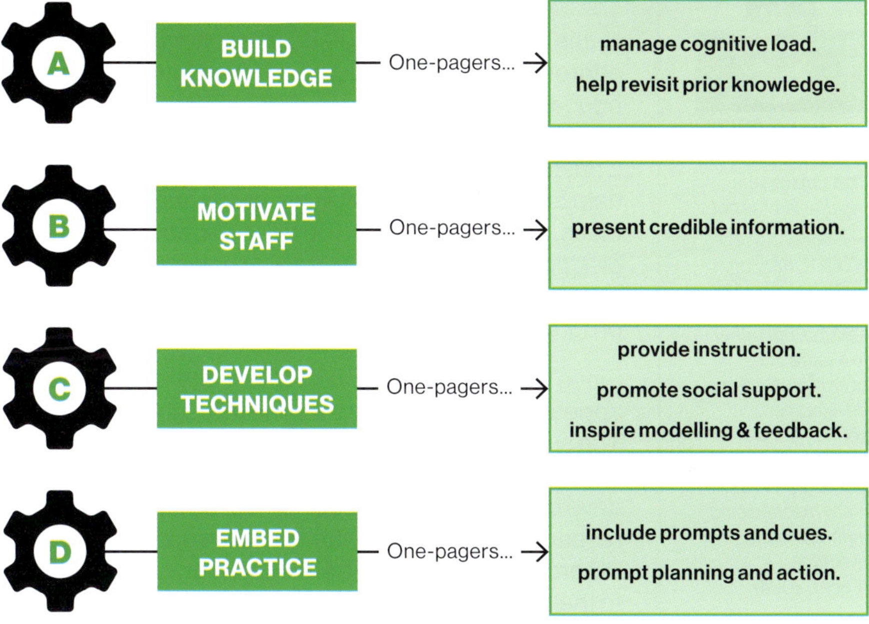

a plantation, Mode B nurtures a non-linear ecosystem where growth is organic and each learner is distinct and unique. Like a wildflower in a manicured garden, it introduces variety and unpredictability to learning.

Educational myths still plague the teaching profession. When scrolling on social media, I often encounter the regular post (and ensuing skirmish) perpetuating misconceptions about what constitutes effective teaching. These myths, while seemingly innocuous, can lead to poor practices. For example, the belief that students have distinct 'learning styles' or that 'direct instruction makes students passive learners' continues to influence classroom practices, despite research debunking these ideas. As Coe et al (2014) explain, effective teaching is rooted in practices supported by robust evidence, not in misconceptions that lack empirical backing. Myths not only divert attention from what truly impacts learning but also risk

DAISY CHRISTODOULOU

Whilst some institutional and structural reform may be valuable, what needs to change most of all is our reliance on defunct ideas. At stake is the education of all our pupils, and particularly the education of our least advantaged pupils.

JON HUTCHINSON

The aim with the mechanisms is not to shoehorn every single one into every professional development session, but rather to ensure the overall professional development sequences are well balanced, incorporating as many mechanisms as is appropriate over time.
(Facer, 2024)

BECKY ALLEN

The problem with workload in teaching is that much of it is driven by accountability structures rather than what is beneficial for learning outcomes.

promoting ineffective strategies that waste valuable time (Jones, 2024a).

In this book, I have dedicated three summaries to addressing nine of the most persistent myths in education, alongside their corresponding truths. Drawing on the work of thought leaders like Daisy Christodoulou, these one-pagers are designed to help teachers critically evaluate commonly accepted ideas, and make informed decisions about their practice. What's more, they're also powerful reminders for professional development leaders designing programmes for their staff.

Since the release of *Teaching One-Pagers* in 2024, the appetite for one-pagers has gone through the roof. The summary format has proven to be an accessible way for educators to access bitesize professional development (PD) and keep abreast of important research. What's more, when used to support school PD programmes, they are also incredibly powerful due to their slim and simple nature. One-pagers address several mechanisms established by the Education Endowment Foundation (EEF) in their 2021 guidance report on 'Effective Professional Development' including managing cognitive load (due to their slim format and design), refreshing prior knowledge and providing prompts and cues (see the diagram on the previous page). As noted in *The ResearchED Guide to Professional Development* (Facer, 2024), the aim with the mechanisms is not to shoehorn every single one into every PD session, but rather to ensure the overall professional development sequences are well balanced, incorporating as many mechanisms as is appropriate over time. This means that one-pagers can be curated and strategically integrated into a school's professional development programme to support long-term teacher growth.

In the following section, **School Stories**, I share how various schools have implemented *Teaching One-Pagers* to support their teachers in reflecting on their practice, building knowledge and engaging with wider reading. Despite all being in early stages of the implementation process, these real-life examples illustrate how schools have used summaries to provide accessible PD opportunities that fit into the day-to-day demands of their schools. After all, workload is a critical barrier to professional development, and schools must find effective ways to alleviate it. As Becky Allen (2017), co-founder of the Teacher Tapp app, aptly states, 'The problem with workload in teaching is that much of it is driven by accountability structures rather than what is beneficial for learning outcomes.' The schools highlighted in this section demonstrate a shift away from this mindset, focusing instead on low-stakes approaches that empower teachers to prioritise their own professional growth.

Like the thriving ecosystems Sherrington describes in *The Learning Rainforest*, great schools are diverse environments where professional development fosters both instructional and personal growth. *Teaching One-Pagers Volume 2* is designed to help busy educators navigate these complexities, equipping them with insights and actionable strategies to cultivate their own rainforest environments where everyone can flourish.

TOM SHERRINGTON'S DESCRIPTION OF THE LEARNING RAINFOREST

There is enormous variety in the range of trees and plants that are thriving in the environment; it is lush, exotic, awe-inspiring, unpredictable, non-linear, evolving, daunting. Each specimen is magnificent in its own right with different organisms occupying their niche in an environment that is self-nourishing. Without the need for artificial interventions, the soil is fertile and the process of evolution is continuous. Whilst each plant has distinctive features and unique requirements, they all co-exist in an equilibrium that develops organically over time in response to changing conditions. However, it is not cosy or safe; this environment is harsh at times. Not everything thrives unaided and, occasionally, invasive specimens inhibit the growth of others. As a result, the plants that flourish are very robust with extensive roots or they are nimble and adapt to change with ease.

SCHOOL STORIES

REAL-LIFE EXAMPLES OF ONE-PAGERS IN ACTION

Professional development (PD) is an essential ingredient for any educational professional. For both staff and students to grow in an optimal *learning rainforest*, where growth is nurtured and challenges are embraced, PD must be a top priority. As Dylan Wiliam (2012) rightly argues, 'Every teacher needs to improve, not because they are not good enough, but because they can be even better.' This is why *Teaching One-Pagers* was created – to empower educators to refine their instruction, deepen their understanding of educational research, and inspire schools to cultivate a shared excitement for continuous growth.

Since the launch of *Teaching One-Pagers*, I have been privileged to work with 28 schools across the globe as part of a case study to integrate evidence-informed summaries into their PD programmes. On the opposite page, you will discover the top reasons why schools chose to sign up. The aim of the yearlong case study is to support busy teachers in becoming more evidence-informed while highlighting how one-pagers can enhance school PD. Throughout this project, schools are guided through the following process:

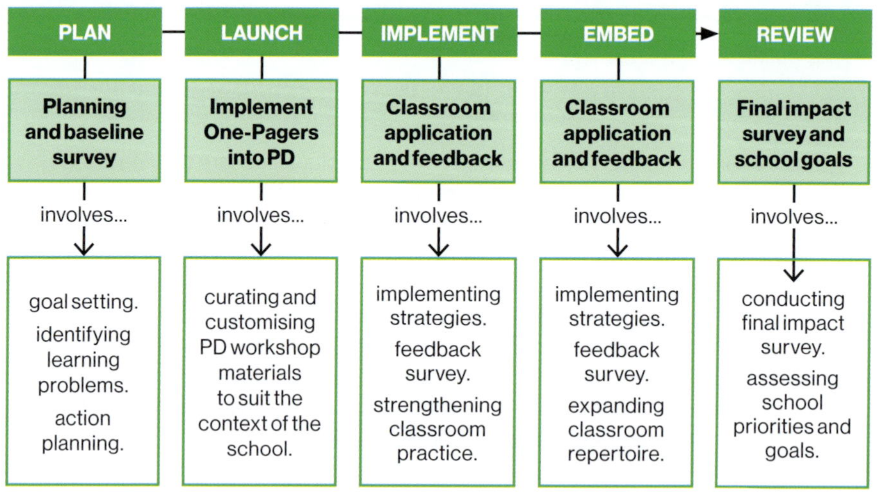

SURVEY FEEDBACK SHOWING REASONS WHY SCHOOLS SIGNED UP FOR THE CASE STUDY

ESTABLISH A PD CULTURE	MEASURE IMPACT OF PD	SUPPORT EXISTING PD	PLAYBOOK CREATION
To improve the love of PD and create a PD culture within the school.	To measure the impact of practices on student outcomes.	To build one-pagers into existing instructional coaching PD.	To help develop a school-wide teaching and learning playbook.

CREATE A PD FRAMEWORK	LINK STRATEGY TO RESEARCH	CREATE SHARED UNDERSTANDING	INFORM PD WORKSHOPS
To establish a solid PD framework for a school with a high staff turnover.	To help align PD with our strategic plan and school vision for learning.	To build a whole-school pedagogy focus and shared understanding.	To support with running short focused PD workshops with teaching groups.

Despite this study being in its early stages at the time of writing this book, I am already witnessing outstanding efforts from passionate PD and school leaders who are driving evidence-informed practices in their schools. As a leader of school PD, I believe collecting data and measuring the progress of implementation is crucial to ensuring strategies are both effective and impactful. In their guidance report on implementation, the EEF (2021a) emphasise that it is vital for schools to 'use implementation data to drive faithful adoption and intelligent adaption'. The schools participating in this study are proactively using surveys and teacher voice to shape their programmes, tailoring evidence-based strategies to meet the unique needs of their staff.

In the following stories, you will see how three schools participating in the study have implemented one-pagers to address their unique learning problems and support their initiatives. These stories provide concrete, real-life examples of how to introduce summaries to staff and the practical PD experiences that make the learning process both interactive and meaningful.

Let's jump in and explore their stories.

DYLAN WILIAM

Every teacher needs to improve, not because they are not good enough, but because they can be even better.

WRITTEN BY NIKKI JONES

PRENTON HIGH SCHOOL FOR GIRLS

SECONDARY SCHOOL, BIRKENHEAD, LIVERPOOL, UK

NIKKI JONES
Assistant Principal

One-pagers deliver clear, actionable strategies backed by research, offering staff the option to explore further while keeping the content concise and easily accessible.

CHERYL BURNS
Raising Standards Lead

The aim of developing an EIP group was to foster professional curiosity and refinement of our teaching practices.

At Prenton High School for Girls, we have taken a bold step towards embedding evidence-informed practices into our teaching and learning framework. As part of our professional development, we have introduced an evidence-informed practice (EIP) team made up of EIP leads across each department to help drive our focus on instructional practices across all curriculum subjects.

WHAT IS THE FOCUS OF YOUR PD?

Through staff and student voice, department self-evaluations and quality assurance processes, it became clear that we needed to focus on increasing cognitive challenge for our students through refining our questioning techniques and retrieval practice activities. This prompted us to focus intensively on these strategies for our PD.

WHY USE ONE-PAGERS?

One of our key priorities has been to make research accessible and actionable for our teachers. Early feedback from our professional development surveys revealed that staff struggled to find time to engage deeply with meaningful PD. One-pagers have been a transformative solution for us. Their concise format allows us to deliver bitesize, research-based insights and practical strategies, particularly on questioning and retrieval practice, without burdening staff with the need to navigate dense academic studies or edubooks.

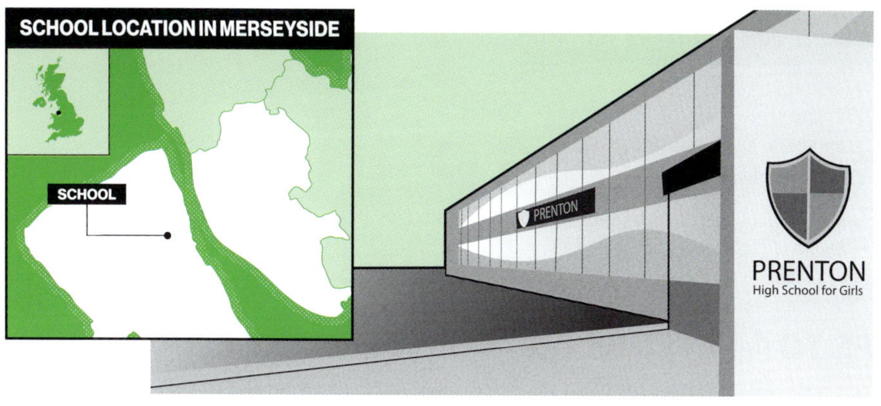

HOW HAVE ONE-PAGERS BEEN IMPLEMENTED?

During INSET days and our termly EIP PD sessions, teachers are given dedicated time to read and engage with our target one-pagers. We ensure that we carve out explicit reading and thinking time in our sessions where subject teams read the one-pagers together in departments or, at times, staff read collaboratively in the main hall where they annotate key information using our scaffolded resources. Focused discussion time follows where staff are guided in discussing ideas or misconceptions based on the research. Following this, we introduce various interactive activities to ensure staff actively participate. For example, our marketplace activity involved multiple stations where EIP leads demonstrated the target strategies such as modelling activities and metacognitive questioning techniques. Teachers stepped into the role of learners, experiencing firsthand what it felt like to engage with the strategies being presented. At each station in the carousel, they worked through activities such as solving maths problems under silent modelling or practising questioning techniques in scaffolded scenarios.

HOW HAVE ONE-PAGERS HAD AN IMPACT?

The implementation of *Teaching One-Pagers* has led to noticeable shifts in teaching practices and has steadily helped staff become more evidence informed. For example, teachers have refined their retrieval techniques to ensure activities promote long-term memory retention. Previously, students often relied on notes, but now teachers recognise the value of healthy struggle and pushing students to retrieve knowledge independently. Strategies like cold calling and the use of mini-whiteboards have also become more widespread, improving student engagement. One-pagers have helped foster a culture of professional curiosity and continuous improvement, supported by collaborative and supportive quality assurance processes.

WRITTEN BY FATEMA KASHIEF

PRISTINE PRIVATE SCHOOL

FS TO A-LEVEL UK CURRICULUM SCHOOL, DUBAI, UAE

FATEMA KASHIEF

Teaching and Learning Lead

The programme follows a structured, reflective model inspired by action research. This ongoing process ensured that strategies are progressively refined and firmly embedded into our classroom practices, while peer discussions build a culture of collaboration and continuous improvement.

Pristine Private School's PD programme provides teachers with bespoke, targeted opportunities to enhance their practice. By introducing a reflective, inquiry-driven process, our teachers are able to engage with research, collaborate with colleagues and refine classroom strategies.

WHAT IS THE FOCUS OF YOUR PD?

Through instructional coaching, teachers participate in an action-research-inspired process where they identify challenges, choose evidence-based strategies to address the challenges, and subsequently evaluate their effectiveness and make adjustments. During our termly Teach Meet sessions, staff share their experiences and exchange ideas, using the one-pager as a talking point. These conversations have helped to strengthen professional dialogue between colleagues.

WHY USE ONE-PAGERS?

Teaching One-Pagers were chosen for their clarity and practicality, offering teachers quick, accessible insights without the burden of dense academic texts. The best bit was that teachers could read about the different educationists' views about a particular strategy in one go. Each summary provides actionable steps tailored to specific pedagogical challenges. For example, one teacher's feedback processes have been enhanced through Dylan Wiliam's formative feedback strategies.

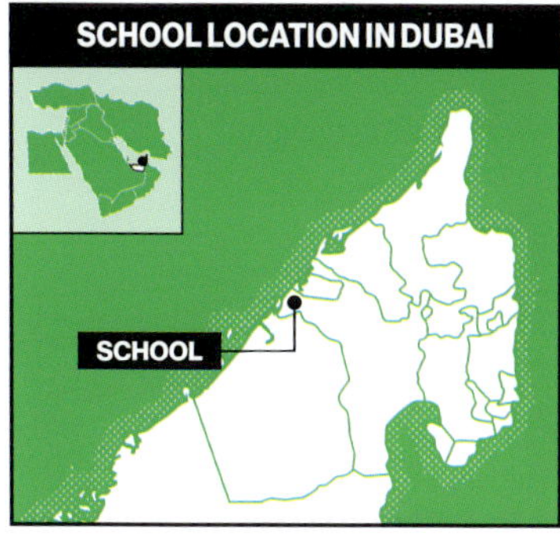

HOW HAVE ONE-PAGERS BEEN IMPLEMENTED?

Our programme follows a structured, reflective model inspired by action research. This ongoing process ensured that strategies are progressively refined and firmly embedded into our classroom practices, while peer discussions build a culture of collaboration and continuous improvement.

1. IDENTIFYING NEEDS: Teachers work with instructional coaches to identify specific challenges, aligning their targets with our school goals.

2. ENGAGING WITH THE RESEARCH: Teachers explore and discuss targeted one-pagers, delving into the research underpinning strategies.

3. TRIAL AND REFLECTION: Teachers trial evidence-based strategies, tailoring their approaches to address their identified challenges.

4. SHARING AND REFINING: During termly Teach Meets, teachers share their experiences, discuss successes and make adjustments.

HOW HAVE ONE-PAGERS HAD AN IMPACT?

The implementation of *Teaching One-Pagers* has resulted in visible shifts in teaching practices and enriched professional dialogue. For example, staff trialling feedback as detective work observed students taking greater ownership of their learning and making significant strides in self-regulation. One English teacher said, 'Feedback puzzles were a game-changer. Students became more engaged in the feedback process, and it helped me create a classroom culture where feedback is a catalyst for growth.' Overall, these experiences have strengthened professional conversations and helped to create a culture where staff trial and adjust their teaching to maximise learning.

WRITTEN BY YAMINA BIBI

SARAH BONNELL SCHOOL

SECONDARY SCHOOL, NEWHAM, LONDON, UK

YAMINA BIBI
Assistant Principal

One-pagers have been a powerful way to discuss and explore a range of research-informed strategies in a concise way, ensuring implementation is practicable and observable for all.

At Sarah Bonnell School, we have an innovative approach to enhancing classroom practice through our focus on 'irresistible teaching' within our SB Lesson Framework. As part of our PD programme, we conduct weekly teaching and learning briefings where classroom-based staff share and discuss evidence-informed strategies to 'improve not prove' their practice.

WHAT IS THE FOCUS OF YOUR PD?

Our journey began with a clear aim: to shift from passive teaching styles to actively engaging students and fostering independent learning. Observations and feedback from learning walks revealed that while instruction was strong, students often acted as passive recipients, requiring more active participation. This insight, coupled with our commitment to cognitive science principles, led us to focus our PD on strategies that increase our pupil participation ratio and encourage student-led learning.

WHY USE ONE-PAGERS?

One-pagers have been a valuable addition to our existing PD programmes, which include *Teaching WalkThrus* and Steplab, providing a concise and impactful way to discuss a range of research-informed strategies. They help avoid overwhelming teachers while ensuring that implementation is both practicable and observable for all.

FIND OUT MORE: www.sarahbonnell.ncltrust.net

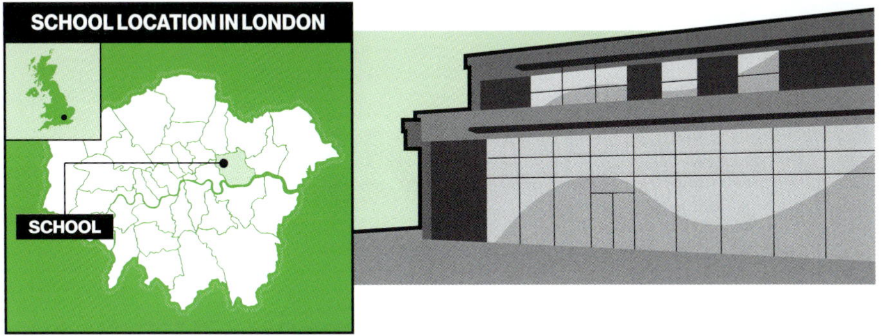

HOW HAVE ONE-PAGERS BEEN IMPLEMENTED?

We implemented structured three-week 'coaching circles' to integrate one-pagers into our PD. These circles are tailored using Steplab instructional coaching data and lesson observations, ensuring alignment with each teacher's specific action steps.

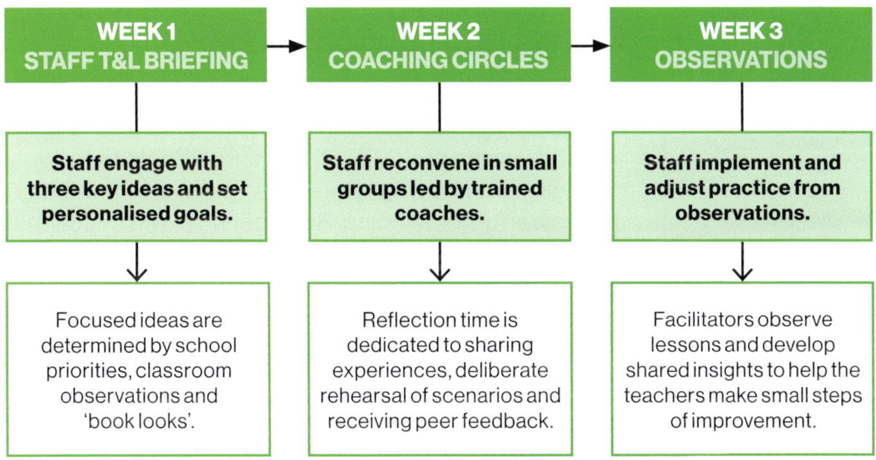

HOW HAVE ONE-PAGERS HAD AN IMPACT?

The implementation of one-pagers has standardised the language around evidence-informed practice, eased the workload for planning teaching and learning briefings, and enabled all classroom practitioners to personalise and refine their approaches. Steplab data shows increased 'shout-outs' and effective action steps linked to one-pager strategies. This consistency has fostered a culture of collaboration and shared purpose across the school. Additionally, staff feedback highlights the effectiveness and efficiency of coaching circles supported by one-pagers.

WRITTEN BY DALE SPICK

TEDDINGTON SCHOOL

SECONDARY SCHOOL, TEDDINGTON, LONDON, UK

DALE SPICK
Assistant Principal

By targeting disengagement, recall practice, ineffective feedback and powerful questioning, we aim to identify where learning falters and implement strategies to strengthen teaching practices, supported by the clarity and practicality of Teaching One-Pagers.

At Teddington School in London, we have taken proactive steps to strengthen our teaching and learning by focusing our professional development on common learning problems identified by our teachers.

WHAT IS THE FOCUS OF YOUR PD?

This year, our school's professional development focused on formative assessment, adaptive teaching and addressing the 'DRIP' in learning. DRIP stands for: disengagement, retrieval practice, ineffective feedback and powerful questioning. By targeting these critical areas, we aim to identify where learning falters and implement strategies to strengthen teaching practices. To support this, we introduced *Teaching One-Pagers* through voluntary PD, offering six-week focus groups, each dedicated to exploring one of these areas in depth over the course of a half term.

WHY USE ONE-PAGERS?

We chose one-pagers as a central tool because of their simplicity and practicality. Teachers already balance heavy workloads, so we wanted a resource that delivers clear and concise information without overwhelming them. The visually engaging format makes complex ideas accessible and provides clarity and consistency. By presenting information in manageable chunks, one-pagers help teachers focus on understanding and applying key strategies effectively.

FIND OUT MORE: www.teddingtonschool.org

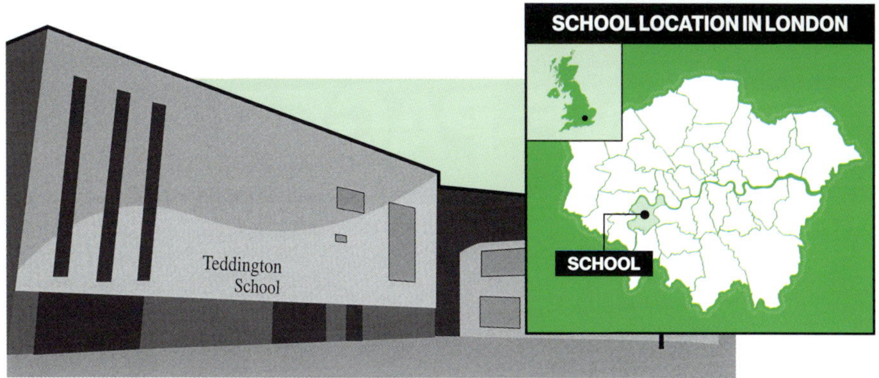

HOW HAVE ONE-PAGERS BEEN IMPLEMENTED?

Each focus group starts with a one-pager on a target idea and details actionable strategies. During the 45-minute training sessions, the one-pager serves as a discussion guide, ensuring all teachers have a shared understanding of the target ideas. This approach aligns with findings from research (McCormick et al, 2014) highlighting that short, focused and practical sessions are effective for engaging busy professionals and encouraging the adoption of new tools and strategies. Teachers also receive two student-facing slides, adapted from the one-pager, which explain the *why*, *how* and *what* behind each approach. These slides are shared with students to build transparency as we believe it is important for students to be part of the journey and therefore need to understand the purpose of our classroom adjustments. At the end of each six-week cycle, we create our own one-pager for staff, summarising feedback and reflecting on the impact of the process.

HOW HAVE ONE-PAGERS HAD AN IMPACT?

DRIP has helped us bridge specific learning gaps. For example, our focus on retrieval practice has improved as we now add more variety to recall activities using a range of low-stakes strategies. Teachers have responded positively to the PD process because they find that it does not overwhelm them or impact their workload. Classroom takeaways have enabled immediate implementation of strategies, while the student-facing slides have helped develop stronger teacher–student connections with a clear focus on helping them learn. One of our Year 10 students said: 'It's helpful to know why we're doing something new; it makes us feel part of the process. We have really improved our practice quizzes.' In future, we plan to scale the use of one-pagers by introducing 'Bright Spot' sign-ups, where staff drop in to observe and learn from colleagues in a non-threatening manner.

THE ONE-PAGER

BOOST SCHOOL PROFESSIONAL DEVELOPMENT

JAMIE CLARK

Since introducing one-pagers in my own school, I've seen teachers' engagement with evidence-informed ideas sky-rocket. Teachers are time-poor, so distilling important ideas into an easily digestible format offers a practical solution.

WHAT ARE THEY AND WHY ARE THEY USEFUL?

The one-pager has proven a popular format for teachers' professional development. Since introducing them in my own school, I've seen teachers' engagement with evidence-informed ideas skyrocket. Distilling important ideas into an easily digestible one-page format offers a practical solution for time-poor teachers. A key reason for their success is that they help to reduce cognitive load by distilling complex information into manageable, bitesize summaries through columns, titles, highlighted sections, call-outs, portraits and diagrams. Research shows helping teachers often requires not adding but taking away; finding ways to free up cognitive resources (Lovell et al, 2024).

SHARED UNDERSTANDING:

Utilise the summaries in this book to promote collaborative discussions and reflections on current practices while identifying common 'learning problems' within your school. Learning problems are focus points (such as 'many of our students are not actively engaged in thinking') and help shape strategic goals. A shared understanding is crucial for developing a unified approach to teaching and learning across the school and helps to narrow down the focus to specific summaries.

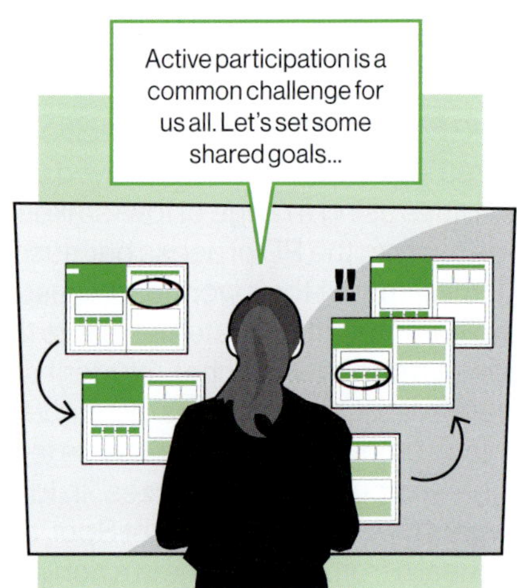

READ MORE: 'Putting Evidence to Work: A School's Guide to Implementation' by the EEF

WHAT ARE THE BENEFITS OF ONE-PAGERS FOR PD?

WIDER READING	**One-pagers** *spotlight* the most important evidence-informed ideas and inspire wider reading so teachers can focus on deeper exploration later.
BUILD KNOWLEDGE	**One-pagers** *serve* as a practical tool for teachers at all experience levels to introduce or refresh pedagogical knowledge.
ACTIONABLE INSIGHTS	**One-pagers** *highlight* evidence-informed classroom strategies and offer actionable steps for teacher to apply immediately in their teaching.
PROFESSIONAL DISCUSSIONS	**One-pagers** *prompt* conversations with colleagues and are a starting point for meaningful discussions on concepts, learning problems and strategies.
SHARED IDEAS	**One-pagers** help to *establish* a shared understanding of educational ideas and unify teams around common goals for professional development.

ONE-PAGERS IMPLEMENTATION: The EEF's School Guide's to Implementation (2019) provides a robust framework for developing sustainable PD. Their approach can be adopted when implementing one-pagers.

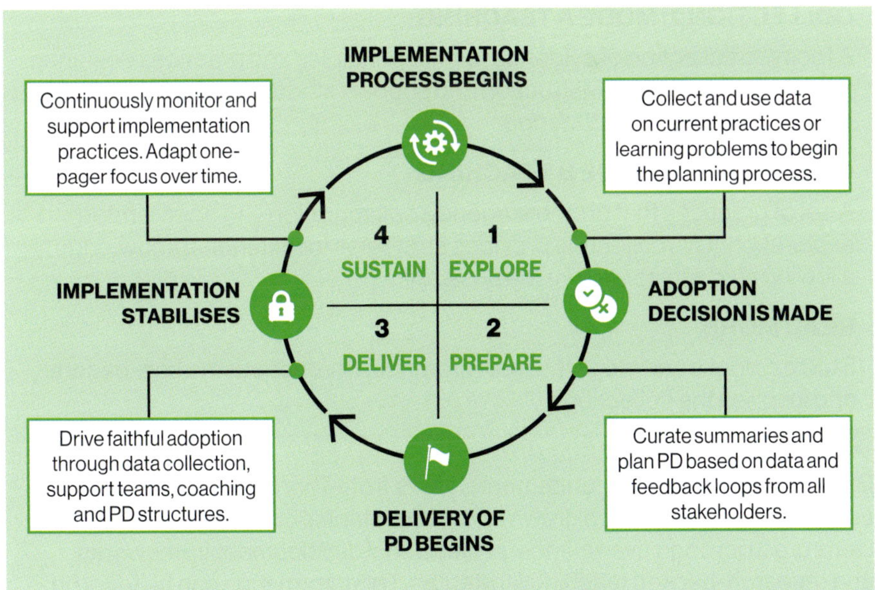

INSPIRED BY PUTTING EVIDENCE TO WORK: A SCHOOL'S GUIDE TO IMPLEMENTATION

READER'S GUIDE

HOW TO NAVIGATE THIS BOOK SUCCESSFULLY

Teaching One-Pagers Volume 2 picks up where its predecessor left off. It is designed especially for convenience and practicality so it can be easily used as a handy reference guide for teachers and as a resource for deep, purposeful professional learning. The content of this book has been organised neatly into three collections, each with a diverse range of summaries relating to the art and science of teaching:

COLLECTION 1: SCHOOL CULTURE

A series of principles and strategic approaches to help guide leaders to *establish the conditions for growth* and inspire a culture of high expectations and excellence in their schools.

COLLECTION 2: MODE A TEACHING

A focused collection of evidence-based principles and practices designed to enhance classroom instruction and support students with *building bodies of connected knowledge*.

COLLECTION 3: MODE B TEACHING

A set of practices that promote agency, collaboration and open-ended exploration. This collection provides strategies for extending knowledge, allowing students to *explore the possibilities*.

READ MORE

Studies, books and blogs that are referenced throughout the one-pagers and inspired the collections.

Despite this book taking fundamental ideas from Tom Sherrington's *The Learning Rainforest*, it also draws upon a substantial body of educational literature from cognitive science, professional development frameworks and research-backed teaching strategies. This information can be found in the 'Read More' suggestions at the bottom of each one-pager.

The individual summaries in *Teaching One-Pagers Volume 2* stick to the same simple format. The '*what, why and how?*' structure provides clarity and ease of use so teachers can understand the concept, the rationale and practical steps for classroom application. Here's a visual breakdown of what is included in each one-page summary in this book:

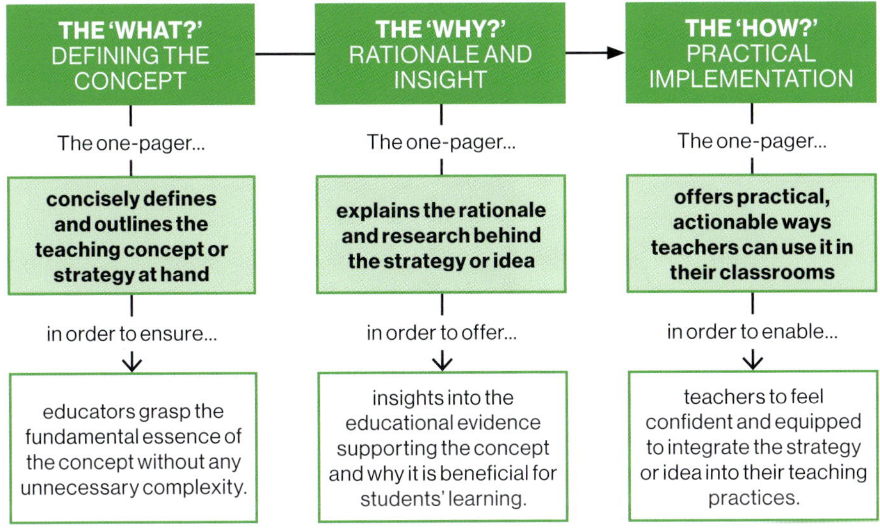

THE 'MORE ABOUT' SUMMARIES

Sometimes one big idea cannot be covered on a single one-pager. As I explained in the first *Teaching One-Pagers*, one-pagers are not intended to be the sole sources of information; they are summaries that add clarity to strategies, encourage deeper reading and inspire action. In this book, I have introduced More About summaries for several of the important ideas that I believe are central to evidence-informed practice. These summaries can be identified by the icon above. They build on previous one-pagers and offer further strategies, research and insights for those looking to delve deeper into those key topics.

Now that you know what to expect from this exciting book, let's dive into **Collection 1: School Culture** and explore how to *establish the conditions for growth*.

JAMIE CLARK

In this book, I have introduced 'More About' summaries that build on previous one-pagers and offer further strategies, research and insights for those looking to delve deeper into those key topics.

SCHOOL CULTURE

A series of strategic principles and practical strategies to help establish the conditions for growth

MODE A TEACHING

A focused collection of evidence-based principles and practices designed to enhance classroom instruction

MODE B TEACHING

A set of practices that foster agency, collaboration and open-ended exploration to deepen and extend knowledge

READ MORE

Studies, books and blogs that are referenced throughout the one-pagers and inspired the collections

Teaching
one
Pagers
2
VOLUME

SCHOOL CULTURE

ESTABLISHING THE CONDITIONS FOR GROWTH

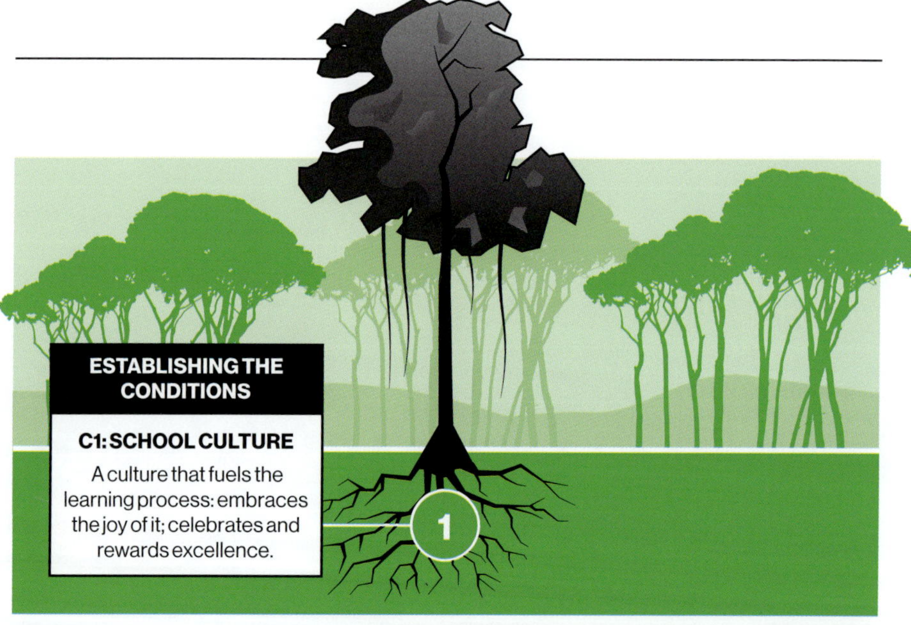

Does your school foster an adaptive culture grounded in purpose, shared values and a sense of belonging that drives both staff and students towards excellence?

In *The Learning Rainforest*, the central tree metaphor highlights that the conditions for growth are created by cultivating a strong school culture. This culture is built on nurturing the right attitudes and habits, which form the essential roots for the growth of excellence (Sherrington, 2017). From experience, this comes down to having a clear purpose that permeates through the whole school and its community. When a school's culture is grounded in a clear sense of purpose, it creates an environment where both staff and students feel a deep sense of belonging and motivation in and outside the classroom. This means it extends beyond external rewards like students' grades or the school's 'outstanding' Ofsted report. In essence, purpose is the *Why* that develops a shared vision and strong culture.

SIMON SINEK'S GOLDEN CIRCLE MODEL ADAPTED FOR SCHOOL CULTURE

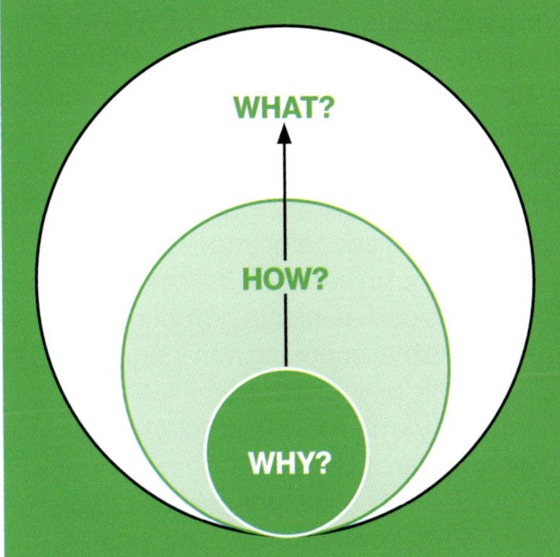

WHAT? (Actions and strategies) represents the visible aspects of the school culture, like curriculum choices, teaching strategies and school events.

HOW? (Principles and practices) shows the principles that guide the school's approach to learning and community.

WHY? (Purpose and values) is the deepest layer, the driving force behind all school decisions and cultural development.

In his book *Start with Why*, Simon Sinek (2009) argues that truly inspiring leaders and organisations operate from a clear sense of purpose, or their *Why*, which forms the foundation of all their actions. He explains that 'great leaders inspire action by giving people a sense of purpose or belonging that has little to do with any external incentive or benefit to be gained'. In his viral 2009 TED Talk *Start with Why: How Great Leaders Inspire Action*, Sinek explains the 'golden circle' model that outlines how successful organisations and leaders communicate. From an education perspective, Sinek's model can be adapted to provide a powerful framework for understanding school culture. The innermost circle of the diagram represents the *Why* – the school's core purpose, mission or vision that guides the organisation in a specific direction. The second layer, *How*, includes the overarching principles and practices that guide how the school achieves its vision. Finally, the outer circle, *What*, stands to represent the classroom actions and tangible strategies the school takes on a daily basis.

During my career, I have experienced the energy and support that come from being part of a thriving school culture with a strong *Why*. At this school, fundamental

SIMON SINEK

Great leaders inspire action by giving people a sense of purpose or belonging that has little to do with any external incentive or benefit to be gained.

LEKHA SHARMA

Having absolute clarity about our collective purpose in schools means that every single person within a school community is moving in the same direction... Our purpose is the sturdy anchor that keeps us grounded.

TOM BENNETT

The key task for a school leader is to create a culture – usefully defined as 'the way we do things around here' – that is understood and subscribed to by the whole school community.

questions were deeply ingrained. Questions like, *Why do we do what we do?*, and *What do we stand for?* were inscribed in the minds of staff and students. We were all rowing in the same direction, united by a common purpose. In contrast, I have also seen the flipside and the negative impact of a poor school climate. In that environment, staff weren't supported in meeting the school's expectations but were instead confined by rigid 'non-negotiables'. As educator and leader Lekha Sharma (2023) points out in her book *Building Culture*, the language we use to communicate purpose is powerful. She explains that imposing non-negotiables can unintentionally stifle dialogue and limit teachers' agency. The language we use plays a crucial role in ensuring that our goals are both clearly communicated and actively embodied. By consistently articulating and reinforcing the school's purpose through a common language, schools can crystalise a sense of shared commitment and collective effort.

In an independent review titled, 'Creating a Culture: How school leaders can optimise behaviour' (2017), behaviour guru, Tom Bennett emphasises the importance of a clear, purposeful school culture, which he defines as 'the way we do things around here'. Despite being aimed at optimising behaviour for learning, the report can arguably be applied more broadly to school ethos. The graphic on the next page represents eight core elements that characterise an excellent school environment with concrete examples of what this looks like in real life. These serve as a handy blueprint for the nitty-gritty actions that underpin a healthy culture.

In the first *Teaching One-Pagers*, I wrote about the power of classroom culture in relation to Michaela Community School in London. Headmistress Katharine Birbalsingh's recipe for academic and pastoral success is built on a foundation of high expectations, unwavering discipline, and a relentless focus on character building. By embedding routines, clear boundaries and instilling a strong sense of personal responsibility, Birbalsingh ensures that students not only excel academically

FEATURES OF EXCELLENT SCHOOL CULTURE CONDENSED BY LEKHA SHARMA

VISIBLE LEADERS	DETAILED EXPECTATIONS	CLARITY OF CULTURE	HIGH STAFF SUPPORT
Leaders actively on duty, present and interacting with staff and students.	Clarity and repetition over the expectations and 'what good looks like'.	Transparency, making clear 'how things are done around here' and 'walking the talk'.	Prioritising professional learning and support for all staff.

ALL STUDENTS MATTER	ATTENTION TO DETAIL	STAFF ENGAGEMENT	CONSISTENT PRACTICES
A child-centred, inclusive approach with high expectations for all students.	Following up on PD and quality assurance to ensure it is being enacted.	Open-door culture where voices are heard and collective decisions made.	Codifying practices and using examples as reference points for staff.

but also develop resilience, respect and a deep commitment to their school. Despite serving mainly disadvantaged students, Michaela stands as a model of a well-structured, purpose-driven school. After connecting with Katharine Birbalsingh virtually, I had the chance to ask about her approach at Michaela. In our conversation, printed on the next page, Katharine's passion for maintaining a strong culture shone through. She continually emphasised the relentless commitment it takes, requiring daily attention to uphold values, beliefs and norms. I learned that leadership at Michaela thrives on focusing on everyday subtle interactions – small signals that reinforce the school's high standards and values in every moment.

In other words, effective leaders intentionally cultivate and refine a specific set of skills. They don't just establish purpose – they also foster a strong sense of belonging and trust within their teams. In *The Culture Code*, Daniel Coyle highlights this point with the assertion: 'It's not something you are. It's something you do.' Building a strong school culture requires a critical-responsive approach made up of constant

KATHARINE BIRBALSINGH

You have to repeat this over and over... Culture is something you nurture daily, constantly talking about it, embedding it in everything you do, and explaining why it's better than other alternatives.

INTERVIEW WITH KATHARINE BIRBALSINGH ABOUT BUILDING SCHOOL CULTURE

JAMIE When building a strong school culture, what values do you believe are most important, and how do you ensure they are embedded daily?

KATHARINE You can build a culture around any set of values, but the key is being relentless. Culture requires daily, sometimes even hourly, attention. It's fragile – one new staff member or student can change it. If you don't control the culture, someone else will, often the kids who consistently misbehave or the most disruptive staff. It's about leadership ensuring consistency, and that starts at the top with the headteacher.

JAMIE How do you see leadership's role in maintaining and shaping culture?

KATHARINE The headteacher is crucial in setting the tone, but it extends to all leaders. Deputies and heads of departments need to take control of their areas too. Leadership is about empowering others to control the culture within their teams. Without this, you risk losing control, and as I often say, culture eats strategy for breakfast.

JAMIE How would you describe the culture at Michaela?

KATHARINE It's a place where high expectations are the norm. If you asked the students or staff, they would likely say it's 'super strict', but that means we love the students enough to push them hard and expect the best from them. There's also a strong sense of belonging; we row together as a team, and that's deeply embedded in everything we do.

JAMIE How do you reinforce this culture across the school?

KATHARINE Constant repetition. Culture is nurtured every day through what we say and do. I meet with staff regularly – briefings, meetings, individual conversations – constantly explaining why we do what we do. It's about narrating the culture, showing examples of what works and what doesn't, and always linking it back to our core values. You have to explain it so much that it becomes second nature for everyone.

JAMIE How do you balance the need for consistency with the need to adapt and evolve the culture over time?

KATHARINE Daily adaptation is a must. I meet with my senior team every morning, and we are constantly reviewing what's working and what isn't. You need to have a clear vision, but culture must adapt to the challenges you face. We tweak things constantly, learning from our mistakes, but always keeping the bigger picture in mind. It's a daily practice of refinement to ensure the culture is delivering on our vision.

input, feedback and adaptation. Just as drivers continuously gather information from the road, adjust their steering and maintain focus, school leaders must actively observe, evaluate and refine their actions to align with the school's purpose. However, in schools, this is more complex. It involves not only the visible aspects of classrooms but also the invisible factors that shape ethos and relationships. The ongoing cycle of observation and adaptation is key to sustaining a thriving school culture. Inspired by the work of Ashbee (2024), this critical-responsive cycle is visualised below.

CRITICAL-RESPONSIVE METHOD INSPIRED BY RUTH ASHBEE

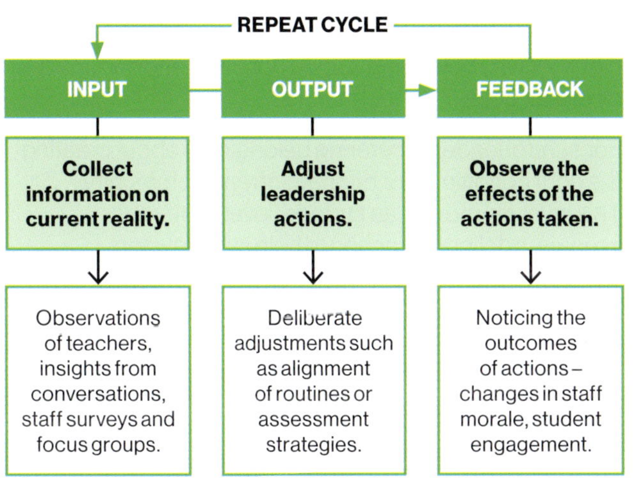

A thriving school culture doesn't just stem from structures and strategies; it grows from a deep sense of belonging within the community. This sense of belonging is essential for both staff and students and has profound implications for wellbeing and performance. Recent research, including Haili Hughes' reflections (2024) on the work of Allen et al (2021), underscores that belonging is not a static feeling but a dynamic process influenced by competencies, opportunities, motivations and perceptions.

DANIEL COYLE

Culture is a set of living relationships working toward a shared goal. It's not something you are. It's something you do.

RUTH ASHBEE

In leadership, as in driving, there are no guarantees: we can never be completely safe from crashing our car, and nor can we be sure of a smooth journey to great culture.

HAILI HUGHES

Encouraging opportunities for collaboration and providing positive reinforcement to cultivate a supportive and motivating school culture also helps. This doesn't just mean cakes in the staff room – collaboration isn't about glossy wellbeing policies; these are often just laminated, not lived!

Belonging in schools is about far more than staffroom cakes or glossy policies – it is about lived experiences and meaningful connections. When belonging is embedded into the culture, it becomes a driver for staff retention, motivation and engagement. Teachers who feel they are a valued part of the community, whose voices are heard and perspectives matter, are far more likely to invest their energy and passion in the school's shared purpose.

From a science of learning perspective, belonging plays a critical role in cognitive and emotional processes. A strong sense of belonging can reduce cognitive load by alleviating concerns about social acceptance, freeing up mental resources for learning and problem-solving. It also builds all-important intrinsic motivation and modulates the stress response, fostering resilience. These benefits highlight why belonging should not be an afterthought but a central focus of school culture.

For school leaders, fostering belonging is about creating the right conditions for connection and community. This involves more than surface-level gestures; it requires deliberate action to help staff develop working relationships. Hughes (2024) points out that 'collaboration isn't about glossy wellbeing policies...these are often just laminated, not lived'. Belonging must be an active process, where opportunities for meaningful collaboration and connection are cultivated.

Four key strategies for school leaders are addressed in the table on the opposite page. As you can see, leaders must make time and space in the busy realities of school life to nourish and consolidate school culture so that it is embodied and owned.

At its heart, belonging is what ties together a strong culture. When staff and students feel that they truly belong, the school becomes a place of growth, support and purpose – a place where every individual feels 'the way we do things around here' is something they are proud to live and breathe every day. As Tom Bennett reminds us, a strong school culture shapes the way people think, feel and act, both in the classroom and beyond.

STRATEGIES TO ESTABLISH A SENSE OF BELONGING

1. BUILDING SOFT SKILLS
Providing training in empathy, active listening and communication skills to equip staff to build meaningful relationships.

2. CREATING OPPORTUNITIES
Establishing spaces in school for collaboration and dialogue where all voices are welcomed and valued.

3. STRENGTHENING MOTIVATIONS
Reinforcing the importance of each individual's role within the school's purpose, helping them to see that their contributions are vital.

4. SHAPING PERCEPTIONS
Actively communicating and reinforcing a shared sense of purpose, making belonging a visible and felt part of everyday life.

The one-pagers that follow in **Collection 1: School Culture** are helpful for schools aiming to establish and maintain the conditions for a successful school culture. The summaries include a range of practices and principles that help establish powerful attitudes, habits and cultural practices that can be applied to any school's overarching purpose (their *Why*).

Before we dive deeper, let's take a moment to step back. The common myths on the next page highlight misconceptions schools often face. Let's examine them.

PART 1/3

MYTHS AND TRUTHS

WHY ARE THESE MYTHS AND TRUTHS IMPORTANT?

In developing a strong school culture, it's important to challenge certain misconceptions that can poison the fertile ground necessary for optimum growth. The three myths on this one-pager often lead schools to chase trends at the expense of establishing solid research-based foundations (that have stood the test of time). It is clear that a school culture reliant on timeless principles including building knowledge and explicit teaching is essential for sustainable growth and success. This one-pager unpacks these myths and offers a more balanced, evidence-based approach to fostering a thriving school environment.

SCHOOLS MUST CHANGE EVERYTHING TO FIT THE 21ST CENTURY

DAISY CHRISTODOULOU

The newer the idea, the more sceptical we should be about teaching it in school, and the older the idea, the more likely it has stood the test of time.

MYTH: In *Seven Myths About Education*, Daisy Christodoulou (2014) critiques the idea that schools must radically change to accommodate the demands of the modern world. This myth assumes that traditional educational methods are obsolete in the face of modern technology and innovation in schools that promote 'soft skills' such as problem-solving, critical thinking and creativity (often associated with discovery learning).

TRUTH: While adapting to change is important, the science of education – structured knowledge, explicit teaching, and well-established pedagogy – remains essential. Educational reform should be balanced, as Tom Sherrington's Mode A and Mode B diet suggests, rather than driven by trends or fads. We are abandoning a focus on the most powerful thing schools can do to improve learning: the systematic teaching of knowledge.

SCHOOLS SHOULD PRIORITISE 'LOOKING UP' OVER KNOWLEDGE

E. D. HIRSCH

It takes knowledge to gain knowledge... The internet has placed a wealth of information at our fingertips. But to be able to use that information – to absorb it, to add to our knowledge – we must already possess a storehouse of knowledge. (2000)

MYTH: Schools should prioritise teaching students to 'just look it up', as modern technologies such as Google and AI give instant access to information, making memorisation and factual knowledge less important. This implies that teaching facts is outdated in a world where students can access information on demand.

TRUTH: Tech has its place and can positively impact learning. However, research shows that relying on tech to replace memory is ineffective because it takes knowledge to gain knowledge. Long-term memory is vital because without a solid base of facts, students struggle to process and connect new information. While the internet offers vast information, students must already possess foundational knowledge to effectively use it (ironic, eh?). Focus on building knowledge through teaching and recall, rather than outsourcing learning to technology!

SCHOOLS MUST ACCOMMODATE STUDENT LEARNING STYLES

HÉCTOR RUIZ MARTÍN

The belief that each person has a distinct learning style, as if our brains have various mechanisms to learn the same type of things, is widespread. However, overall, the evidence does not support the concept of learning styles. (2024)

MYTH: Schools must tailor their teaching to individual learning styles, such as visual, auditory or kinaesthetic, (often referred to as VAK) to maximise learning. This belief suggests that students learn best when instruction matches their preferred way of processing information, and failing to do so hinders their academic success.

TRUTH: Research has debunked the effectiveness of learning styles, showing no evidence that tailoring instruction to individual preferences improves learning. The most effective teaching practices are those that align with how the brain processes and retains information. Schools should cultivate a culture grounded in evidence-based practices that focus on the science of learning and memory. Schools should prioritise strategies like direct instruction, retrieval practice and scaffolding, which have been proven to enhance understanding and retention.

PART 1/3

THE LEARNING RAINFOREST

ESTABLISHING THE CONDITIONS FOR GROWTH

TOM SHERRINGTON

Each of the specimens in the learning rainforest is represented in the wonderful array of trees with their complex roots, trunk and branch systems that give them strength and structure and glorious canopies where their character finds expression.

WHAT IS IT AND WHY IS IT IMPORTANT?

The Learning Rainforest intertwines Sherrington's personal values and experiences with key educational research to establish guiding principles for effective teaching and thriving teaching culture. The first part of his tree metaphor explains the importance of establishing fertile conditions for growth and is broken down into three main areas: fostering the attitudes and habits needed as a basis for students to achieve excellence, establishing clear behaviour routines and relationships, and finally, designing a knowledge-rich curriculum where skills are structured in a way that supports long-term retention. The summaries in this section are underpinned by these ideas. First, let's look at *establishing the conditions* in more depth.

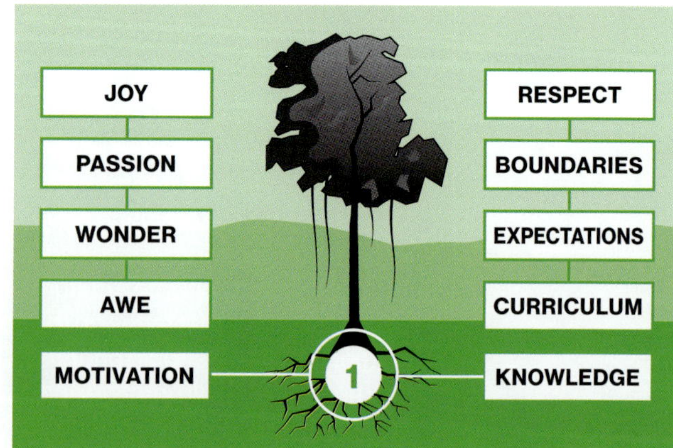

READ MORE: *The Learning Rainforest* by Tom Sherrington

ATTITUDES AND HABITS FOR EXCELLENCE:

Sherrington's first set of principles reflects his experience and insights gained from years in the classroom. He emphasises that to cultivate fertile conditions for growth, teachers must inspire a genuine joy for learning and passion for their subject. Central to his approach is establishing a shared curiosity with students to help build a culture where 'awe and wonder' are part of daily life and students are motivated to excel. These values form the roots of the learning rainforest, providing the essential foundation for all growth and achievement.

RELATIONSHIPS AND BEHAVIOUR:

In Sherrington's view, effective relationships are built on 'mutual respect', with high expectations as the standard. Teachers should foster positivity, show genuine care and ensure students always know where they stand. Clear boundaries are established through consistent routines and habits that inspire excellence. Sherrington advocates for straightforward yet impactful classroom management strategies, such as reinforcing expectations with positive language, using non-verbal cues, and maintaining a calm, authoritative presence (aka being the adult!).

PLANNING THE CURRICULUM: Creating the right conditions for growth includes implementing a well-structured curriculum. Sherrington explains pedagogy and curriculum are deeply intertwined, making it essential for schools to plan and design the curriculum thoughtfully and in advance. Cognitive science research supports this approach, showing that 'knowledge sticks to knowledge', meaning that information is more easily retained when connected to prior knowledge. Schools should organise content so that students can learn in manageable chunks, gradually building schemas in their long-term memory.

SCHOOL CULTURE PRINCIPLES

HIGH EXPECTATIONS

NURTURE A CULTURE OF ACADEMIC RIGOUR

DOUG LEMOV

One consistent finding of academic research is that high expectations are the most reliable driver of high student achievement, even in students who do not have a history of successful achievement.

WHAT IS IT AND WHY IS IT IMPORTANT?

In *Teach Like a Champion*, Lemov underscores that high expectations are essential for cultivating a rigorous academic culture. Research (CESE, 2020) supports this, stating that when teachers hold high academic expectations, it positively impacts student outcomes, engagement and wellbeing. Setting ambitious yet achievable standards encourages students to strive beyond their comfort zones, build resilience and develop a sense of pride in their progress. High expectations are more than rules; they are a mindset. When teachers establish and maintain these standards consistently, students thrive academically, behaviourally and socially. As Archer and Hughes (2011) explain, 'I believe you can do it' must always be paired with, 'Here's how you can do it'.

HOW DO WE IMPLEMENT IT?

EMBRACE CHALLENGE:

Research highlights that the most effective teachers instil in every student an expectation of success (OECD, 2013). On a practical level, teachers can do this by exuding enthusiasm and embracing challenge in every lesson. Make adjustments to language to ensure it communicates belief in students' abilities and emphasises that challenge is a good thing.

READ MORE: *Teach Like a Champion (Chapter 4 Academic Ethos)* by Doug Lemov

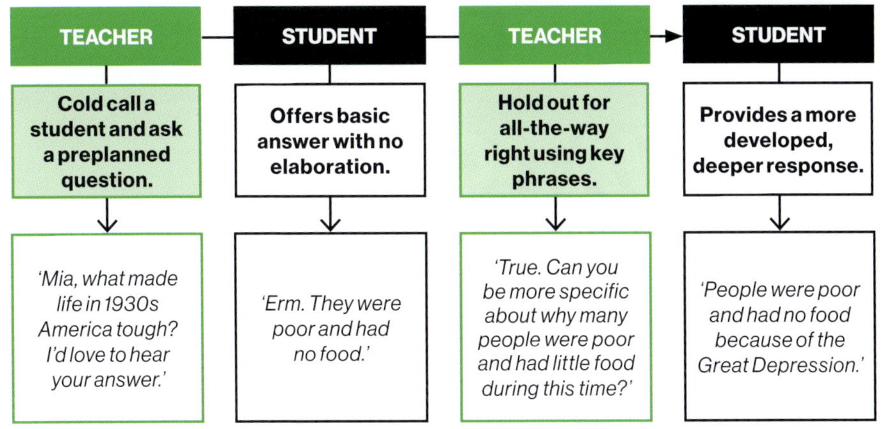

USE THE RIGHT IS RIGHT TECHNIQUE: Doug Lemov's 'Right is Right' technique from *Teach Like a Champion* (2021) emphasises the importance of teachers maintaining high standards for student responses by insisting on complete and accurate answers. When listening to students' responses, avoid affirming partial or middle-tier responses. Refraining from 'rounding up', where a teacher adds missing details to a student's answer. Instead, Lemov recommends to aim higher by 'holding out' until the student's answers is 'all-the-way right'.

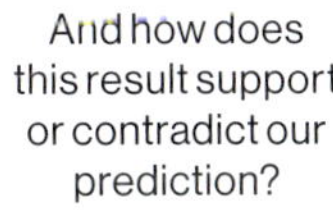

DIG FOR DEEPER ANSWERS: When posing a question to students, ask follow-up questions to deepen their understanding and push them towards mastery. As Lemov (2010) explains, 'The sequence of learning does not end with a right answer.' Ask students to explain how they arrived at their answers, use more precise vocabulary, or apply concepts in a different context to reinforce their understanding and promote a growth-focused mindset.

TAILOR THE CONTENT: Adjust instruction to meet the needs of all students. Pitching it up ensures all learners are challenged and thinking. John Hattie (2012) reinforces this by explaining that effective differentiation requires 'designing challenges calibrated to the learning goals of individual students'. Offer tiered tasks, scaffolding and clear success criteria to ensure all students are stretched, supported and encouraged to excel.

SCHOOL CULTURE PRINCIPLES

MOTIVATION

IMPLEMENT INTRINSIC DRIVERS FOR SUCCESS

PEPS MCCREA

Motivation matters. Especially in school. When pupils are motivated, they pay more attention, put in more effort, persist longer and work more independently.

WHAT IS IT AND WHY IS IT IMPORTANT?

Though it takes time and deliberate effort, building motivation has the power to transform culture. Contrary to popular belief, success breeds motivation, not the other way around! Schools must optimise the opportunities for success as often as possible. In *Motivated Teaching*, Peps Mccrea (2020) argues that motivation is a specific response to the situation, not a general trait. In other words, culture is key. To drive motivation, schools must not only deliver quality instruction and well-designed curricula but also pull the right levers to make the love of learning attractive for students.

HOW DO WE IMPLEMENT IT?

USE CORE DRIVERS: Peps Mccrea's Motivation for Learning framework can help schools think about the way they influence effort and attention to help establish a thriving culture where students are motivated to succeed.

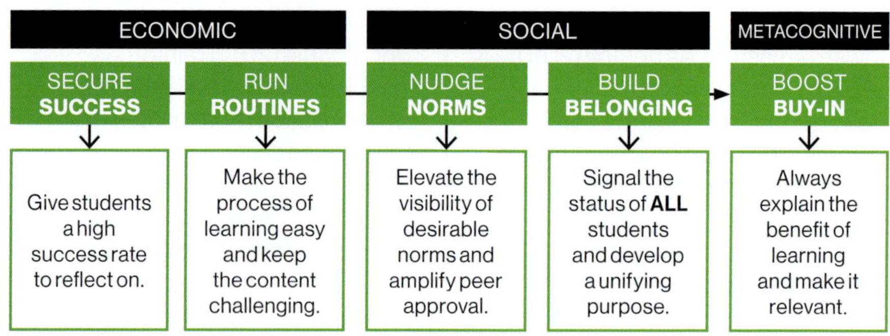

READ MORE: *Motivated Teaching* by Peps Mccrea

1 RAINFOREST
2 DESERT
3 TUNDRA

Base your short answer response on one biome of your choice...

PROVIDE CHOICE IN THE CURRICULUM WHEN IT MATTERS:

Offering students meaningful choices can significantly boost motivation, but only when the choices align with their interests, goals and values (Katz et al, 2006). Providing too many or irrelevant options can overwhelm and demotivate students. Allowing students some autonomy while maintaining focus makes it more likely students will experience higher rates of success.

PROMOTE INTEREST AND VALUE IN YOUR SUBJECT: The amount of importance students assign to the content of the lesson will determine their motivation to learn it (Wigfield et al, 1992). Author of *How Do We Learn*, Héctor Ruiz Martín (2024) argues that teachers can boost student interest by demonstrating genuine subject passion and connecting the material to students' interests. By showing the real-world relevance and value of what is being learned, teachers can make the content more meaningful and applicable to real life.

BUILD SELF-EFFICACY:

Self-efficacy (SE) is a student's belief in their ability to complete a task successfully. As Urhahne and Wijnia (2023) explain, 'Students who have higher self-efficacy are more likely to persist through challenges and perform better academically, as they believe their efforts can lead to success.' To build self-efficacy, schools can prioritise evidence-based instruction such as formative feedback, setting achievable goals and aiming for mastery.

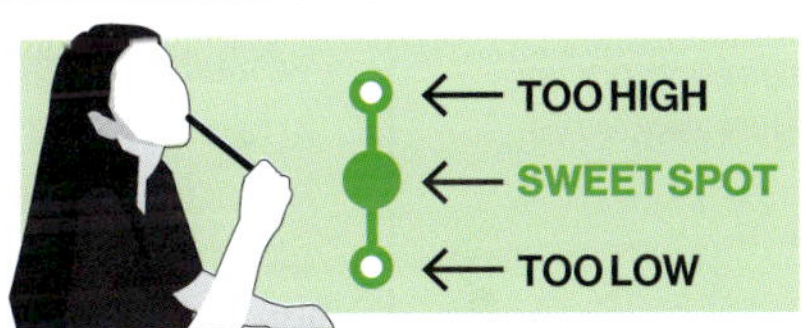

HIT THE 'SWEET SPOT':

Optimal motivation is achieved when the stakes are neither too high nor too low. This 'sweet spot' can lead to optimal memory function, decision making, motivation, learning and performance (Mccrea, 2024a). To apply this across a school, departments should design curriculum tasks that are challenging but achievable. Introducing low-stakes competitions or time-bound challenges also add excitement without the high-stakes fear of failure.

SCHOOL CULTURE PRINCIPLES

CURRICULUM DESIGN

BUILD A KNOWLEDGE-RICH LEARNING SEQUENCE

E. D. HIRSCH

Learning to learn is not an abstract skill. It entails already having the preparatory knowledge that enables further learning to occur. (Dunlosky, 2013)

WHAT IS IT AND WHY IS IT IMPORTANT?

In the context of building a strong school culture, curriculum design plays a crucial role in shaping not only what students learn but also how they engage with knowledge over time; a well-designed curriculum should focus on building a secure knowledge platform allowing students to reach the next level. Research (Sweller, 1994) shows 'the more knowledge students have in long-term memory, the easier it is to attain new knowledge that builds on their existing knowledge base'. Schools should sequence content progressively, increasing in complexity while helping students connect new learning to prior knowledge and avoiding cognitive overload. Having a broad and deep set of schemas in long-term memory can reduce cognitive overload, as students can recall information from schemas to link concepts and process new information in working memory (Willingham, 2021).

HOW DO WE IMPLEMENT IT?

MAKE IT KNOWLEDGE-RICH: According to research, knowledge is the foundation of learning. As E. D. Hirsch (2000) explains, 'Learning to learn is not an abstract skill. It entails already having the preparatory knowledge that enables further learning to occur.' With this in mind, a curriculum should focus on building a deep and coherent body of knowledge, ensuring students have the factual basis to help connect new information (NI).

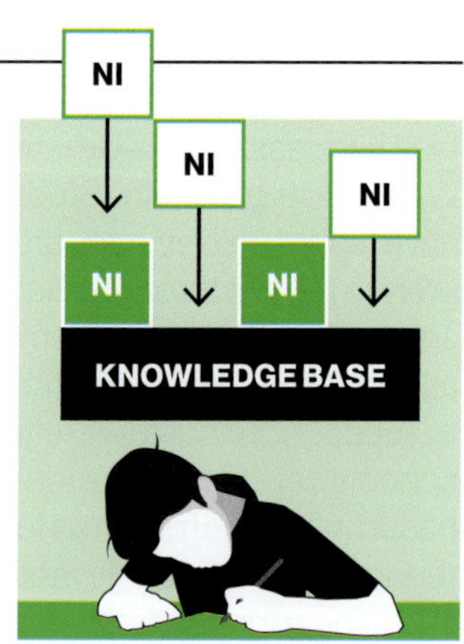

READ MORE: *Why Knowledge Matters* by E. D. Hirsch

AN EXAMPLE SEQUENCING OF A KNOWLEDGE-RICH CURRICULUM FOR KS3 ENGLISH (UK)

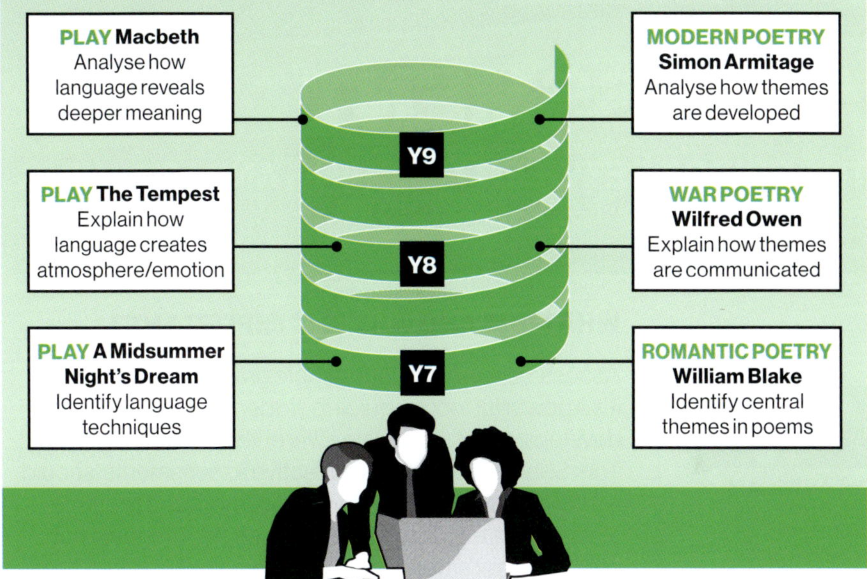

SEQUENCE KNOWLEDGE: Subjects should sequence content so that lessons build on one another in small, manageable steps with opportunities for students practice after each step (Rosenshine, 2012). This helps students avoid cognitive overload and retain information in long-term memory. Knowledge coherence across subjects also enhances learning by connecting key disciplinary ideas (Surma et al, 2025). For instance, studying war poetry in English alongside WWI in history.

BALANCE CORE AND THE 'HINTERLAND':
In addition to core knowledge, Tom Sherrington advocates for the inclusion of what he calls 'hinterland' knowledge – contextual information that enriches the curriculum alongside the core material to be taught. This broader context helps students engage more deeply with the material by providing opportunities and experiences that give meaning to the foundational knowledge. For study of *Animal Farm*, the hinterland could involve studying the Russian Revolution and the rise of totalitarianism.

PAUL KIRSCHNER

As students develop more complex schemas, they are increasingly able to recognise links between pieces of information and understand how concepts are related.

(Chi et al, 1981; Kirschner at al, 2020 from AERO guide)

SCHOOL CULTURE PRINCIPLES

ASSESSMENT

THE BRIDGE BETWEEN TEACHING AND LEARNING

DYLAN WILIAM

Assessment provides the link between teaching and learning. As such, it should be part of every lesson that teachers plan.

WHAT IS IT AND WHY IS IT IMPORTANT?

Assessment is more than simple grading and reporting; it's a powerful tool for guiding student learning and developing metacognitive awareness. According to Tom Sherrington (2021a), effective assessments 'should reinforce standards, guide improvement and promote student agency'. This means assessments should not only test what students know (summative) but also provide actionable feedback, helping them understand their strengths and areas for improvement (formative). Assessment should include self-reflection and encourage students to set meaningful goals that support their progress. When assessments are embedded thoughtfully, they build confidence and motivation and create a cycle of learning and growth.

HOW DO WE IMPLEMENT IT?

FORMATIVE ASSESSMENT:

Formative assessment plays a central role, providing teachers with continuous insights into students' progress towards mastering the curriculum and developing independence. Most assessment should be formative and give actionable feedback on how to improve. This type of assessment allows teachers to adjust instruction in real time, meeting students where they are and addressing gaps in knowledge before moving forward.

MORE FORMATIVE THAN SUMMATIVE

80%	20%

READ MORE: *Student Assessment* by Dylan Wiliam, Doug Fisher and Nancy Frey

LONG CYCLE	MEDIUM CYCLE	SHORT CYCLE
Measures...	Measures...	Measures...
student progress towards mastery of curriculum standards.	**progress towards mastery of focused unit goals.**	**student understanding during instruction to inform decisions.**
6–10 WEEKS OR MORE Common formative assessments, interim and benchmark assessments.	**2–6 WEEKS** Practice tests, short responses linked to unit goals or success criteria.	**REAL TIME** Checks for understanding (exit tickets, questioning, whole class responses).

FORMATIVE ASSESSMENT CYCLES: We assess to make our teaching more responsive to our students' learning needs, increase student engagement and strengthen our students' memories. Wiliam et al (2024) have developed a structured time frame that teachers can use to gather evidence with and from students, enabling them to make more informed instructional decisions.

SHARED LANGUAGE FOR SCHOOL ASSESSMENT INSPIRED BY MICHAEL CHILES (2024)

PURPOSE	Assessment must test the knowledge learned in the curriculum.
MEANINGFUL	Assessment must be connected to core knowledge of each subject.
CUMULATIVE	Assessment must check for knowledge retention over time.
RELIABLE	Assessment must generate data to move learners forward.

ALTERNATE THE ZONES: When designing assessment opportunities, it's important to balance what Briceño (Ted at Work, 2023) calls the learning zone and performance zone. The learning zone is a low-stakes environment where students focus on skill development, practice and learning from mistakes. In contrast, the performance zone is where students apply what they have learned in high-stakes settings, such as exams. Developing a balanced assessment approach means dedicating ample time to the learning zone, ensuring students are prepared for success.

THE LEARNING ZONE

Focus on growth

Making mistakes

Deliberate practice of skills

Seeking feedback

THE PERFORMANCE ZONE

Execution under pressure

Showcasing competence

Producing tangible results

Applying expertise

SCHOOL CULTURE PRINCIPLES

MASTERY LEARNING

BUILD FLUENCY, INDEPENDENCE & AUTOMATICITY

WHAT IS IT AND WHY IS IT IMPORTANT?

Learning occurs when information is encoded into long-term memory. Through repeated practice, students can achieve automaticity – where knowledge or skills are so well ingrained that they can be recalled and applied effortlessly. When students build extensive, schemas (networks of knowledge), they can access and use this information with greater efficiency (Tse et al, 2007). Mastery learning supports this by structuring units of work so that each set of tasks focuses on a specific learning objective, requiring students to master each task before moving on. Research by the EEF (2021b) indicates that mastery learning can lead to significant gains, adding an average of five months' progress over a year.

KURT ENGELMANN

Mastery itself leads to faster learning as students have a solid basis of acquiring new skills and knowledge. (2024)

HOW DO WE IMPLEMENT IT?

CONSOLIDATE LEARNING: Moving information from working memory to long-term memory is known as consolidation. This process is best achieved by providing students with ample time for guided and independent practice. Mastery learning approaches are normally implemented over the course of an academic year, as taking more time with a topic or scheme of work requires flexibility in curriculum planning. Spacing practice over time, rather than cramming, also allows students to revisit material to strengthen memory retention.

READ MORE: *Explicit Instruction* by Anita Archer and Charles Hughes

CHUNK TASKS WITH SPECIFIC LOs: Identify clear learning objectives that students need to achieve and break skills down into chunks. Design lesson activities that explicitly teach the necessary skills in and understandings needed for mastery. During each task, clearly communicate the learning objective and model what mastery looks like. Sequencing these tasks in a logical progression ensures that each one builds on previously learned objectives.

GIVE IMMEDIATE AFFIRMATIVE AND CORRECTIVE FEEDBACK: Formative assessment is key for achieving mastery as it helps track student progress after each task. An effective way of doing this is by informing students whether the answer is correct or incorrect and what can be done to improve future performance (Hattie et al, 2007). Affirm correct responses and address misconceptions by giving corrective feedback during instruction.

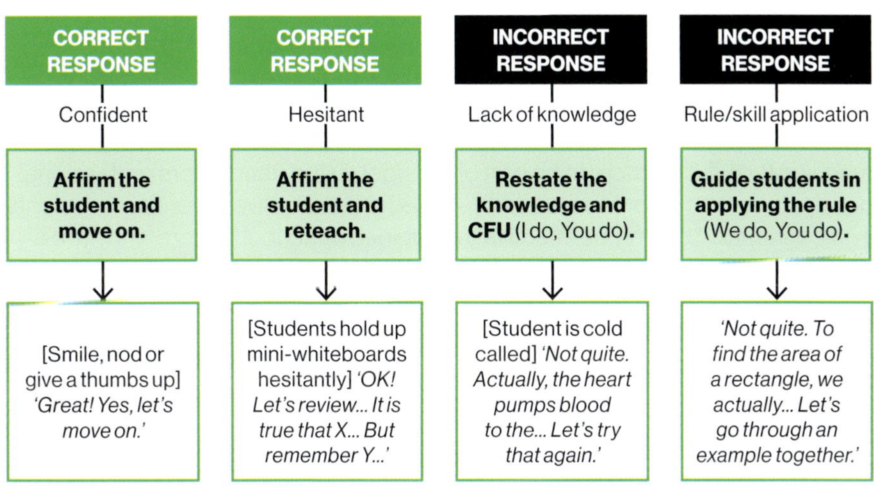

TYPES OF FEEDBACK BY ANITA ARCHER AND CHARLES HUGHES (2011)

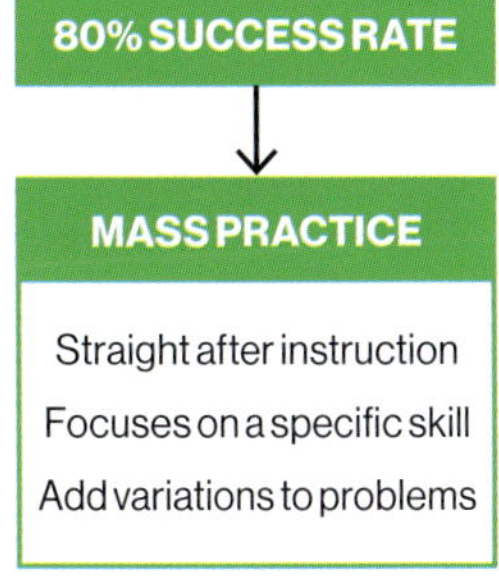

ALLOW TIME FOR INDEPENDENT PRACTICE: Once a skill or concept has been modelled and at least an 80% success rate has been achieved, implement an initial mass practice opportunity. Mass practice is done straight after instruction and allows all students to attempt a single skill or procedure with lots of different example-problems. This helps students to consolidate their skills so they become concrete and stick firmly in long-term memory.

SCHOOL CULTURE PRINCIPLES

PROFESSIONAL DEVELOPMENT

DEVELOPING AN EVIDENCE-INFORMED CULTURE

WHAT IS IT AND WHY IS IT IMPORTANT?

The recent surge in educational research has significantly transformed the teaching practices of many educators. The EEF (2021a) explain, 'The quality of teaching is not fixed: teachers can be improved, and they can be improved via effective professional development.' To continue growing and refining your teaching toolkit, it is crucial to be part of a school culture that fosters professional development and embraces research-based ideas. The five essential ingredients in this summary can only be effectively combined by school leaders who have a clear strategic vision and framework committed to teacher development.

SARAH COTTINGHATT

A teacher with a good understanding of how we learn can better understand the problems they are trying to solve and choose better solutions that are more likely to lead to learning. (2022a)

HOW DO WE IMPLEMENT IT?

COMMON GOALS: Establishing a strong evidence-informed culture requires a shared understanding between everyone working within the school. Staff should clearly define and communicate what constitutes effective teaching and the principles guiding it. For instance, a school-wide commitment to high challenge might focus PD on lesson design regarding key research; for example, Bjork and Bjork's concept of 'desirable difficulties' in relation to retrieval practice activities (2011).

SCHOOL PD GOAL

For example...

We expect excellence from **ALL** students, setting high challenges that make learning challenging and promotes hard thinking.

This informs...

PD FOCUS AREA: Desirable difficulties

READ MORE: 'Effective Professional Development Guidance Report' by the EEF

KNOW HOW LEARNING HAPPENS: True evidence-informed teaching requires educators to grasp how learning occurs, drawing on cognitive science models like Daniel Willingham's 'Simple Memory Model'. Understanding cognitive aspects, such as the limits of working memory and how long-term memory works, enables teachers to apply research with nuance and insight.

BUILD TRUST AND AUTONOMY: Fostering an environment that encourages educators to share challenges and learn together is essential. Building a culture where professional relationships prioritise development over accountability enhances growth. Activities such as instructional coaching, edu-book clubs and informal classroom visits promote trust and collaboration. Implementing a coaching programme, for instance, should address teachers' individual needs, allowing them autonomy over key strategies to meet their goals.

TAILOR YOUR SCHOOL PD:
Professional development must be customised to the specific needs and challenges faced by each school. This ensures that strategies are both based on evidence and directly applicable to classroom issues. For instance, PD sessions might focus on integrating formative feedback to bridge learning gaps in specific year groups, employing methods like whole-class feedback to reduce teacher workload. These strategies necessitate ongoing assessment and fine-tuning so that PD evolves in response to its effectiveness over time.

AGREE ON THE STRATEGIES:
Teachers informed by evidence develop a variety of key teaching strategies that reflect the school's strategic goals. These strategies should be research-backed yet flexible, allowing for customisation to fit individual teaching styles and the needs of different classrooms. For instance, to enhance accountable questioning, Mr Smith may use 'cold calling' but also lets students write down their responses first, reducing stress and fostering a supportive atmosphere. Schools should create their own evidence-informed guides and 'playbooks'.

SCHOOL CULTURE PRINCIPLES

SUPPORTING SEND

BUILD A PREDICTABLE LEARNING ENVIRONMENT

BECKY FRANCIS

The evidence tells us that teachers should instead prioritise familiar but powerful strategies, like scaffolding and explicit instruction, to support their pupils with SEND. (2020)

WHAT IS IT AND WHY IS IT IMPORTANT?

Building a positive school culture is essential for ensuring that all students, including those with special educational needs and disabilities (SEND), feel supported and able to thrive. Research from the EEF (2020) explains that consistent and predictable routines play a crucial role in reducing anxiety for students with SEND, as they provide a sense of safety and help students anticipate what will happen next. Clear expectations help students feel secure so they can focus. Inconsistent routines can lead to frustration and heightened anxiety, undermining students' ability to focus and progress. By maintaining stable routines, teachers build a predictable environment that empowers students with SEND to succeed confidently in both behaviour and task completion.

WHAT DOES RESEARCH FROM THE EEF (2020) SAY?

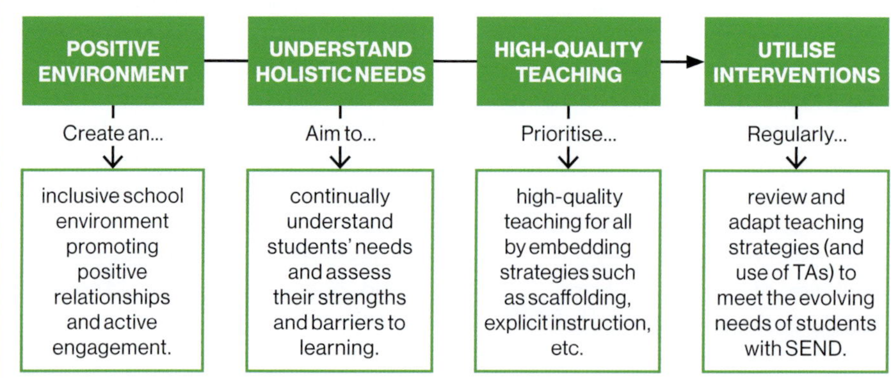

READ MORE: *A Little Guide for Teachers: SEND in Schools* by Amjad Ali

HOW DO WE IMPLEMENT IT?

FOCUS ON HIGH-QUALITY TEACHING: High-quality teaching is the foundation for supporting SEND students. According to the EEF, good teaching for SEND students involves using evidence-based strategies like scaffolding and explicit instruction. Teachers should incorporate flexible grouping, cognitive strategies like dual coding, and metacognitive strategies, such as prompting students to reflect on their learning processes. These approaches are effective not only for SEND students but for all learners.

PROVIDE TARGETED INTERVENTIONS: Small-group or one-on-one support can significantly improve learning outcomes. Select interventions based on thorough assessments of students' needs and ensure that these programmes are integrated with classroom learning. During interventions use the following effective and practical strategies:

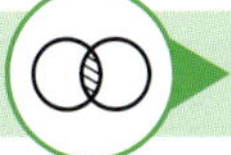

VERBALISE YOUR THOUGHTS	INVITE THEM TO REPEAT	BREAK THE MATERIAL DOWN	DO GROUP INTERVENTION
When modelling, explain your thinking out loud as you go.	Ask the student(s) to repeat your instructions back to you.	Present work in chunks and plan to revisit prior learning.	Break students into small groups depending on their needs.

USE COMPARATIVES	USE GRAPHIC ORGANISERS	LEVERAGE ASSISTIVE TECH	ADJUST THE ENVIRONMENT
Compare similar or opposing ideas using vocabulary and visuals.	Plan using visual scaffolds, concept maps and card sorts.	Use digital tools like text-to-speech to reduce cognitive load.	Plan for noise management, seating and make sensory areas.

CULTIVATE A POSITIVE LEARNING CULTURE: Research (EEF, 2020) shows that a consistent, supportive environment helps SEND students feel secure and confident in their learning. A structured routine reduces anxiety, especially for students with communication and interaction difficulties. Teachers can foster this environment by using clear, predictable language and promoting positive relationships; seating adjustments and noise management, for example, can improve focus and participation in lessons.

SCHOOL CULTURE PRACTICES

ROUTINES

INVEST TIME TO BUILD LASTING HEALTHY HABITS

DOUG LEMOV

Routines give students a clear model of how to execute common tasks successfully and clear working memory for high-order tasks.

WHAT IS IT AND WHY IS IT IMPORTANT?

A routine is a sequence of actions triggered by a specific cue, occurring with minimal cognitive effort. Research shows that forming a habit takes about 66 days of consistent repetition within a stable context, although simpler actions may become automatic sooner (Gardner et al, 2012). In the classroom, consistent routines – such as signalling for attention or using mini-whiteboards for whole-class responses – allow students to internalise behaviours more quickly. This helps to free up space in working memory so that students can focus cognitive attention on learning. Schools should invest time to strengthen routines by having all staff use the same procedures, cues and action sequences.

HOW DO I IMPLEMENT IT?

INTRODUCE ROUTINE TYPES: Doug Lemov (2021) outlines three types of routine central to helping students internalise actions and form shared habits. Ultimately, when such routines are automated, students can save their cognitive energy for engaging with the material rather than the process of learning.

ACADEMIC ROUTINES	PROCEDURAL ROUTINES	CULTURAL ROUTINES
Enable students to properly engage in learning activities.	**Enable students to manage class materials and transitions.**	**Enable students to feel they belong through shared values and norms.**
Cold Calling, Think-Pair-Share, Choral Response	Do Now, Threshold, Exiting Class, Mini-Whiteboards	SLANT/STAR, Peer Feedback, Active Listening

READ MORE: *The Teaching and Learning Playbook* by Michael Feely and Ben Karlin

HOW PROCEDURES ARE USED TO CREATE FAMILIAR ROUTINES (LEMOV, 2021)

SYSTEM: CHECK ALL STUDENTS' UNDERSTANDING

PROCEDURE 1	PROCEDURE 2	PROCEDURE 3	PROCEDURE 4	PROCEDURE 5
Cue attention (*'1,2,3', 'Eyes on me.'*)	Pose question (*'What is the name of...'*)	Give think time (*'You have 20 seconds to...'*)	Give write time ('Write and hide your answer').	Show answers (*'Show me in 3, 2, 1...Go!'*)

BECOMES ROUTINE: SHOW ME (MINI-WHITEBOARDS)

PRACTISE THE PROCESS: In *Teaching One-Pagers,* we looked at introducing and embedding routines by providing a clear rationale and explicitly teaching them to students. Another crucial element to note is that deliberate practice can foster automaticity (Feldon, 2007). Do this by breaking down the routines and practising each procedure in isolation. Provide actionable feedback throughout.

FOSTER BELONGING: Peps Mccrea (2024b) explains routines 'act as a collective ritual which can foster belonging'. In other words, they make students feel safe. Lemov's 'Threshold' routine emphasises the importance of belonging because it involves teachers standing at the door to greet students as they enter, building rapport and setting clear expectations before they even step into the classroom. Warmly address them by name and remind them of the first steps upon entry: '*Morning, Holly. Sit down quietly and start the Do Now. Thank you.*'

ACKNOWLEDGE AND PRAISE: Teachers can support students in understanding and successfully following classroom routines by providing specific praise about expected behaviours. Acknowledge when expectations have been met and use praise when expectations have been exceeded. 'Brilliant job, everyone. I am very pleased with how you entered.' (AERO, 2023a)

JAMES CLEAR

You start to realise how much a product of your environment any human is, and so if you can prime the environment to make the next action easy, then you put yourself in a much better position. (2023)

SCHOOL CULTURE PRACTICES

CLASSROOM MANAGEMENT 1

PRINCIPLES AND ROUTINES FOR BEHAVIOUR

WHAT IS IT AND WHY IS IT IMPORTANT?

Effective classroom management is the bedrock of a positive and productive school culture. When teachers consistently implement routines, use consistent language and develop high expectations, they create an environment where learning can thrive. By managing behaviour effectively, teachers reduce disruptions, increase student engagement and promote respect, all of which help create a calm and focused classroom. Schools can build a consistent classroom management culture using strong principles, tools and routines.

HOW DO I IMPLEMENT IT?

1. **CRACKING BEHAVIOUR IS A CODE**
   Identify factors influencing each student's behaviour.
2. **DEVELOP EFFECTIVE HABITS**
   Build and deliberately practise classroom management routines.
3. **START WITH HIGH EXPECTATIONS**
   Set firm behavioural standards from day one.
4. **MASTER YOUR OWN BEHAVIOUR**
   Stay calm and consistent in your own emotions and actions.
5. **BEHAVIOUR IS A CURRICULUM**
   Plan and model behaviour just like you would with academic content.
6. **IT'S WHAT YOU SAY AND HOW!**
   Take note of your tone, posture and non-verbal signals.
7. **SUCCESS IS THE BEST MOTIVATOR**
   Break tasks into steps and check for understanding to foster success.
8. **SEEK EXAMPLES OF EXCELLENCE**
   Observe and learn from high-performing teachers.
9. **LET THEM KNOW THEY MATTER**
   Create an environment of support and trust so students feel they belong.
10. **BANK POSITIVITY WITH STUDENTS**
    Actively build positive relationships through praise.

READ MORE: *The Classroom Management Handbook* by Mark Dowley and Ollie Lovell

ENTRY ROUTINES: A well-established entry routine is essential for creating a calm, organised and focused classroom environment. This routine involves teachers greeting students at the door with a friendly welcome, setting a positive tone right from the start. As students enter, they are provided with clear, concise instructions about what to do next, whether it's beginning a Do Now activity or preparing materials for the lesson. Teachers should narrate and praise students who follow the instructions promptly, reinforcing positive behaviours. This process ensures students are prepared to engage and ready to start learning without delay.

OLLIE LOVELL

Classroom management is about... consistent routines, high expectations and relationships. (Lovell et al, 2024)

DEFUSE DEBATES: When a student challenges a request, such as asking to put away headphones, teachers should avoid engaging in back-and-forth arguments. Instead, use partial agreement phrases like 'maybe so', to acknowledge the student without conceding the debate. Focus on primary behaviours and tactically ignore minor reactions like eye-rolling. Offer directed choices that provide the student with clear options for compliance. Say, 'You can either do X or [consequence]', while calmly restating the school expectations.

GAINING ATTENTION: Teachers should develop a consistent method for signalling when they need students to focus, whether it's using a verbal cue like 'eyes on me', a hand signal or a countdown. These signals should be practised and reinforced regularly so that students respond immediately and know exactly what is expected. By calmly waiting until everyone is attentive and using positive narration for those following instructions, teachers create a focused, respectful and calm learning environment.

TIGHT TRANSITIONS: Tight transitions between classroom activities are vital for minimising disruption and keeping the momentum of learning. To achieve this, teachers should clearly communicate what students need to do, how long they have to transition and what the next task involves. Rehearsing this process using visual timers or countdowns helps create urgency without stress, while narrating and acknowledging students who transition efficiently can reinforce positive behaviour.

SCHOOL CULTURE PRACTICES

CLASSROOM MANAGEMENT 2

PRINCIPLES AND ROUTINES FOR BEHAVIOUR

MARK DOWLEY

We have distilled key behaviour management principles and provided the tools and routines needed to create a calm... classroom. (Dowley and Lovell, 2024)

WHAT IS IT AND WHY IS IT IMPORTANT?

Consistent classroom management nurtures safety and belonging, encouraging students to take risks and move beyond their comfort zones. Bill Rogers (2024) explains that effective behaviour management requires teachers to establish clear, respectful boundaries while consistently holding students accountable: 'Building a positive classroom environment is about more than just setting rules; it's about fostering mutual respect.' This involves using precise, assertive language that prompts reflection rather than compliance. Structured routines and clear expectations can help to establish a calm atmosphere where positive relationships can thrive.

HOW DO I IMPLEMENT IT?

School-wide tools and routines can enhance classroom culture, even if not perfectly executed, ultimately boosting student learning (Gill et al, 2016).

PRIMARY NOT SECONDARY	**Focus on the primary behaviour you want. Ignore secondary behaviour.** *'I've been clear about your behaviour, Jon.'* [e.g. tactically ignore eye rolling]
NARRATED COUNT	**A count with descriptions of behaviour.** *'Listening in 3, pens down, 2, all eyes on me in...1.'*
ATTENTIONAL CUE	**A cue or routine used to quickly and efficiently gain attention.** *Teacher: '1, 2', Students: 'Eyes on you.'*

READ MORE: *Classroom Behaviour* by Bill Rogers

PLANNED AND CLEAR INSTRUCTION: The key to improving student behaviour is helping them succeed through clear, explicit instruction. This approach involves breaking down complex tasks into manageable steps, using structured routines, and incorporating frequent checks for understanding. By providing clear expectations and scaffolding students' efforts, teachers create an environment where students are more likely to experience success. This success builds confidence and, in turn, motivation, creating a positive classroom atmosphere that supports learning and engagement.

MOVING A STUDENT: When proactive strategies fail, moving a disruptive student to a new seat is an effective way to maintain classroom order. Begin by using descriptive and direct language, clearly explaining the behaviour that needs to stop. Offer a directed choice, allowing the student to either remain in their seat quietly or move. If the behaviour persists, calmly instruct the student to move, using partial agreement to deflect excuses and allow take-up time for compliance, setting a timer if needed. Ignore minor disruptions, like sighing, and acknowledge positive behaviour once the student complies. Escalate further if necessary.

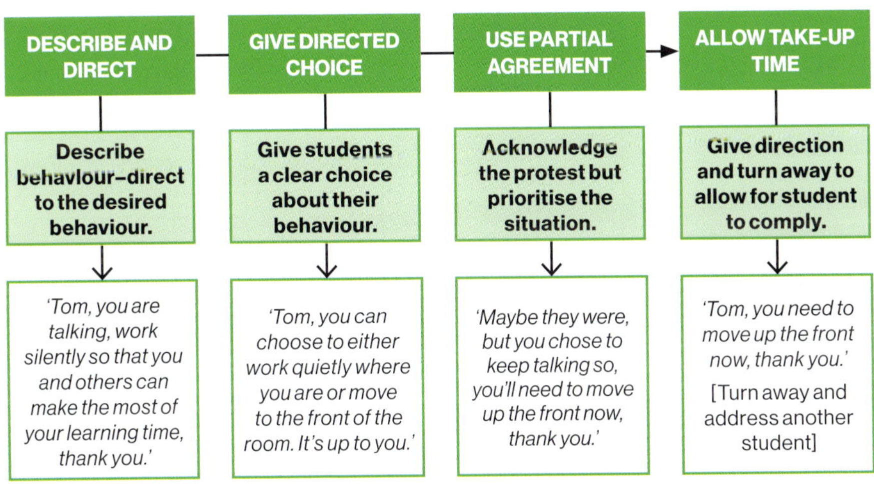

AFTER CLASS CONVERSATIONS: If a pattern of poor behaviour arises or there is a significant incident, a follow-up conversation after class can be essential. These conversations serve three key purposes: to provide students with an opportunity to reflect on their behaviour; clarify the standards that need to be met; and maintain a positive relationship. By using techniques like partial agreement and guiding students through reflection on the impact of their behaviour, teachers can help students and commit to better behaviour.

SCHOOL CULTURE PRACTICES

POSITIVE BEHAVIOURS

ON-THE-SPOT BEHAVIOUR MANAGEMENT MAP

BILL ROGERS

Behaviour leadership involves guiding students rather than controlling them. Stay calm, clear, and consistent and recognise that positive behaviour is as crucial as addressing negative behaviour. (TES Magazine, 2017)

BEHAVIOUR 1
TALKING

Students talking over the teacher.

Always use...

POSITIVE LANGUAGE

Give clear and respectful directions and corrections and expect compliance:

'Settling down now, everyone. Thank you.'

'Let's focus now. I need everyone to have their pens down and eyes this way. Thanks.'

Utilise... (→ Partial agreement)

Ensure to use...

DESCRIPTIVE LANGUAGE

Affirm desired behaviours and *describe* any unwanted behaviours:

DO SAY: *'A number of students are talking.'*

DO NOT SAY: *'Why are you still talking, Mason?'*

If necessary... (→ Take-up time)

BEHAVIOUR 2
RUDENESS

Student answers back or argues.

Always use...

PARTIAL AGREEMENT

Use phrases like when/then, maybe/but:

'Maybe you weren't talking but I need you two on task. Thanks.'

If necessary give...

TAKE-UP TIME

Take your eyes off the student, move away and give them time to take up your direction.

If necessary...

TACTICALLY IGNORE

Unless serious, tactically ignore secondary behaviours such as sighing, eye rolling, tutting, etc.

READ MORE: The ERRR Podcast #031 Featuring Bill Rogers by Ollie Lovell

HOW DO I IMPLEMENT IT?

Renowned educator Bill Rogers, known for his practical and effective strategies, reframes traditional approaches by focusing on low-stakes, relationship-building methods that foster a positive learning environment. His techniques emphasise guiding students towards behavioural awareness and self-regulation without escalating confrontations. This concept map outlines on-the-spot actions to take when behaviour issues arise.

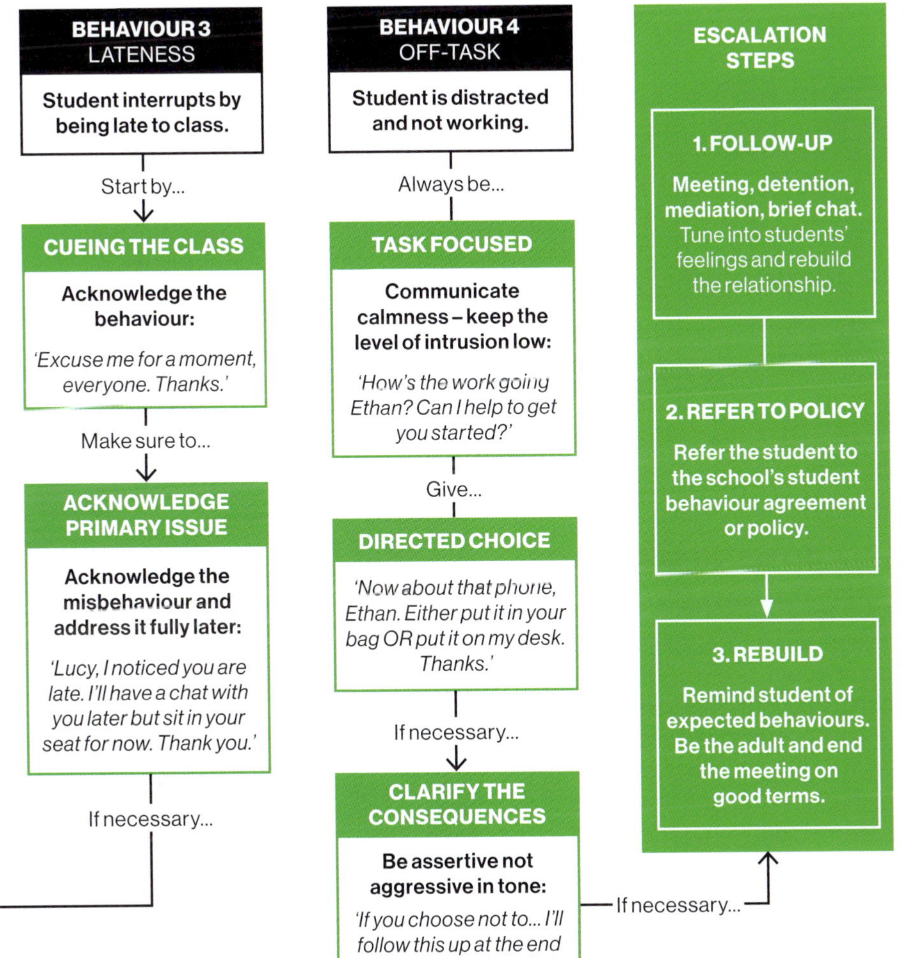

SCHOOL CULTURE PRACTICES

BUILDING TEAMS

ESTABLISH BELONGING, PURPOSE AND TRUST

SAM CROME

Effective teamwork leads to purpose, belonging, trust, learning, and, ultimately, high performance.

WHAT IS IT AND WHY IS IT IMPORTANT?

In his book *The Power of Teams*, author and educator Sam Crome (2023) explains that schools must strive to apply evidence-informed methods to create a thriving team culture. When built on psychological safety, trust and a shared purpose, school teams can achieve higher success, cohesion and wellbeing. To row seamlessly in the same direction, educators can codify traits of high-performing teams and apply it within a school context. These elements include goal setting, roles, communication and systems to help teams operate efficiently and thrive.

HOW DO WE IMPLEMENT IT?

FOLLOW THE PRINCIPLES:

Team building is an essential component in developing a school culture where vision and purpose are aligned and upheld. Sam Crome outlines five essential ingredients that are crucial to a team's ongoing success, all of which are actionable and grounded in evidence from education and industry.

1. **TEAM BELONGING**
   Psychological safety, belonging and trust
2. **TEAM ALIGNMENT**
   Purpose, values and goals
3. **TEAM OPERATIONS**
   Knowledge, roles, mental models, meetings
4. **TEAM DYNAMICS**
   Motivation, conflict, cohesion, wellbeing
5. **TEAM DEVELOPMENT**
   Learning, coaching, debriefs, leadership

READ MORE: *The Power of Teams* by Sam Crome

BUILD BELONGING: Belonging is key to creating effective, cohesive school teams and is the underpinning component of the model. A sense of belonging stems from psychological safety, trust and shared purpose. When teachers feel supported and valued, they are more likely to collaborate openly, take risk and invest in their roles. Cultivate this mindset and give colleagues autonomy to take risks and share their ideas – 'belonging before performance' (Crome, 2023).

ENSURE ALIGNMENT: Establishing a shared sense of purpose, values and goals helps guide the actions and decisions of teams. Over-communicate your shared vision and sense of purpose into your team's daily work to build motivation.

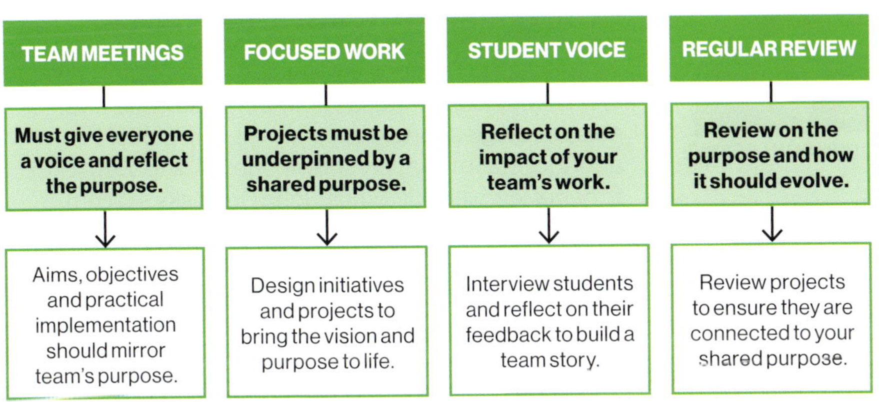

MAINTAIN OPERATIONS: Team members should build expertise related to their specific roles, as teams work better when everyone understands and shares their expert knowledge. Additionally, structure meetings effectively and ensure clear communication by using streamlined tools like Microsoft Teams or OneNote, which also promote sharing and collaboration.

ADDRESS TEAM DYNAMICS:
Develop autonomy and competence by supporting colleagues on their professional journeys to help build their motivation. Address conflicts constructively by promoting open, respectful dialogue and regularly check in on wellbeing by encouraging feedback and support.

SUPPORT TEAM DEVELOPMENT:
Successful teams are committed to learning and growing together (Eastwood, 2021). PD boosts morale and effectiveness. Schedule PD sessions on relevant skills and team goals, and encourage collaborative learning through peer coaching and reflective debriefs.

SCHOOL CULTURE PRACTICES

STUDY STRATEGIES

TEACH RESEARCH-BASED LEARNING STRATEGIES

JOHN DUNLOSKY

Teaching students how to learn is as important as teaching them content because acquiring both the right learning strategies and background knowledge is important – if not essential – for promoting lifelong learning.

WHAT IS IT AND WHY IS IT IMPORTANT?

As educators, it's important to guide students not only in what they learn but also in *how* they learn. Effective study strategies can significantly improve students' ability to retain and apply knowledge, leading overall to better learning outcomes. John Dunlosky's (2013) paper Strengthening the Student Toolbox unpacks this on a practical level because it outlines a set of effective strategies students can use. Establishing a healthy study culture is crucial for developing student independence. Schools should actively teach, promote and reinforce awareness of these strategies through school assemblies, parent information evenings, and pastoral care sessions. By integrating and embedding these effective learning strategies into the fabric of the school culture, we can help students develop strong study habits to support lifelong learning.

HOW DO I IMPLEMENT IT?

APPLY DIFFERENT STRATEGIES: Dunlosky categorises common learning strategies into three groups. While none of these strategies are inherently 'bad', some are more beneficial than others and are best suited for specific contexts.

MOST EFFECTIVE	PROMISING STRATEGIES	LESS USEFUL
Practice testing	Interleaving practice	Rereading and highlighting
Distributed practice	Elaborative interrogation	Summarisation
	Self-explanation	Key word mnemonic

READ MORE: *Dunlosky's Strengthening the Student Toolbox in Action* by Amarbeer Singh Gill

TEACH THE SIX EFFECTIVE STRATEGIES FOR LEARNING: Explicitly teaching learning strategies is an effective way of helping students to develop positive study habits so that they can retain information, understand complex concepts, and apply knowledge effectively. The Learning Scientists, a group of cognitive psychological researchers including Dr Yana Weinstein and Dr Megan Sumeracki (n.d.), emphasise that 'these strategies are effective because they are backed by decades of cognitive science research'.

DISTRIBUTED PRACTICE	RETRIEVAL PRACTICE	ELABORATION
Get students to spread out study sessions over time rather than cramming all at once.	Get students to actively recall information from memory, such as through self-quizzing.	Ask students to explain ideas in their own words and make connections between different ideas.

INTERLEAVED PRACTICE	CONCRETE EXAMPLES	DUAL CODING
Mix different topics or types of problems within a single study session to see inherent differences.	Use tangible examples to help students understand and remember abstract concepts.	Combine verbal information with visual elements, like diagrams or charts.

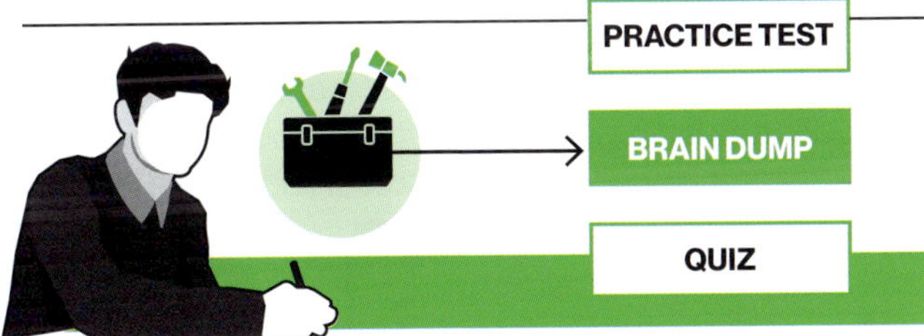

EMBED THE MOST EFFECTIVE STRATEGIES: Implementing retrieval practice, also known as practice testing, encourages consistent and effortful recall. Amarbeer Singh Gill (2024) emphasises the importance of starting with low-stakes quizzes or quick recall activities that allow students to retrieve information without the pressure of being graded. For example, begin lessons with a short retrieval exercise, where students write down everything they remember about a previously covered topic (brain dump). This can be followed by peer discussions or teacher feedback to correct any misunderstandings and reinforce correct information.

AMARBEER SINGH GILL

When you're using these strategies, it's not about labeling them; it's about understanding the problem you're trying to solve in your classroom and then choosing the right approach.

SCHOOL CULTURE PRACTICES

RESPONSIVE COACHING

EVIDENCE-INFORMED INSTRUCTIONAL COACHING

JOSH GOODRICH

Helping teachers to change... is not about simply giving teachers new things to do... but about successfully helping them to replace old habits with new ones.

WHAT IS IT AND WHY IS IT IMPORTANT?

Instructional coaching involves one teacher working with another teacher to help them take small, personalised steps to improve their practice (Steplab, 2022). It's often referred to as responsive coaching as it helps educators to develop and embed mental models and habits based on regular observation and feedback cycles with incremental 'action steps'. This method is focused on the following core ingredients used by coaches with teachers: *See it* (model the technique), *Name it* (name the strategy with concrete language), and *Do it* (using planning and rehearsal so it is successfully enacted) (Goodrich, 2024).

HOW DO I IMPLEMENT IT?

REMOVE THE BARRIERS: Building a great coaching programme requires tackling four barriers: creating an open environment for feedback; providing thorough training for coaches; designing efficient systems that fit the school's routine; and maintaining responsive leadership for ongoing improvement.

BUILDING CULTURE	Build trust with an open-door culture separate from managing performance.
TRAINING STAFF	Develop a shared vision of great teaching; train the coaches before.
SYSTEM DESIGN	Implement structures to support coaching (e.g. repurposed meetings).
RESPONSIVE LEADERSHIP	Collect and assess data, recognise effort, and expand the coaching team.

READ MORE: *Responsive Coaching* by Josh Goodrich

DIAGNOSE WITH QUESTIONS: For teachers to make meaningful progress, they need clear and precise guidance on their next steps. Responsive coaching involves asking diagnostic questions to assess the teacher's mental model. If their understanding is weak, use a more directive approach such as suggesting 'A good next step might be X'. If their mental model is partial or nearly there, ask guiding questions to help them refine their thinking. When the teacher shows a strong mental model, step back and allow them to proceed independently.

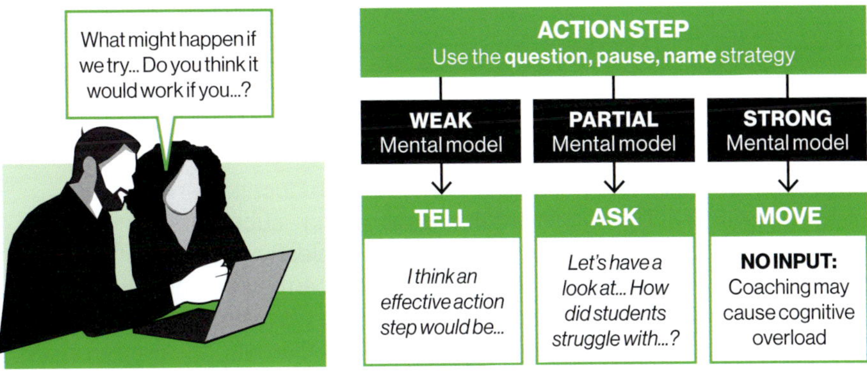

COLLECT EVIDENCE AND SET ACTION STEPS: Action steps are precise and granular changes teachers make to improve their practice. They are intentionally small because breaking down complex tasks into manageable chunks helps to free up working memory (Lovell et al, 2024). When coaching, it is important to focus suggested action steps on specific 'learning problems' and goals. Choosing action steps relies on evidence-based discussions. To move beyond general impressions, collect specific examples from the classroom, such as student work, observation notes, or recorded lessons.

USE IMPACT LANGUAGE: In coaching conversations, it's crucial to shift from opinion-based feedback to impact-focused language. This means replacing phrases like 'I loved how you did...' with 'It was effective when...' or 'What was the impact of...?' This approach centres the conversation on what benefits student learning rather than on pleasing the coach.

REHEARSE ACTION STEPS: Rehearsal enables teachers to practice in a low-stakes environment before implementing it in the classroom. Get teachers to repeat the step multiple times, and give feedback between each round. This allows them to refine their technique, build confidence and achieve mastery before facing the complexities of the actual classroom.

SCHOOL CULTURE PRACTICES

SEND AND WRITING

KEY STRATEGIES TO FREE-UP WORKING MEMORY

WHAT IS IT AND WHY IS IT IMPORTANT?

Writing can be challenging for students with special educational needs and disabilities (SEND). The cognitive demands of writing – such as recalling information, organising ideas, and communicating clearly – can overwhelm working memory. As Kellogg (2008) notes, writing can be as mentally taxing as playing a game of chess. When students struggle with tasks like spelling or handwriting, their working memory becomes overburdened, leaving less capacity for higher-level processes like planning and revising. By automating transcription skills, composition skills and executive function abilities, teachers can help free up students' working memory, enabling them to focus on content generation and self-regulation. This summary outlines strategies to support students with conditions such as dysgraphia, dyspraxia, dyslexia and ASD.

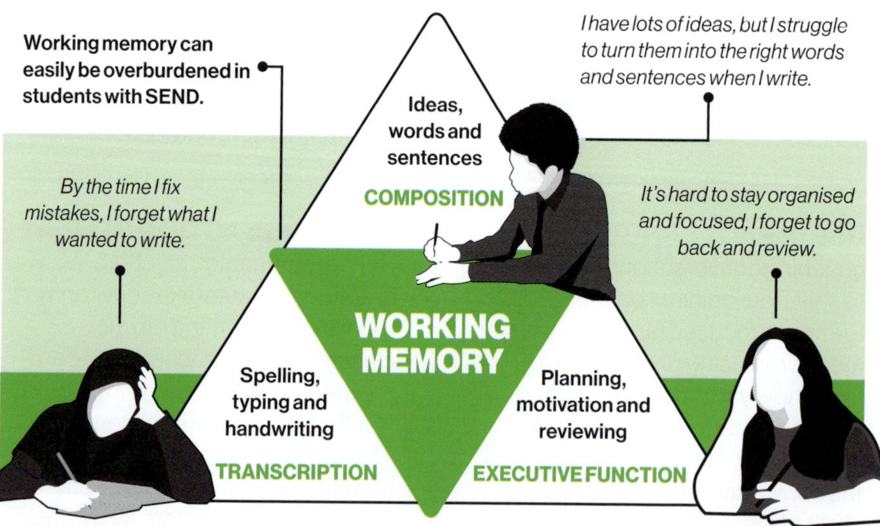

THE SIMPLE VIEW OF WRITING Diagram initially developed by Berninger et al (2002)

READ MORE: 'Special Educational Needs in Mainstream Schools Guidance Report' by the EEF

HOW DO WE IMPLEMENT IT?

STUDENTS WITH DYSGRAPHIA: Dysgraphia affects language and motor skills, causing challenges like difficulty forming letters, inconsistent spacing, poor pencil grip and illegible handwriting. To address these issues, implement strategies such as structured checklists, using assistive technologies, including 'text-to-speech' tools, and utilising AI-generated images and other visual aids to support comprehension and language expression.

MARTIN FERGUSON

Writing is a demanding process for pupils with SEND, requiring the integration of transcription, composition and executive function skills, which heavily tax working memory. Knowing reading age data helps tailor instruction to meet each pupil's specific needs and provide appropriate support.

STUDENTS WITH DYSPRAXIA: Dyspraxia affects motor skills, leading to difficulties with handwriting and coordination. Students may struggle with forming letters, holding a pencil and producing neat, legible writing. Dyspraxia often coexists with other learning differences, such as dysgraphia. Common signs include clumsiness and delayed hand dominance. To support students, teachers can provide sentence starters, allow extra time for writing tasks, use keyboards or word processors, and offer alternative methods for students to complete assignments without writing.

STUDENTS WITH DYSLEXIA: Dyslexia affects students' ability to process phonological information, making writing tasks difficult due to challenges with spelling, letter reversals and handwriting fluency. These difficulties slow the writing process and can impact the clarity of written expression. Effective strategies include breaking words into syllables, using multi-sensory tools like flashcards and reinforcing spelling rules with mnemonics.

STUDENTS WITH ASD: Students with autism spectrum disorder (ASD) often experience difficulties with written expression due to challenges with abstract thinking, imagination and perspective-taking. To guide the writing process, teachers can link writing tasks to their interests, provide story starters, use images for inspiration and employ tools like mind mapping, peer planning, modelled examples and scaffolds.

SUMMARY

One of the most crucial lessons from *The Learning Rainforest* is how schools can create the fertile conditions necessary for growth. Sherrington explains that these conditions are prerequisites for successful learning. By focusing on purpose, positive habits, relationships and well-structured curricula, schools can nurture a thriving school culture where both staff and students flourish. These principles serve as the 'roots' of a strong culture to help drive excellence and long-term success.

To make these ideas more accessible, I have condensed the key concepts into five straightforward takeaways (also visualised in the diagram opposite). These takeaways have inspired my own approach to leadership and influenced my classroom practice.

TAKEAWAY 1: CLEAR PURPOSE

Establish a shared sense of purpose that motivates staff and students, fostering belonging and driving excellence beyond external rewards.

TAKEAWAY 2: POSITIVE ATTITUDES AND HABITS

Cultivate curiosity, a passion for learning, and awe in the classroom to inspire a culture of excellence and lay the foundation for growth.

TAKEAWAY 3: RELATIONSHIPS AND ROUTINES

Develop mutual respect and high expectations through consistent behaviour routines to create a structured, supportive environment for everyone.

TAKEAWAY 4: CONTINUOUS ADAPTATION

Adopt a critical-responsive approach by observing, evaluating and adjusting actions based on input and feedback to align with the school's purpose.

TAKEAWAY 5: KNOWLEDGE-RICH CURRICULUM

Design well-structured, balanced curricula that build on prior knowledge, helping students to achieve mastery and create long-term memory schemas.

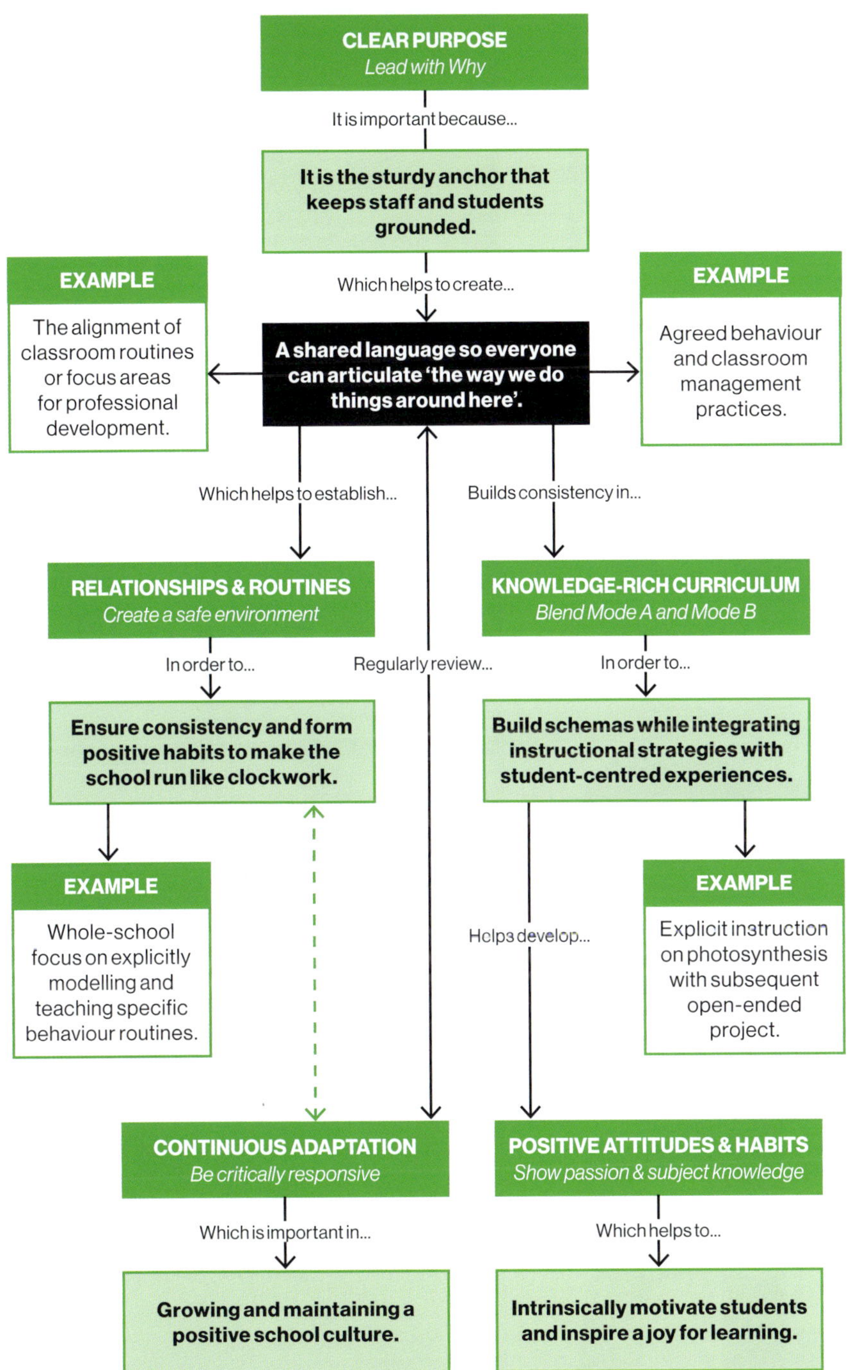
CLEAR PURPOSE
Lead with Why
It is important because...
It is the sturdy anchor that keeps staff and students grounded.
Which helps to create...
A shared language so everyone can articulate 'the way we do things around here'.
EXAMPLE
The alignment of classroom routines or focus areas for professional development.
EXAMPLE
Agreed behaviour and classroom management practices.
Which helps to establish...
Builds consistency in...
RELATIONSHIPS & ROUTINES
Create a safe environment
KNOWLEDGE-RICH CURRICULUM
Blend Mode A and Mode B
In order to...
Regularly review...
In order to...
Ensure consistency and form positive habits to make the school run like clockwork.
Build schemas while integrating instructional strategies with student-centred experiences.
EXAMPLE
Whole-school focus on explicitly modelling and teaching specific behaviour routines.
Helps develop...
EXAMPLE
Explicit instruction on photosynthesis with subsequent open-ended project.
CONTINUOUS ADAPTATION
Be critically responsive
POSITIVE ATTITUDES & HABITS
Show passion & subject knowledge
Which is important in...
Which helps to...
Growing and maintaining a positive school culture.
Intrinsically motivate students and inspire a joy for learning.

SCHOOL CULTURE

A series of strategic principles and practical strategies to help establish the conditions for growth.

MODE A TEACHING

A focused collection of evidence-based principles and practices designed to enhance classroom instruction

MODE B TEACHING

A set of practices that foster agency, collaboration and open-ended exploration to deepen and extend knowledge

READ MORE

Studies, books and blogs that are referenced throughout the one-pagers and inspired the collections

Teaching
one
Pagers
2
VOLUME

MODE A TEACHING

TEACHER-LED INSTRUCTION TO BUILD KNOWLEDGE

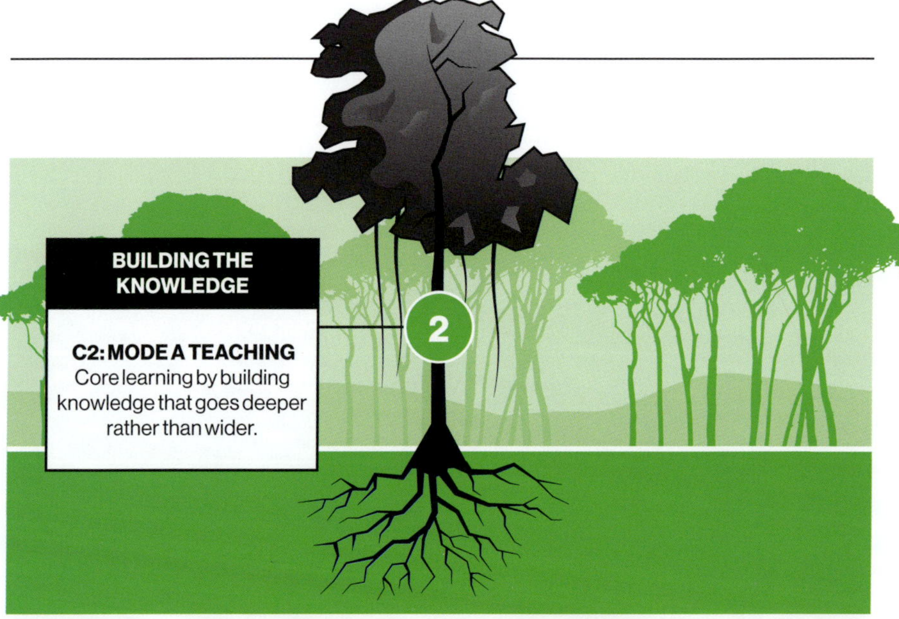

Does your classroom practice focus on structured, evidence-informed strategies that build knowledge, reduce cognitive load and ensure long-term student success?

Mode A teaching lies at the heart of Sherrington's *The Learning Rainforest*. Once a strong school culture is firmly rooted, Mode A provides the structure and strategies needed to build a solid foundation of knowledge and skills for students to thrive.

Essentially, Mode A defines teacher-led practices that promote thinking, reduce cognitive load and build schemas (networks of interconnected knowledge). If learning occurs when knowledge is transferred to long-term memory, then Mode A teaching is the engine that drives this process. Its emphasis on explicit instruction actively engages students through what I refer to as the 'expert teaching principles', which are: *challenge, explaining, modelling*, *questioning*, providing *feedback* and facilitating *practice*. These principles, highlighted in the first *Teaching One-Pagers*, are revisited and explored in greater depth throughout this collection.

Explicit teaching is critical for gradually guiding novice learners through the learning process, building fluency and developing independence. In their research, Kirschner et al (2006) explain: 'Novices benefit more from explicit instruction because it allows them to focus on learning the content rather than expending cognitive resources on discovering it themselves.' In other words, explicit teaching focuses attention and guides mental effort accordingly, providing students with the building blocks to construct solid knowledge structures.

Mode A teaching is anchored in a well-established body of research. The table below represents some of the most influential theories and principles from cognitive science that have influenced my own practice. They are a recommended starting point for teachers looking to become more 'evidence-informed'.

TOM SHERRINGTON

Beyond the early years, a lot of the time, if not most of the time, teachers are trying to teach specific knowledge and skills to their novice students. This requires good instructional methods; these are the staples of knowledge building in very many subjects and contexts: this is Mode A. (2018a)

CONCEPTS	KEY THINKERS	MAIN IDEAS
LEARNING AND MEMORY	Daniel T. Willingham's *Why Don't Students Like School?*	The important role of memory, attention and thinking to help teachers design effective instruction.
EXPLICIT INSTRUCTION	Barak Rosenshine's Principles of Instruction	Principles of effective teaching, focusing on clear explanations, guided practice and regular checks for understanding.
DESIRABLE DIFFICULTIES	Bjork and Bjork's Desirable Difficulties	Introducing challenges in the learning process enhances long-term retention, even if it feels harder at first.
COGNITIVE LOAD	John Sweller's Cognitive Load Theory	The brain processes and stores information, and the importance of minimising cognitive load to maximise learning.
FORMATIVE ASSESSMENT	Dylan Wiliam's Formative Assessment	The use of ongoing assessment to provide feedback, adjust teaching strategies and ensure that students are moving forward.

NATHANIEL SWAIN

When teachers start to teach in a way that incrementally guides students through the learning process, they systematically add knowledge, skills and tools to their students' mental toolboxes. (2024)

PAUL KIRSCHNER

Knowledge isn't merely the accumulation of disconnected or meaningless facts. When experts begin to master any domain... they acquire and construct interconnected and organised schemata of knowledge about that discipline. (2009)

Daniel Willingham's 'Simple Model of the Mind' visualised in the diagram on the opposite page, perfectly represents how learning occurs – and why it sometimes doesn't. In essence, the diagram shows that when students engage in hard thinking, they actively process information in *working memory*, which is finite and can only hold a small amount of information at once. When students think, they draw on prior knowledge stored in *long-term memory*, connecting it to new ideas and applying it meaningfully. This process builds schemas, which must be retrieved to ensure they are strengthened and permanently encoded.

Crucially, when working memory is overloaded, students struggle to process and retain new information. In my early days of teaching, I did this without even realising it by cramming PowerPoint slides with unnecessary visual decorations and too much text. The result of this was opposite to what I expected: disengaged faces and a stunted understanding of what was being taught.

Cognitive load theory is about maximising learning by designing instruction to account for the limits of students' working memory (Sweller, 1994). This means lessons must be deliberately designed to minimise extraneous cognitive load – removing distractions and unnecessary complexity – and focus on intrinsic cognitive load, the essential effort required to understand the content. Strategies such as chunking information and using worked examples are critical in helping students manage cognitive demands.

LIMITATIONS OF WORKING MEMORY BY AERO (2023b)

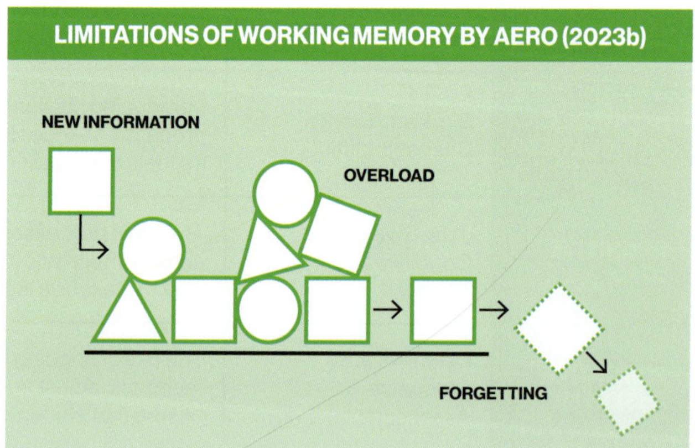

ADAPTED FROM OLIVER CAVIGLIOLI'S DIAGRAM 'THE SIMPLE MODEL OF THE MIND'

HOW LEARNING HAPPENS (AND SOMETIMES WHY IT DOES NOT)

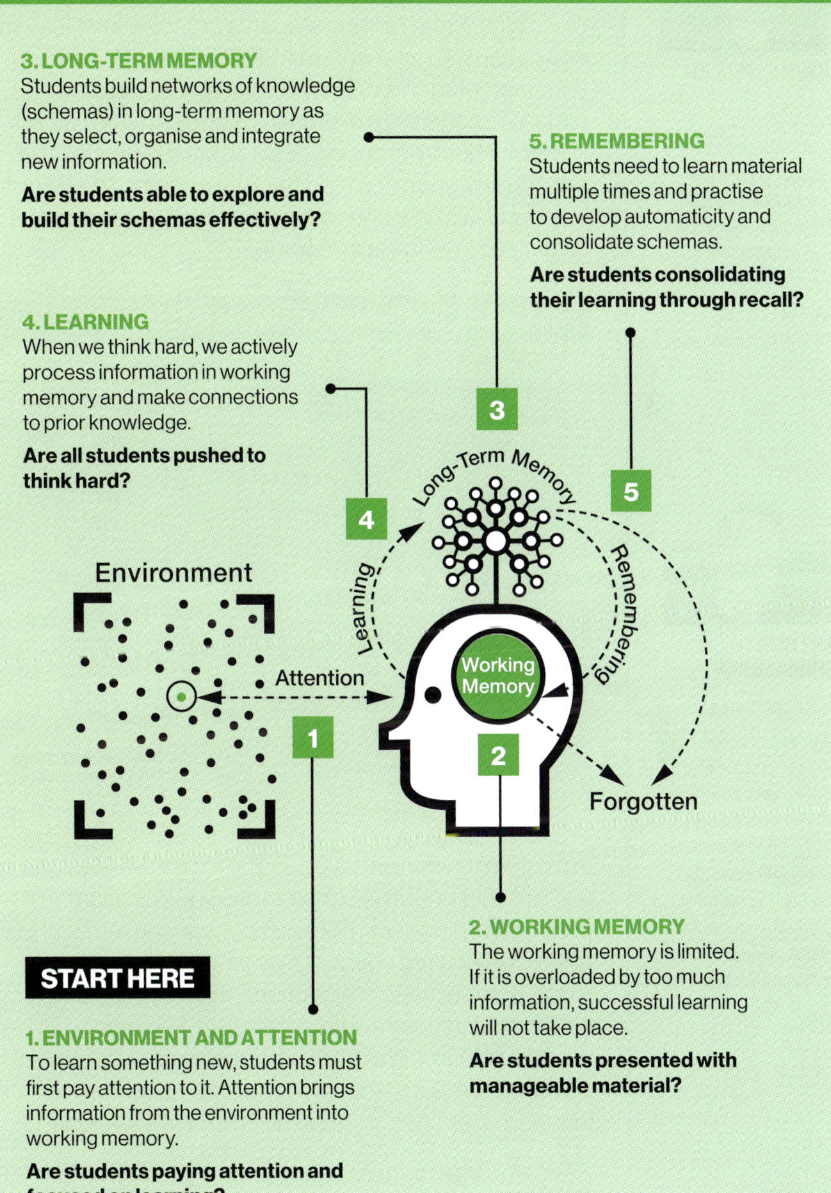

JOHN SWELLER

Instructional procedures that reduce cognitive load and enhance schema acquisition are essential for effective learning. (1988)

ARTHUR SHIMAMURA

Throughout the learning process it is critical to establish meaningful chunks of new information and relate them to existing knowledge... Psychologists refer to these knowledge structures as schemas. (2018)

Schemas are central to effective learning. These webs of connected knowledge in long-term memory help students easily relate and integrate new information. According to research, explicit (Mode A) teaching is more effective in helping students organise their learning into coherent frameworks (AERO, 2023b). By building schemas, students move from perceiving isolated facts to recognising relationships and patterns within a subject. This progression helps students transfer and apply knowledge across different contexts. The diagram below shows how connections are built, extended and organised in long-term memory.

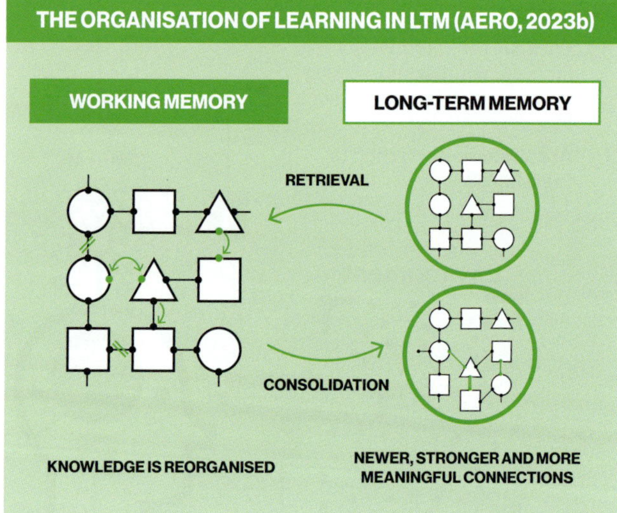

In my own teaching, I have seen how carefully designed lessons that prioritise schema-building can assist in making learning stick. For example, varying retrieval tasks and incorporating concept mapping into topics helps to strengthen these connections, making it easier for students to access and integrate their knowledge. When we design learning experiences that deliberately build schemas, we set students up for success, ensuring their learning is retained for application in new situations.

Research from cognitive science is a game-changer for teachers. It ensures teaching remains learning-focused rather than devolving into activity for activity's sake.

For me, the main takeaway from the research (in particular Willingham's 2021 work) is that teachers should design lessons that directly promote challenging cognitive work. No fluff, no distractions – just deliberate, purposeful teaching! This means reviewing each lesson with a focus on what the student is likely to think about. By identifying what students need to process in working memory, we can tailor the stepping stones required to achieve the desired outcomes.

Let's take a closer look at an example of how this might play out in a typical secondary school English class. Imagine the class are learning about the impact of rhetorical devices in persuasive speeches. The teacher might break this learning sequence into three blocks based on the following learning objective: identify rhetorical devices, analyse their use in a persuasive speech, and explain the effects these devices have on the audience.

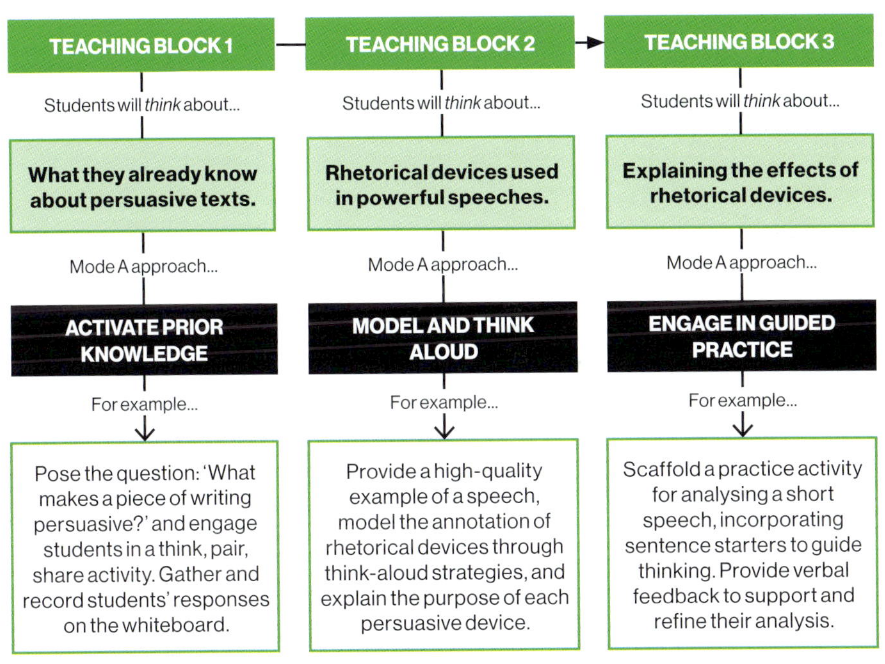

Every teacher needs to embed effective Mode A into their practice, as it's a universal requirement for effective teaching across all subjects in the curriculum. In **Collection 2: Mode A Teaching**, the one-pagers are structured into principles (overarching concepts) and practices (actionable classroom strategies). Each summary is crafted with the science of learning in mind, focusing on how to optimise learning by leveraging insights into human cognitive architecture.

PART 2/3

MYTHS AND TRUTHS

WHY ARE THESE MYTHS AND TRUTHS IMPORTANT?

Building deep knowledge is at the heart of the rainforest metaphor, serving as the essential framework for all learning. When students develop well-structured schemas (networks of interconnected information) they are better equipped to understand and retain new knowledge. Echoing the work of E. D. Hirsch, Cottingham (2022b) points out, 'If we've got really good prior knowledge of something, it acts like mental Velcro, allowing us to learn more quickly.' Mode A teaching is crucial for building foundational schemas. Here are some debunked myths about Mode A instruction, thinking and the importance of schema building.

DIRECT INSTRUCTION MAKES STUDENTS PASSIVE LEARNERS

PAULO FREIRE

Knowledge emerges only through invention and re-invention, through the restless, impatient continuing, hopeful inquiry human beings pursue in the world, with the world, and with each other. (1996)

MYTH: Teachers should not simply transmit knowledge for students to memorise and regurgitate. Educational theorist Paulo Freire argues against what he calls the 'banking model' of education, where students are seen as passive recipients of knowledge deposited by the teacher. Instead schools should base education around discussion, discovery and inquiry where students learn from their world, their experiences and each other.

TRUTH: The truth is that teacher-led instruction is highly effective. Research from cognitive science explains that the act of thinking plays a critical role in memory and learning – 'memory is the residue of thought' (Willingham, 2021). This means that what students think about during instruction directly influences what they remember. Mode A teaching involves strategies that engage students' cognitive attention and push them to think hard.

WE SHOULD TEACH TRANSFERABLE SKILLS

DANIEL WILLINGHAM

Research from cognitive science has shown that the sorts of skills that teachers want for students – such as the ability to analyse or think critically – require extensive factual knowledge. (2006)

MYTH: Schools should prioritise teaching transferable skills, such as critical thinking, problem-solving, and creativity, under the belief that they can be applied across all subjects. This perspective suggests that teaching generic skills independently of subject knowledge better prepares students for the real world, as these skills are timeless, unlike specific content knowledge.

TRUTH: In reality, teaching transferable skills in isolation is flawed. Research shows that skills like critical thinking are deeply tied to subject-specific background knowledge. Schools should focus on building a strong foundation of factual knowledge, as this enables students to apply critical thinking and problem-solving more effectively. Evidence-based practices, such as direct instruction and cumulative knowledge building, ensure that students can transfer and apply their skills effectively.

PROJECTS AND ACTIVITIES ARE THE BEST WAY TO LEARN

PAUL KIRSCHNER

Direct, strong instructional guidance is most often found to be superior to minimal guidance for teaching both basic and advanced skills. (et al, 2006)

MYTH: This belief suggests that hands-on, discovery and project-based learning helps students understand and retain information better than more traditional, teacher-led instruction. Advocates argue that engaging students in active projects promotes deeper learning and prepares them for real-world problem-solving.

TRUTH: Research shows that while projects and activities can be beneficial, they are not inherently the most effective way to teach new content. Kirschner et al state, 'Minimal guidance during instruction is significantly less effective and efficient than guidance specifically designed to support the cognitive processes necessary for learning.' The most effective strategies include direct instruction and methods that support how the brain processes information. Schools should prioritise Mode A practices and utilise Mode B opportunities selectively.

PART 2/3

THE LEARNING RAINFOREST

MODE A: BUILDING THE KNOWLEDGE STRUCTURE

TOM SHERRINGTON

Beyond the early years, a lot of the time, if not most of the time, teachers are trying to teach specific knowledge and skills to their novice students. This requires good instructional methods; these are the staples of knowledge building in very many subjects and contexts: this is Mode A. (2020)

WHAT IS IT AND WHY IS IT IMPORTANT?

At the heart of the learning rainforest metaphor is the importance of building interconnected knowledge (schemas) through structured, Mode A instructional teaching. Mode A centres on research-backed practices that emphasise teacher-led instruction, such as explaining concepts clearly, modelling thought processes, and demonstrating what success looks like. This also includes providing students with ample time to practise and build fluency, enabling them to independently solidify their knowledge and skills over time. Sherrington stresses that in his context, a 80% Mode A and 20% Mode B is the right balance. Teachers should adjust this according to their own contexts.

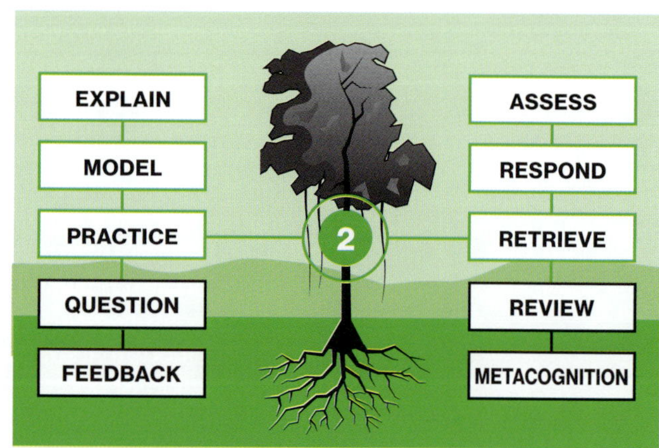

READ MORE: *Teaching WalkThrus* series by Tom Sherrington and Oliver Caviglioli

EXPLAIN, MODEL, PRACTICE: In this section, Sherrington underscores the importance of teachers having secure subject knowledge and the skill to explain concepts artfully, using techniques like storytelling, analogies and visuals. Great teachers, he argues, make their thought processes visible and carefully break down examples to support the limitations of students' working memory. Underpinning all of this is the necessity of guided practice, which helps students build fluency before they attempt tasks independently.

QUESTIONING AND CFU: Building knowledge requires effective strategies for checking for understanding (CFU), with Sherrington emphasising the use of questioning techniques to explore *what* students understand rather than simply *if* they do. Techniques like probing questions and think, pair, share are powerful tools for cognitively engaging all students in the learning process. Similarly, Sherrington advocates for whole-class response systems, such as mini-whiteboards, which allow teachers to instantly gather data on students' understanding across the class in a single hit.

QUESTION, FEEDBACK, ASSESS: Effective feedback is crucial in meeting the needs of learners, with Sherrington highlighting the value of specific verbal or written feedback that moves students forward. He highlights the importance of strategies and routines that support students in retaining information, ensuring it is embedded in long-term memory. Drawing on Rosenshine's principles, Sherrington emphasises the power of retrieval practice and structured reviews – daily, weekly and monthly – to make learning truly 'stick'. These ideas are explored in depth throughout Collection 2: Mode A, offering practical summaries and insights. Let's dive into these core principles and impactful practices!

MODE A PRINCIPLES

THE SCIENCE OF LEARNING

FOCUS PEDAGOGY ON COGNITIVE ARCHITECTURE

WHAT IS IT AND WHY IS IT IMPORTANT?

The 'science of learning' (SoL) studies how people learn and how to improve the learning process. The field combines ideas from psychology, neuroscience, education and cognitive science to understand the brain and how learning works in order to create better teaching strategies. Nathaniel Swain calls the recent SoL boom in schools an 'educational renaissance' because educators are embracing and transforming their instructional approaches by applying and refining evidence-based ideas in their classrooms. These practices take into account cognitive architecture and rely on explicit instruction, continuous checking for understanding and guided practice to help optimise learning.

DANIEL WILLINGHAM

Understanding is remembering in disguise. If you understand why a fact is true, you're more likely to remember that fact. (2021)

WHAT ARE THE MAIN PRINCIPLES?

EXPLICIT TEACHING: Explicit teaching is a fundamental aspect of SoL because it aligns with how the brain learns best. Stepping back too much in the learning process can lead to inequities, as cognitive overload halts learning while insufficient challenge leads to disengagement. Explicit instruction offers clear guidance, worked examples, and checking for understanding (CFU). Being aware of the forgetting curve is vital, and strategies like interleaving, spaced practice and retrieval practice are powerful. Techniques such as daily review, multiple-choice questions and 'Do Now' activities enhance retrieval and retention, with Rosenshine's principles emphasising frequent review of forgotten material at spaced intervals to ensure long-term retention.

READ MORE: *Harnessing the Science of Learning* by Dr Nathaniel Swain

ENCODING AND RETRIEVAL DIAGRAM INSPIRED BY AERO

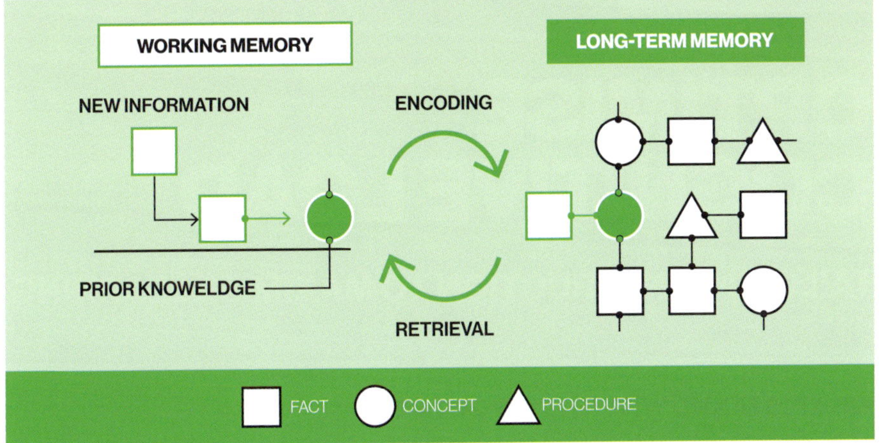

BUILDING SCHEMAS: Working memory is where learning starts – it processes new information and combines it with what students already know from long-term memory. But it has its limits: it can only hold information while students stay focused. Repeated exposure helps consolidate this new knowledge into long-term memory. Long-term memory is vast and interconnected, storing facts, skills and experiences that can be recalled and built upon. Teaching in small, manageable steps helps avoid overloading working memory, making it easier for students to consolidate learning.

NOVICES VS EXPERTS: The SoL highlights the crucial differences between novice and expert learners. Novices require explicit and detailed guidance, and frequent feedback to grasp new concepts and build foundational skills based on the limitations of working memory. On the other hand, experts benefit from opportunities to apply their deep understanding, engage in complex problem-solving, and extend their learning independently. Recognising these differences means educators can tailor their teaching approaches, ensuring novices receive the cognitive support they need while providing experts with the challenges that guide further growth and mastery of other knowledge and skills.

MODE A PRINCIPLES

OPTIMISE COGNITIVE LOAD

TAILORING INSTRUCTION TO MAXIMISE LEARNING

WHAT IS IT AND WHY IS IT IMPORTANT?

Cognitive load theory (CLT) explores how the cognitive load, or mental effort, required to process information impacts learning. To learn something new, knowledge must first be processed in working memory (WM) before being transferred and stored in long-term memory (LTM) in the form of 'schemas'. If WM is overloaded, there is a greater risk that the content being taught will not be understood by the learner. This knowledge of the human brain is critical for teachers because it helps to design instructional strategies that optimise the load on students' working memories to help maximise learning.

WHAT ARE THE MAIN PRINCIPLES?

Learning can be slowed down or even stopped if our WM is overloaded, such as when we have to process too much new information at once. To overcome this, we can achieve a cognitive balance by reducing extraneous load (bad cognitive load) as much as possible and optimise intrinsic load (good cognitive load).

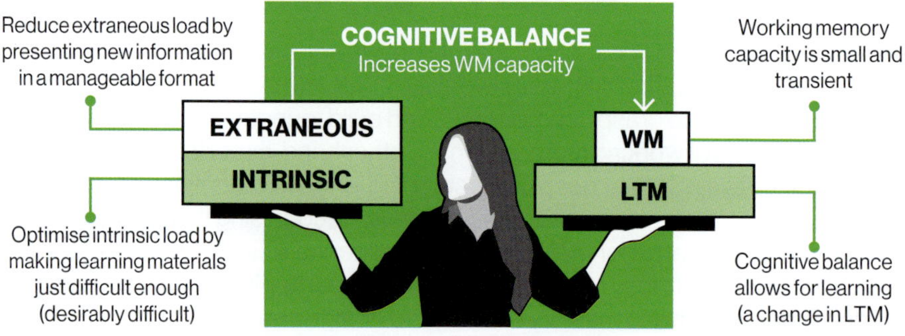

READ MORE: 'Cognitive Load During Problem Solving: Effects on Learning' by Professor John Sweller

WHY COGNITIVE OVERLOAD HAPPENS AND HOW TO OVERCOME IT (BUSCH ET AL, 2023)

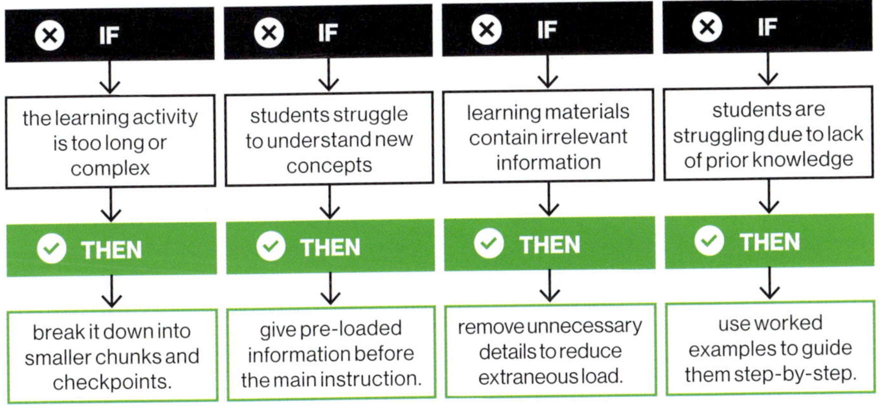

PRE-LOAD NEW INFORMATION: Pre-load new information by introducing key concepts and vocabulary before the main instruction. By familiarising students with foundational or important knowledge early on, pre-loading optimises intrinsic load and prepares them for more complex material, setting the lesson for deeper understanding and integration of new information. This can be done by vocabulary lists or advanced organisers.

CHUNK NEW INFORMATION: Chunking is an essential strategy to minimise cogntive load. Chunking involves breaking down complex information into smaller, bitesize pieces, making it easier for students to process and understand. This prevents cognitive overload by ensuring that learners are not overwhelmed with too much information in working memory all at once.

JOHN SWELLER

Cognitive load theory has been designed to provide guidelines intended to assist in the presentation of information in a manner that encourages learner activities that optimise intellectual performance. (1988)

ACTIVATE PRIOR KNOWLEDGE: Tailoring lessons to students' existing knowledge is crucial for optimal learning. This method of instruction encourages students to construct new knowledge based on their previous experiences and understanding, leading to more meaningful and lasting learning. By adjusting the complexity of tasks based on students' knowledge and abilities, you can optimise intrinsic load to ensure the level of challenge is desirably difficult.

MODE A PRINCIPLES

RETRIEVAL PRACTICE 7 PRINCIPLES

MAKING RETRIEVAL PRACTICE WORK EFFECTIVELY

WHAT IS IT AND WHY IS IT IMPORTANT?

Retrieval practice – actively recalling information rather than passively reviewing it – is one of the most well-supported, evidence-based learning strategies. Professor Carl Hendrick believes, despite its effectiveness, many schools struggle with its application. Hendrick highlights the growing trend where schools mandate retrieval practice at the start of every lesson but too often it fails to deliver the intended impact. This highlights a crucial point: effective implementation requires more than just routine – it demands that teachers have a deep understanding of the underlying principles. In his 2025 blog post, *Making Retrieval Practice Actually Work,* Hendrick outlines the following key principles.

ROBERT BJORK

The very conditions that produce forgetting: spacing, change of context, reducing cues... are the very things that enhance learning when you in fact, get a chance to study the material again. (2014)

WHAT ARE THE MAIN PRINCIPLES?

1. DON'T FORGET THE POWER OF FORGETTING:
When we retrieve information after a period of partial forgetting, our brains engage in a more effortful reconstruction process that actually strengthens the long-term memory trace. This means it is important to space learning events before returning to the material.

2. ENSURE IT'S USED AS A LEARNING EVENT:
Retrieval should be used to enhance learning, not just to measure it. Keep activities low-stakes to avoid inducing student anxiety and adding unnecessary pressure. The point is not so much to find out what students have learned but to be a learning event in and of itself.

READ MORE: 'Making Retrieval Practice Actually Work' blog by Professor Carl Hendrick

3. PROVIDE ENOUGH CHALLENGE: Giving quizzes where the first retrieval is very soon after learning can create the 'illusion of competence'; this is where students recall easily on that first attempt but later performance suffers. The initial retrieval needs to be sufficiently challenging to be effective. Design retrieval activities that encourage deep processing and hard thinking.

4. SPACE OUT RETRIEVAL : Hendrick explains that retrieval practice is most effective when it's distributed over time. Frequent, short quizzes or retrieval activities over time are more beneficial than a single, lengthy review session right before a test. Spacing strengthens *retrieval strength* (how easily information can be accessed at a given moment) and storage strength (how well information is consolidated into long-term memory).

JEFFREY D. KARPICKE

Learning is altered by the act of retrieval itself. Every time a person retrieves knowledge, that knowledge is changed, because retrieving knowledge improves one's ability to retrieve it again in the future. (2012)

5. CONNECT THE LEARNING: Retrieval practice should be done in context and meaningfully integrated into the curriculum so that it is aligned with learning objectives. Hendrick explains that our memories don't store information in isolation – they encode it within context and meaning. Connecting retrieval to prior knowledge (PK) is key.

6. TEACH HOW TO RETRIEVE: Students do not naturally know how best to utilise retrieval practice. Explicitly introduce students to these, such as elaboration (explaining concepts in their own words), generative retrieval (creating their own questions) and concept mapping (visually organising knowledge from memory).

7. KEEP IT LOW-STAKES: High-stakes tests and the fear of failure can create a negative feedback loop. Students may start to avoid challenging tasks or learning opportunities that could lead to errors. Frequent, low-stakes retrieval is key. Make retrieval practice a regular and integrated part of instruction but with low or no stakes attached so students can become more comfortable with it.

MODE A PRINCIPLES

EXPLICIT GUIDANCE

THE KEY ADVANTAGES OVER DISCOVERY LEARNING

WHAT IS IT AND WHY IS IT IMPORTANT?

Explicit guidance has been shown to be more effective than self-discovery or inquiry-based models, a conclusion supported by extensive research from Kirschner, Sweller and Clark. These educational psychologists argue that while minimally guided approaches are popular and appealing, they often fail to account for the limitations of human cognitive architecture. This summary explores five key reasons why explicit guidance leads to better learning outcomes, drawing on the principles of cognitive load theory, guided instruction, and the importance of foundational knowledge, particularly for novice learners.

PAUL KIRSCHNER

Minimal guidance during instruction is significantly less effective and efficient than instructional approaches that place a strong emphasis on guidance of the student learning process.

WHAT ARE THE MAIN PRINCIPLES?

GUIDE STUDENTS' LEARNING: Guided instruction offers immediate and corrective feedback, essential for effective learning. In self-discovery models, feedback is often delayed, allowing misconceptions to persist and potentially be embedded in long-term memory. Explicit guidance ensures that learners receive timely support, reinforcing correct understanding.

SUPPORT NOVICE LEARNERS: Novice learners benefit significantly from explicit guidance as they often lack the prior knowledge to navigate complex tasks independently. Kirschner, Sweller and Clark argue that self-discovery models can frustrate novices and lead to cognitive overload, while explicit instruction provides a clear and supportive pathway.

READ MORE: 'Why Minimal Guidance During Instruction Does Not Work' by Kirschner et al

JOHN SWELLER

Cognitive load theory suggests that free exploration of a highly complex environment may generate a heavy working memory load that is detrimental to learning.

MINIMISE COGNITIVE LOAD: Explicit guidance minimises cognitive load on learners by providing structured information, which prevents the working memory from becoming overwhelmed. According to Kirschner, Sweller and Clark (2006), self-discovery methods often lead to cognitive overload, hindering effective learning and long-term retention.

EXPLICIT GUIDANCE: TYPICAL LEARNING STRUCTURE

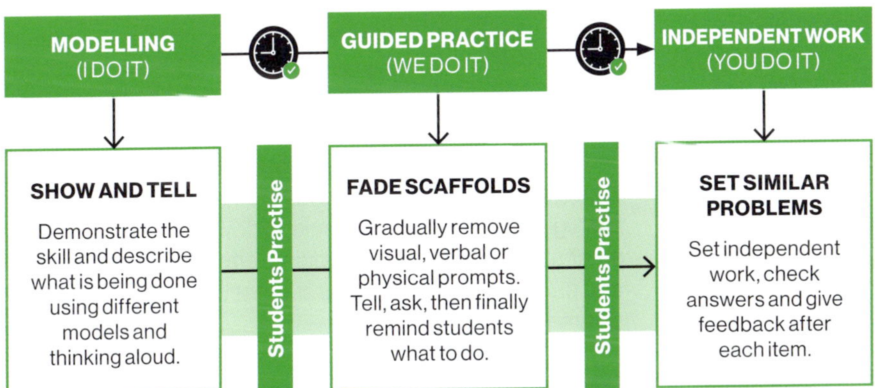

THROUGHOUT EACH LESSON: Involve students. Monitor performance. Provide feedback.

EFFICIENCY IN LEARNING:

Explicit guidance is more efficient, reducing the time required to learn new concepts and skills. Kirschner, Sweller and Clark (2006) highlight that structured approaches direct learners' attention to relevant information, making the learning process faster and more effective.

BUILDING KNOWLEDGE:

Foundational knowledge is crucial for higher-order thinking and problem-solving. Explicit instruction ensures that learners have a solid understanding of basic concepts before advancing. This foundational knowledge is necessary for engaging in complex cognitive tasks.

MODE A PRINCIPLES

PRINCIPLES OF INSTRUCTION 1–5

ROSENSHINE'S 10 RESEARCH-BASED STRATEGIES

BARAK ROSENSHINE

The most effective teachers ensured that students efficiently acquired, rehearsed and connected knowledge by providing a good deal of instructional support.

WHAT IS IT AND WHY IS IT IMPORTANT?

Barak Rosenshine's (2012) 'Principles of Instruction' offers a comprehensive synthesis of decades of research, providing educators with 10 foundational strategies to enhance teaching and learning. Grounded in research from cognitive science and observations of master teachers, these principles serve as a blueprint for effective instruction and serve to represent the Mode A approach perfectly. Principles 1 to 5 in the framework emphasises the significance of understanding cognitive limitations, highlighting the need for breaking down information into small steps, frequent questioning, effective use of models, and guided practice to foster deeper understanding and skill mastery.

WHAT ARE THE FIRST FIVE PRINCIPLES?

1. DAILY REVIEW: Daily review aids students in connecting new concepts with existing knowledge, making learning more durable and meaningful. By engaging students in regular review, through activities like retrieval practice quizzes, homework correction tasks, and addressing common misconceptions as a class, students rehearse and enhance their skills to the point of automaticity. This form of daily practice makes it easier for students to acquire and assimilate future knowledge into their existing schemas.

 READ MORE: 'Principles of Instruction' by Barak Rosenshine

2. SMALL STEPS: Rosenshine explains that our working memory is limited and can only process a few pieces of information at once. Since too much information swamps working memory, teachers should strive to break down curriculum concepts and key processes into small manageable steps and allow for focused practice after each step. Breaking down information facilitates better understanding and gives teachers insights into students' knowledge gaps.

---

3. QUESTIONING: Frequent questioning is an effective method of engaging all students actively with new content and linking it to their existing knowledge. Utilising a broad range of questioning techniques (such as 'cold calling') allows teachers to assess all students' understanding and promotes a culture of active participation. Questioning strategies also help to deepen students' grasp of the material by requiring them to apply and articulate their learning either to the teacher or a peer.

---

4. MODELS: Rosenshine suggests that providing models and worked examples significantly aids students in problem-solving by offering essential cognitive support. This includes teacher demonstrations and step-by-step explanations, which help reduce students' cognitive load. Effective modelling also includes think-alouds where the teacher externalises their thinking process. Modelling is key in helping novices develop expertise by unveiling the expert's underlying thought processes.

---

5. GUIDED PRACTICE: Guided practice is vital in the learning process as it ensures students actively engage with new material through sufficient rehearsal, crucial for transferring information to long-term memory. It involves the teacher spending significant time asking questions, checking understanding and correcting errors as students practise the new material. This process of practice and feedback is key for teachers in diagnosing any common errors and adjusting their teaching.

MODE A PRINCIPLES

PRINCIPLES OF INSTRUCTION 6–10

ROSENSHINE'S 10 RESEARCH-BASED STRATEGIES

BARAK ROSENSHINE

Effective teachers spend more time guiding students' practice of new material... the material will be forgotten unless there is sufficient rehearsal. (2012)

WHAT IS IT AND WHY IS IT IMPORTANT?

Principles 6 to 10 in Rosenshine's recommendations stress the importance of continuous assessment and scaffolding to ensure effective learning. These approaches are central to Mode A pedagogies because they are staples of robust knowledge building. By regularly checking student understanding and providing structured support, teachers can identify learning gaps and offer timely interventions. This helps students build a solid foundation of knowledge, which is essential for mastering more complex concepts. Real-time feedback and adjustments to teaching strategies and scaffolding provides the necessary support for students to progress from guided to independent learning.

WHAT ARE THE SECOND FIVE PRINCIPLES?

6. CHECK UNDERSTANDING: Checking for understanding (CFU) underscores the importance of regular assessment to ensure students grasp new material effectively. Frequent CFU is critical, as it contributes to processing information into long-term memory and helps teachers identify and rectify misconceptions early. Strategies include using 'TAPPLE' (page 132), probing questions, encouraging students to summarise concepts, and fostering discussions that require students to defend their specific viewpoints.

 READ MORE: *Rosenshine's Principles in Action* by Tom Sherrington

7. HIGH SUCCESS RATE: Ensuring students achieve a high success rate during instruction is crucial, with Rosenshine's research advocating for an optimal success rate around 80%. This benchmark balances challenge and attainability, indicating that students are not only learning the material successfully but are also being sufficiently challenged. Teachers can use tools such as mini-whiteboards to quickly check for levels of success from the entire class to decide upon their next steps.

8. SCAFFOLDS: Temporary supports assist students in mastering challenging concepts. These scaffolds include strategies such as live modelling, think-alouds, sentence starters, and checklists, which are designed to guide students through the learning of new information. Effective teachers introduce these supports, gradually phasing them out as students gain fluency. Scaffolds and supports ensure that students are neither overwhelmed by complexity nor under-challenged by simplicity.

9. INDEPENDENT PRACTICE: Following teacher-led instruction and guided practice, students should engage in independent practice to help reinforce their learning. Rosenshine explains that practice is essential for achieving fluency, allowing for automatic recall that frees up working memory for more complex cognitive tasks. Independent practice should involve the same material as the guided practice. During this process, teachers should actively monitor and circulate the classroom.

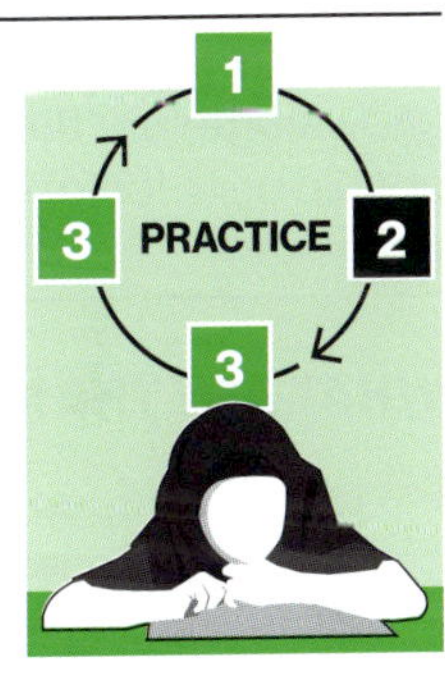

10. WEEKLY/MONTHLY REVIEW: Rosenshine emphasises the importance of regular reviews, extending beyond daily checks to include weekly and monthly formative assessments. This advanced strategy, termed 'successive relearning', involves spacing out retrieval practice over time to achieve mastery. Such reviews involve retrieval practice, strengthen connections between new and old knowledge and ensures learning is transferred to long-term memory.

MODE A PRINCIPLES

DESIRABLE DIFFICULTIES

DESIGNING MORE CHALLENGING CLASSROOMS

WHAT IS IT AND WHY IS IT IMPORTANT?

Desirable difficulties are instructional strategies that may seem challenging or counterintuitive at first but ultimately enhance long-term learning. These methods, based on research by Bjork and Bjork (2011), emphasise that making learning slightly more difficult can improve students' ability to remember and apply knowledge over time. This contrasts with traditional methods that focus on immediate performance, which may lead to short-lived understanding and achieve immediate results. True learning focuses on retaining and applying knowledge over the long haul. The ultimate goal of our classroom practice should be to foster long-term retention, even if students struggle more initially.

WHAT ARE THE MAIN PRINCIPLES?

Performance does not equal learning. True fluency is developed through consistent and sustained practice over time, rather than short-term efforts. Effective learning often involves a process of forgetting and relearning, which strengthens memory retention. Three main ideas of desirable difficulties are:

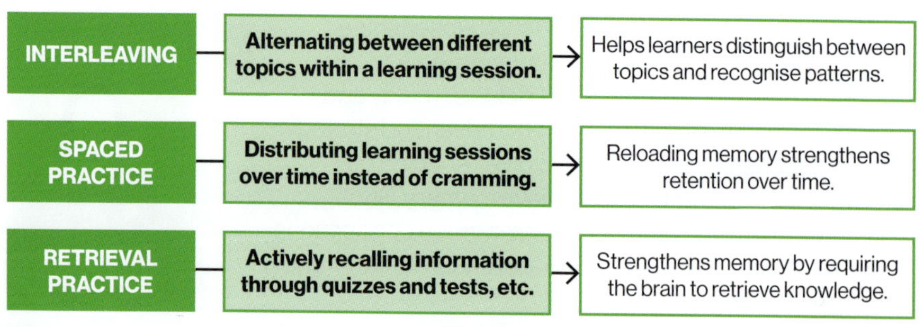

READ MORE: *Bjork & Bjork's Desirable Difficulties in Action* by Jade Pearce and Isaac Moore

INTERLEAVING Natural enemy = blocking: Unlike blocking, interleaving is mixing together different types of items, problems and questions (Karpicke and O'Day, 2024). This helps students see similarities and differences between concepts and group similar information together. The trick is not to interleave subjects but mix up concepts or topics. For example, in maths, finding the area of a circle, triangle and square in a single lesson rather than working with one shape per lesson.

SPACING Natural enemy = cramming: Unlike cramming, spacing is a learning strategy that means doing little and often. Ebbinghaus's forgetting curve shows that if students re-encounter learning materials after a delay, it helps to strengthen retention of information in long-term memory. With this in mind, teachers must plan to embed spacing into the curriculum so that students can revisit and retrieve information multiple times. Reteaching complex concepts is also important.

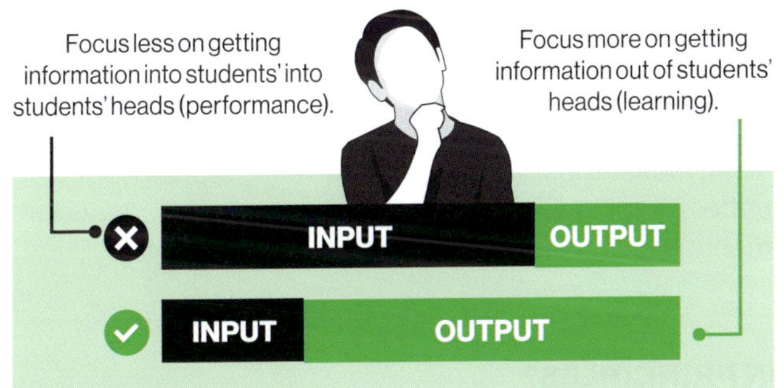

JADE PEARCE

Desirable difficulties have the power to improve both teacher instruction and students' independent study and so have a dramatic impact on learning and outcomes. (2024)

RETRIEVAL PRACTICE Natural enemy = rereading, highlighting: Unlike being presented or engaging with information such as notes, retrieval practice involves pulling out information from memory. Low-stakes (yet challenging) testing strategies involve quizzing, asking factual questions and free recall (brain dumps, multiple-choice questions). This helps learning to take place, which is also described as a permanent change in long-term memory .

MODE A PRINCIPLES

EXPLICIT DIRECT INSTRUCTION

THE POWER OF THE WELL-CRAFTED, WELL-TAUGHT LESSON

JOHN R. HOLLINGSWORTH

Every time you tell the whole class to do something, they become engaged. And the way to keep students engaged is to keep asking them over and over again to do things while you teach.

WHAT IS IT AND WHY IS IT IMPORTANT?

John Hollingsworth and Silvia Ybarra (2017) explain that 'explicit direct instruction' (EDI) is a structured set of teaching practices that help teachers form highly effective lessons. These lessons are designed to clearly instruct students, ensuring they all receive the necessary information while being highly engaging and interactive. EDI can be considered an important approach for learning because it helps to address common learning gaps and misconceptions, ensuring that all students have a solid understanding of the material. By using clear, focused instruction and frequent checking for understanding, EDI is interactive, supporting students in managing cognitive load and mastering content.

WHAT ARE THE MAIN PRINCIPLES?

The main eight principles of EDI emphasise the importance of modelling, guided practice and independent practice, allowing students to gain independence.

1. LEARNING OBJECTIVE
2. ACTIVATE PRIOR KNOWLEDGE
3. CONCEPT DEVELOPMENT
4. GUIDED PRACTICE
5. RELEVANCE (THE 'WHY?')
6. CLOSURE
7. INDEPENDENT PRACTICE
8. PERIODIC REVIEW

READ MORE: *Explicit Direct Instruction (EDI)* by John R. Hollingsworth and Silvia E. Ybarra

ENGAGEMENT NORMS: Engagement norms include practices such as tracked and choral reading, pair-shares, and holding up whiteboards to show answers. The norms help to establish a culture of participation and engagement by asking the whole class to do something at the same time. The norms also focus on reading, vocabulary use, listening, speaking and remembering. What's more, they are also effective for classroom management by guiding students on when to pay attention and actively engage in the lesson.

PRONOUNCE WITH ME
Explicitly show students how to say key vocabulary.

TRACK WITH ME
Get students to touch/look at words as you read.

READ WITH ME
Cue students to read chorally along with you at same time.

GESTURE WITH ME
Add physical movements to convey meaning (hand, fingers).

PAIR-SHARE ROUTINE
Direct students to explain to their partners.

ATTENTION SIGNAL
Stop students talking and turn to listen with a familiar signal.

SHOW-ME BOARDS
Engage the entire class to do something using whiteboards.

COMPLETE SENTENCES
Respond out loud in full sentences with a 'public voice'.

TEACHER-LED GUIDANCE:

A crucial component of EDI is setting a learning objective. Learning objectives include a concept (big idea) and a skill (verb) such as 'identify', 'write' or 'describe'. In conjunction with learning objectives, 'activating prior knowledge' (AKP) is used to reveal a connection between something students already know and the new content they are going to learn. When prior knowledge is explicitly activated, it's easier for students to learn new content.

MODELLING AND PRACTICE:

Another large component of EDI is teacher-led modelling, where the teacher demonstrates the specific skills and processes. This step involves the teacher thinking aloud, showing each step of a task, and explaining the reasoning behind each action. Following modelling, the teacher asks students, 'How did I solve the problem?' After students work a problem, the teacher asks for the answer and then enquires, 'How did you solve the problem?'

MODE A PRINCIPLES

CHALLENGE

ENGAGE STUDENTS IN HEALTHY STRUGGLE

SHAUN ALLISON

Challenge in education is the provision of difficult work that causes students to think deeply and engage in healthy struggle. (2015)

WHAT IS IT AND WHY IS IT IMPORTANT?

The Pygmalion Effect, explored by Robert Rosenthal and Lenore Jacobson (1968), reveals that the subtle and often unconscious ways teachers convey their beliefs – through feedback, attention and encouragement – can shape students' self-perception and growth. Integrating challenge across the curriculum, rather than viewing it as an isolated component of individual lessons, is key for learning and motivation. Showing exemplary work and embracing a language of growth (e.g. 'if it's not excellent, it's not finished') can inspire students to strive for excellence.

HOW DO I IMPLEMENT IT?

CHALLENGE EVERYONE: In every lesson, pitch content at a high level to ensure all students are challenged. Avoid limiting students' potential by assuming that only 'more able' learners can handle challenging material. Be responsive to students' needs in real time. For instance, if students are writing an essay on Lady Macbeth, provide tailored support or extension tasks to stretch or scaffold learning as required.

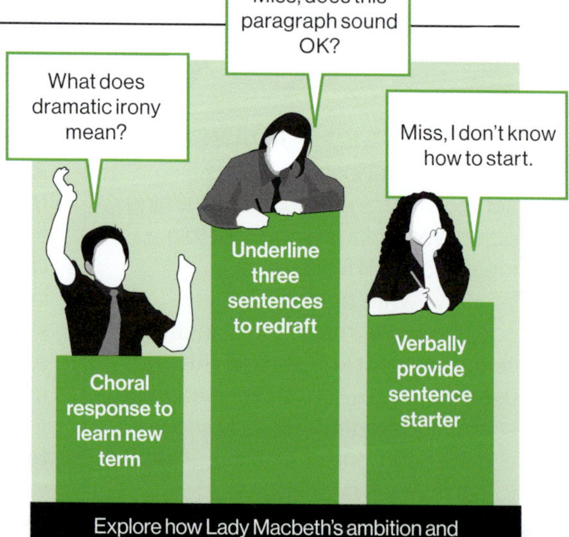

READ MORE: *Making Every Lesson Count* by Shaun Allison and Andy Tharby

SET A CLEAR LEARNING OBJECTIVE: Ensure learning objectives are concise and aspirational for all students. Keep in mind the highest attainers when constructing them. For example, instead of saying, 'Understand how photosynthesis happens', use 'Describe and explain the process and chemical nature of photosynthesis'. This revised objective sets a clear expectation and emphasises the challenge of both describing and explaining the concept.

RAISE THE BAR: Set work that is slightly above students' expected knowledge and skills. By exposing students to content at a level usually considered above (or beyond) expectations, we anchor in challenge. For example, in a Year 7 biology unit on the skeletal system, explore how the skeleton and muscles work together for movement. Subsequently, go beyond naming bones to studying muscle pairs and force measurement (Year 9 level).

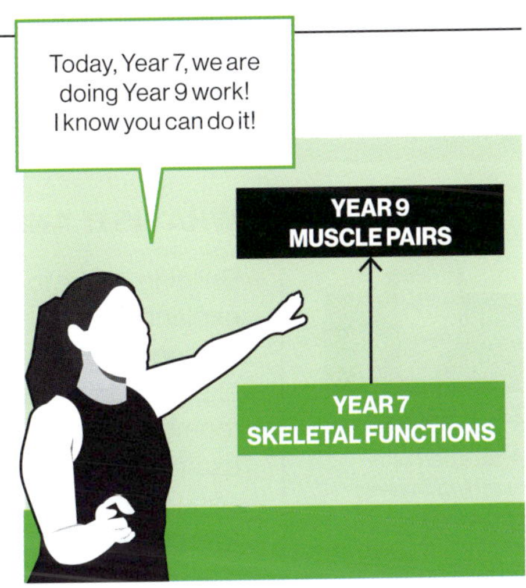

BUILD SUBJECT KNOWLEDGE: A deficit in subject knowledge can be a barrier to student achievement. When a teacher has solid subject knowledge, they are naturally able to challenge students and encourage them to 'think hard' (Coe et al, 2014). Develop subject knowledge by testing your own responses to exam questions, focus on common misconceptions and brainstorm topics with colleagues.

USE GROWTH LANGUAGE: According to Carol Dweck (2007), in a growth mindset, challenges are exciting rather than threatening. Reinforce that belief that effort leads to improvement. Encourage students to view mistakes as learning opportunities rather than failures so they are more willing to tackle challenging tasks. Say, 'This problem is tough but gives us a great chance to grow and improve.'

MODE A PRINCIPLES

EXPLANATION

MAXIMISE CLARITY AND REDUCE COGNITIVE LOAD

ZACH GROSHELL

A core part of teaching involves conveying information, getting your point across, and explaining things in a way that works for all. (2024)

WHAT IS IT AND WHY IS IT IMPORTANT?

Building on the foundations of effective and precise explanation from the first book, there are additional strategies to help teachers improve the clarity of their explanations. Research-backed methods like dual coding (combining words with visuals) and implementing worked examples help bridge understanding gaps and reduce cognitive load. Furthermore, working with colleagues to create consistent explanations, examples and non-examples across subjects, and using shared resources like PowerPoint templates or team-developed lesson plans, ensures consistency. What's more, the rehearsal of explanations can have a massive impact on clarity.

HOW DO I IMPLEMENT IT?

In his book, Ros Atkins (2023) breaks down the anatomy of good explanation:

1. **SIMPLICITY**
   Is this the simplest way I can say this?
2. **ESSENTIAL DETAIL**
   What detail is essential to include?
3. **COMPLEXITY**
   Are there elements I don't understand?
4. **EFFICIENCY**
   Is this the most succinct I can say this?
5. **PRECISION**
   Am I saying exactly what I want to say?
6. **CONTEXT**
   Why does this matter to students?
7. **NO DISTRACTIONS**
   Are there visual/verbal distractions?
8. **ENGAGING**
   Where might attention waver?
9. **USEFUL**
   Have I answered potential questions?
10. **CLARITY OF PURPOSE**
    Above all else: what am I explaining?

READ MORE: *Just Tell Them: The Power of Explanations and Explicit Teaching* by Zach Groshell

REHEARSE YOUR EXPLANATIONS: Prepare your explanations in advance, much like you would plan a lesson. Consider not only what to say but also how to illustrate it, as 'multimedia learning occurs when a learner builds a mental representation from words and pictures that have been presented' (Mayer, 2001). Be mindful of the 'curse of knowledge' – assume minimal prior knowledge and build understanding step by step. If artistic ability is a challenge, use simple drawings or stick figures; clarity is more important than complexity.

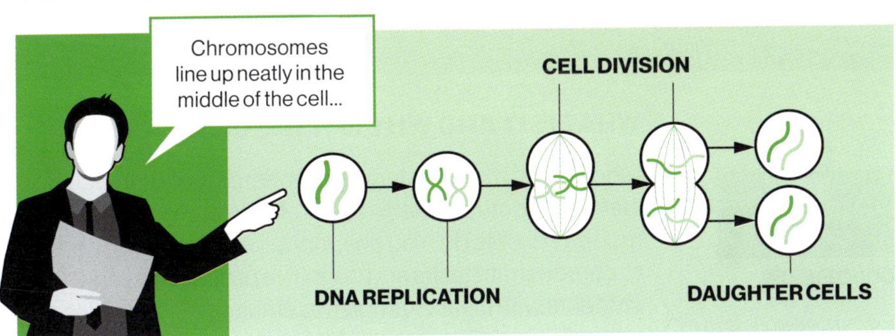

PAIR WORDS WITH VISUALS: According to dual coding theory, presenting verbal explanations alongside clear, relevant images allows for more effective information processing because it leads to what Paul Kirschner calls 'double-barrelled learning'. However, avoid cluttered or irrelevant visuals, as they can overwhelm cognitive capacity. When using diagrams highlight specific elements to guide students' focus and identify and emphasise important ideas.

EXPLAIN WORKED EXAMPLES:
Worked examples are step-by-step demonstrations of how to solve a problem or understand a concept. They help students see the process, not just the end result. Research shows that worked examples are particularly useful for novice learners, as they reduce cognitive load and provide a clear pathway to follow. To maximise their impact, break down each step, use simple language, and ensure students understand the reasoning behind each part of the example.

AVOID THE REDUNDANCY EFFECT:
According to research, presenting the same information both verbally and in writing can overload students' working memory (Mayer, 2001). To avoid this, keep explanations clear and simple by focusing only on the essential words and visuals. Reduce decorative graphics and excessive text on slides. Instead direct attention to relevant images or diagrams by pointing or using arrows. Use concise phrases or bullet points rather than full sentences to maintain clarity throughout.

MODE A PRINCIPLES 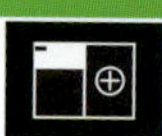

MODELLING

GRADUALLY SHIFT THE COGNITIVE WORK

DOUG FISHER

Explanation alone is insufficient; students need to see it for themselves. (2013)

WHAT IS IT AND WHY IS IT IMPORTANT?

Modelling is a key strategy that underpins effective guided learning. Rooted in the gradual release of responsibility model ('I do, We do, You do'), modelling allows teachers to demonstrate tasks and cognitive processes, providing students with clear examples to emulate before moving into independent practice. When a student attempts to learn new information without being explicitly taught, their working memory can quickly become overloaded, interfering with the ability to store, recall and apply what they are learning (Kirschner et al, 2006).

HOW DO I IMPLEMENT IT?

THE GRADUAL RELEASE MODEL: The gradual release of responsibility (GRR) model of instruction suggests that cognitive work should shift slowly and intentionally from teacher modelling, to joint responsibility between teachers and students, to independent practice and application by the learner (Pearson et al, 1983). Fisher and Frey (2013) outline four related components of the GRR that can be practically applied over a day, week, month or longer. Use this method to support novice learners to become capable thinkers and build mastery through expert guidance.

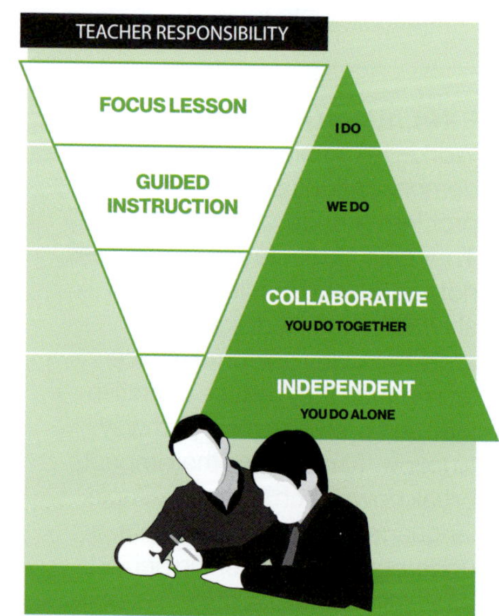

 READ MORE: *Five Ways to Secure Progress Through Modelling* blog by Tom Sherrington

THE MODELLING PROCESS: In his popular blog, Tom Sherrington (2022) outlines five steps to enhance student progress through effective modelling.

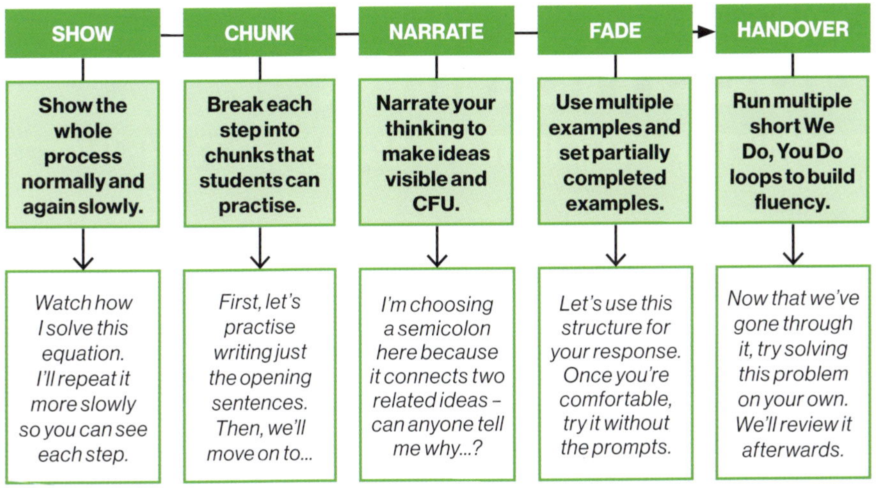

USE QUESTIONS, PROMPTS AND CUES: Frey and Fisher (2010) show that teacher modelling involves more than showing how to complete a task; it requires a deliberate use of questioning, prompting and cueing to engage students' thinking and metacognitive processes. Encourage active participation using different question types: elaboration ('Can you tell me more about that?'), clarification ('Why did you choose that answer?') and elicitation ('Who?', What?, 'Why?).

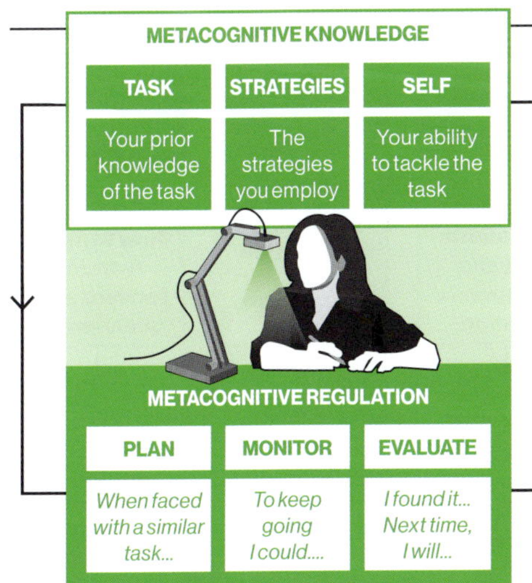

MODEL SELF-KNOWELDGE: The EEF (2023) emphasises the importance of teachers modelling self-knowledge. By openly reflecting on their own thought processes, teachers can plan and action effective thinking-aloud strategies to help students become aware of their strengths and areas for improvement. Map out your approach to planning, monitoring and evaluating so you can speak it aloud in class.

MODE A PRINCIPLES 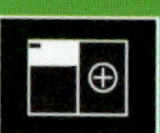

QUESTIONING

PROMOTE PARTICIPATION AND HARD THINKING

WHAT IS IT AND WHY IS IT IMPORTANT?

As Willingham (2021) explains, 'students remember what they think about'. Through strategic questioning, teachers can focus students' attention and engage them in deep thinking. In addition to techniques like cold calling and whole-class participation strategies discussed in the first book, the following ideas help establish a powerful questioning culture that moves beyond surface-level answers, encouraging students to explain and connect their knowledge.

HOW DO I IMPLEMENT IT?

POWERFUL QUESTIONING PRINCIPLES INSPIRED BY MICHAEL CHILES (2023)

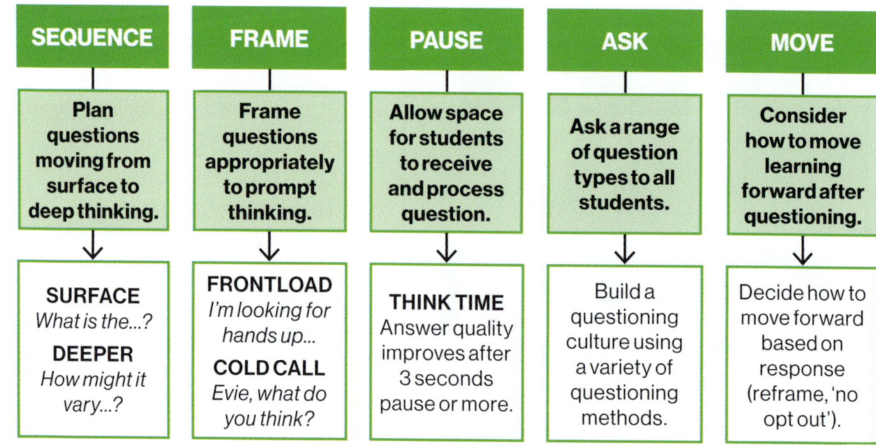

READ MORE: *Powerful Questioning* by Michael Chiles

PLAN DIFFERENT QUESTION TYPES: Plan effective questions in advance:

DIVERGENT	No specific answer and can be used to encourage students to think more broadly about a specific topic. For example: 'How else could we solve this problem?'
PREDICTIVE	Prompt students to anticipate what might happen next or speculate on possible outcomes. For example: 'What do you think will happen if we change this variable?'
FUNNEL	A series of guiding questions that start broadly and become increasingly specific. For example: 'What do you notice about...?', 'How does this part relate to...?'
ORGANISING	Help students to structure their thoughts, categorise information and clarify relationships. For example: 'What are the main parts of this process or topic?'

ASK PROCESS QUESTIONS: Rosenshine (2012) says that more effective teachers ask process questions. This involves prompting students to explain their reasoning or describe the steps they used to reach an answer. Focusing on *how* they reached their answer improves metacognition: 'Thanks, Fin, that's right – what method did you use?'

CALL AND RESPONSE: The call and response strategy is an effective method to encourage whole-class participation as students answer questions in unison (Lemov, 2021). This builds energy and helps reinforce key knowledge through repetition. Involving the entire class also increases attentiveness and reduces off-task behaviour.

FRONTLOAD PARTICIPATION: Frontloading instructions, as explained by Adam Boxer (2022), means giving students clear instructions on how to respond before actually asking the question. By setting these expectations upfront, it can prevent moments of confusion or noisy transitions. For example, if you want students to answer on mini-whiteboards or raise their hands, clearly state this first, before asking the question. This 'means of participation' helps students understand exactly what to do. Additionally, waiting for 'golden silence' – the quiet focus before responses begin – is useful to ensure students are attentive and ready, which leads to more thoughtful and engaged answers.

DANIEL WILLINGHAM

Here's how you should think about memory: it's the residue of thought, meaning that the more you think about something, the more likely it is that you'll remember it later.

MODE A PRINCIPLES 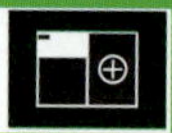

PRACTICE

REMOVE THE CEILING AND FOCUS YOUR SUPPORT

WHAT IS IT AND WHY IS IT IMPORTANT?

Providing support during practice is a key method of assisting all students to reach ambitious goals and is also an essential element of Mode A teaching practice. When engaging students in guided or independent practice, scaffolding is essential. Scaffolding can be either designed in advance (designed-in scaffolding) or provided in real-time to address immediate student needs (contingent scaffolding) (Hammond et al, 2005). Rosenshine (2012) suggests that effective instruction involves 'providing scaffolds for difficult tasks' with the aim of gradually withdrawing these supports as learners develop competence. As students gain confidence and proficiency through frequent practice, scaffolds should be deliberately faded out to promote independence and self-sufficiency.

HOW DO I IMPLEMENT IT?

ALWAYS FADE SCAFFOLDS:
Fading scaffolds refers to the smooth transition from full teacher support to minimal guidance, allowing students to build fluency by practising independently. The process involves the reduction of modelling, explanation and demonstration, shifting responsibility to the student. Regularly monitor student progress to assess scaffold effectiveness and gradually reduce or remove the scaffold as proficiency improves.

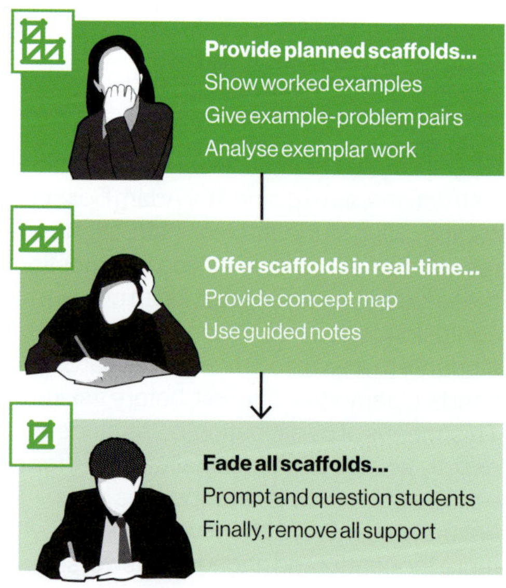

 READ MORE: *Example-Problem Pairs* blog by Greg Ashman

PRACTICE WITH GUIDED NOTES: Guided notes are pre-prepared summaries with blanks for students to complete with key information. As an effective scaffolding technique, they help students focus on the most essential concepts by requiring students to fill in the blanks. Write a guided notes sheet with key terms, vocabulary and important elements intentionally removed. Adjust the level of support accordingly throughout the practice phase until students no longer require the structure.

GREG ASHMAN

Research found that for an example to be most effective, it had to be accompanied by a problem to solve. The most efficient method of studying examples and solving problems was to present a worked example and then immediately follow this example by asking the learner to solve a similar problem.

USE EXAMPLE-PROBLEM PAIRS: An example-problem pair gets students to first study a worked example and then immediately attempt a similar problem on their own. Problem pairs bridge the gap between instruction and independent problem-solving, helping to manage cognitive load and support mastery (Ashman, 2016). Present a worked example alongside a minimally different problem on a whiteboard or PowerPoint slide. Putting these problems side-by-side allows teachers to emphasise key aspects of the solution process, making it easier for students to understand and apply each step.

CREATE WRITING SCAFFOLDS: Writing scaffolds provide structured support for students by offering prompts such as sentence stems, sentence starters or picture prompts. These scaffolds help students begin sentences, formulate responses, guide discussions, and demonstrate cause-and-effect relationships. Introduce sentence stems, starters, or picture prompts on handouts or display them on a PowerPoint slide.

USE TEMPLATES: Templates offer students a structured framework for tasks by outlining specific features and guiding their responses, reducing cognitive load and allowing them to focus on content. For instance, a template for writing a technical description of an animal might include sections for classification, appearance, behaviour and habitat. Encourage students to refer to the template and adjust support as they build fluency.

MODE A PRINCIPLES

FEEDBACK

IMPROVE THE LEARNER NOT THE WORK

KATE JONES

Feedback is the beating heart of the classroom... Without feedback pupils will continue to make the same mistakes, misconceptions will linger and can become entrenched in long-term memory. (2024b)

WHAT IS IT AND WHY IS IT IMPORTANT?

Feedback, when delivered thoughtfully, can be a powerful catalyst for learning and growth. However, as research by Hattie and Timperley (2007) highlight, its impact can be either positive or negative, depending on how it is understood and applied. To make it effective, teachers should ensure that feedback is purposeful, actionable and focused on improving the learner. A common issue, as noted by Kirschner and Neelen (2018), is that 'learners often don't do much with given feedback'. Overcoming this challenge involves delivering feedback that motivates students to engage with and apply it meaningfully using a kit-bag of effective written and verbal approaches.

HOW DO I IMPLEMENT IT?

A safe and supportive classroom is key for encouraging students to engage with and act on feedback. When students feel secure, they are more receptive to constructive input and motivated to learn from it. As Hendrick and Macpherson (2017) highlight, 'Students will often only respond to feedback if they believe that improvement is possible. Therefore, fostering a belief in their ability to grow becomes an integral part of the challenge.' The following principles help to build a positive feedback culture.

1. **ACTIONABLE STEPS** Focus on next steps rather than flaws.
2. **TIMELY BUT SPACED** Time feedback to enhance retention.
3. **MOTIVATIONAL** Foster growth and effortful learning.
4. **POSITIVE AND CONSTRUCTIVE** Balance strengths with areas for growth.
5. **CLEAR AND UNDERSTANDABLE** Ensure it is clear and links to goals.

 READ MORE: *Feedback* by *Kate* Jones

TIME FEEDBACK EFFECTIVELY: Align the timing of feedback with principles of spaced learning by giving feedback at intervals that allow students to process and make improvements before revisiting the material. Cepeda et al (2008) suggest that feedback, like study sessions, shouldn't be too immediate nor too delayed. After introducing a new concept, wait some time to provide feedback, strategically spacing it to reinforce learning when initial understanding starts to fade but before it is forgotten. Thoughtful timing can leverage retrieval effects.

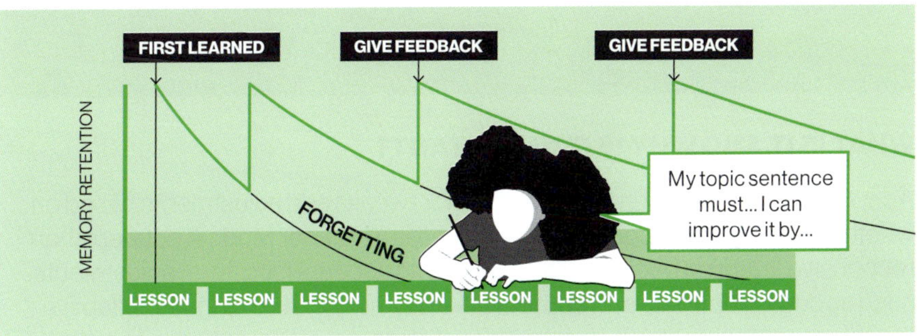

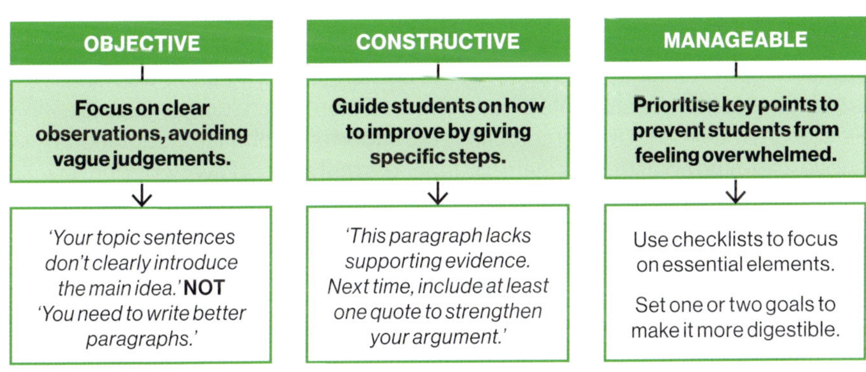

GIVE WRITTEN FEEDBACK: Peps Mccrea (2023) explains that written feedback that is objective, constructive and manageable can be effective for guiding student progress. It should be concise and focus on key points that students can act upon without overwhelming them.

GIVE VERBAL FEEDBACK: Interact with students during lesson time and offer feedback in the moment. This responsive method is workload-friendly and conveys tone and emotion to help feedback become positive and motivational. Address the transience of information by getting students to act on feedback straight away. This ensures that feedback is processed and applied immediately.

MODE A PRINCIPLES

ADAPTIVE TEACHING

REMOVE THE CEILING AND PLAN YOUR SUPPORT

WHAT IS IT AND WHY IS IT IMPORTANT?

Adaptive teaching is when teachers plan for tweaks and adjustments based on whether students are coping with learning. It is a broader Mode A concept than responsive teaching because it also takes into account long-term adjustments, such as curriculum, data and collaborative planning with colleagues. Adaptive teaching represents a shift from traditional classroom differentiation to a more inclusive approach that ensures all students are provided with the opportunity to succeed. Teaching to the top and providing a single explicit instructional goal helps to cultivate a classroom culture of high expectations that does not cap students' opportunities or aspirations. The cornerstone of adaptive teaching is being responsive to students who might need more scaffolding or support. Research by Corno (2008) emphasises the importance of 'microadaptations'; subtle, real-time adjustments made by teachers that support every student in reaching shared learning goals. These include strategies such as pre-teaching concepts, checking for understanding or flexible grouping for specific tasks.

HOW DO I IMPLEMENT IT?

This simple comparison by the Huntington Research School (2023) outlines the main differences between adaptive teaching and differentiation.

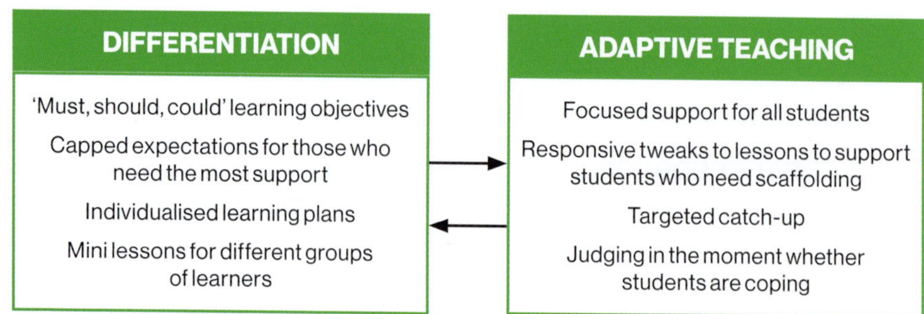

READ MORE: 'On Teaching Adaptively' by Lyn Corno

PLAN FOR MICROADAPTATIONS: Alex Quigley (2023) explains 'there are a number of activities teachers can use before, during and after teaching a topic that will help them to diagnose students' levels of understanding and make timely microadaptations'. Some of these simple formative strategies include:

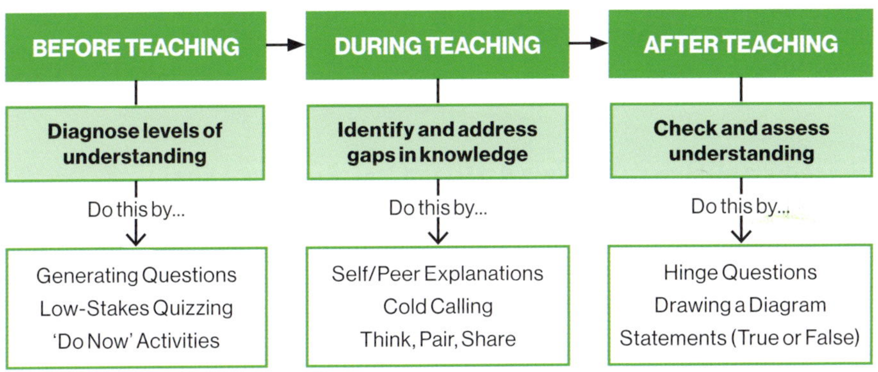

FLEXIBLE GROUPING: Often, we need to revisit topics to make sure everyone understands. Be ready to change groupings in class to help with this. Flexible groupings emphasises the importance of observing students' performance in real-time to identify their strengths and areas for improvement. It might involve seating students together who need to address a particular misconception or pairing students with differing levels of understanding to promote peer tutoring.

PLAN ADJUSTMENTS: Prepare to change the direction of instruction by making quick adjustments and reteaching the misunderstood content. Plan to reintegrate these concepts into future lessons by presenting the information in different ways and checking for understanding.

ALEX QUIGLEY

If you ask teachers exactly what adaptive teaching looks like in action, the answers will not typically be confident or consistent. This is a problem, because if adaptive teaching is to live up to the hype, and not become a passing fad, we need to be able to define what it is, what it isn't and how it works in practice.

MODE A PRINCIPLES

RESPONSIVE TEACHING

STRATEGIES TO ELICIT EVIDENCE IN REAL-TIME

WHAT IS IT AND WHY IS IT IMPORTANT?

Responsive teaching is not a new concept; it involves consistently gathering evidence in real-time to inform a teacher's next steps in the classroom. This approach requires teachers to anticipate and plan for moments to check for understanding and engage students in thinking and rehearsal activities. Dylan Wiliam's seminal work, *Embedded Formative Assessment*, outlines these principles in detail. However, responsive teaching primarily focuses on short-term, lesson-by-lesson assessment and action. The importance of responsive teaching lies in its ability to provide insights into students' thinking, allowing teachers to make necessary adjustments and understand their prior knowledge. Additionally, responsive teaching plays a crucial role in securing students' attention by actively involving them in the learning process.

HOW DO I IMPLEMENT IT?

Responsive teaching involves building familiar routines to check for understanding (CFU). Plan ahead and select techniques informed by the possible outcomes that may arise throughout the lesson. The main principles of responsive teaching are based on the regular eliciting of evidence to guide instructional decisions, the anticipation and preparation for various contingencies, and the ability to make immediate adjustments to enhance learning.

1. PLAN FOR CONTINGENCIES
2. REGULARLY ELICIT EVIDENCE
3. INTERPRET STUDENTS' THINKING
4. MAKE INFORMED DECISIONS
5. ADJUST TEACHING ON THE FLY

LISTEN: 'Bron Ryrie Jones on Responsive Teaching' on the Knowledge for Teachers Podcast

BUILD IN TURN AND TALK: Turn and talk is an effective technique to ensure all students are participating and building fluency. It buys the teacher time to make informed decisions on their next steps. For example, you might say: 'Tell your partners a sentence with the words: photosynthesis and chlorophyll – go!'

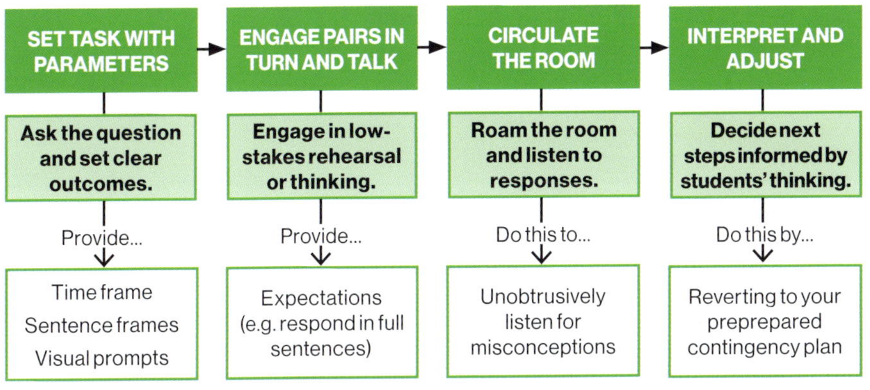

LOW-STAKES WRITTEN RESPONSES: Keeping student responses low stakes helps to build confidence and fluency. Short written activities such as cloze exercises (where students fill in missing words), and 'stop and jot' tasks using mini-whiteboards enable students to quickly demonstrate their thinking. Develop 'pause points' into your classroom routines so students get familiar with regular checks for understanding.

CHECK WITH CLOSED QUESTIONS: Closed questions are a quick way to elicit evidence of learning:

CONTENT CHECK
'Did you find the main idea in the text we just read?'
PROCEDURAL KNOWLEDGE
'Do we isolate the variable on one side in this equation?'
COMPREHENSION CONFIRMATION
'Is the character development in *Macbeth* linked to his ambition?'
PREDICTIVE INSIGHT
'Will a heavier object fall faster in a vacuum?'

BRON RYRIE JONES

A hallmark of responsive teaching is the routine, regular, embedded eliciting of evidence in order for the teacher to make better founded decisions about what to do in real time in classrooms. (2024)

MODE A PRINCIPLES

FORMATIVE ACTION

THE FIVE CORE PRINCIPLES TO TRANSFORM LEARNING

HILLY DROK

Formative action is a pedagogical method that ensures teachers and students can get a better handle on the student's learning process... so that it becomes clear what the next step in the process should be. (2024)

FLEMMING VAN DE GRAAF

Formative action makes it quicker, easier and more precise to check if what has been explained by teachers has actually been mastered. (2024)

WHAT IS IT AND WHY IS IT IMPORTANT?

Formative action is a teaching method developed by the Formative Action School in the Netherlands and uses ongoing assessment to gather real-time feedback on student learning. This pedagogical approach enables teachers to make informed decisions about what material to cover and how to adjust their instruction, while actively engaging students in their learning journey toward mastery. The process is goal-orientated, emphasising the learning journey and making cycles of improvement towards a set goal. Ultimately, this approach fosters student autonomy and helps learners to develop independence and self-efficacy as they progress. A major component of formative action is to ensure feedback from the teacher or the student 'lands' and promotes hard thinking and actionable steps forward.

WHAT ARE THE FIVE PRINCIPLES?

1. FA IS NOT ASSESSMENT BUT PEDAGOGY:
Formative action is not merely a one-off assessment tool but a comprehensive and ongoing pedagogical approach. The formative action method focuses on understanding and improving the learning process rather than grading students with summative assessments. Ultimately, formative action helps determine whether students have understood the material so that you can identify the next steps in your instruction and guide learners towards mastery.

READ MORE: 'Five Core Principles for Formative Action' blog by the Formative Action School

2. FA IS NOT GOING GRADELESS BUT CONSTRUCTIVE ALIGNMENT:

This means aligning learning goals, teaching activities and assessments to ensure a clear focus in the learning process. During the learning process, the emphasis should be on using formative action to provide meaningful feedback that guides students towards achieving the set learning goals. Start by formulating observable goals on what students should master independently and build in interim checkpoints for your students to check their progress towards mastery.

---

3. FA IS NOT DATA COLLECTION BUT TIME-SAVING IN PRACTICE:

Formative action is a time-saving process and is not designed to increase teacher workload. Conventional methods of collecting data on where students stand can be time-consuming and can detract from the crucial task of acting on the data. Ensure you move on when at least 80% of students give the right answer and provide additional instruction to the remaining students. Utilise CFU methods such as diagnostic questions to collect real-time data.

4. FA IS NOT TRANSMISSION BUT TRANSFORMATIVE FEEDBACK:

For learning to be effective and long-lasting, students need to engage in hard thinking, as this helps the information stick in long-term memory. Transformative feedback is feedback given during the learning process that encourages students to think and take concrete steps to improve their work. The aim of formative action is to empower students to seek feedback in order to build independence and self-regulation skills.

---

5. FA IS NOT A FULL CURRICULUM BUT A CLEAR ROADMAP:

Teachers can often feel too overwhelmed to implement formative action effectively because they have too much content to cover in their curriculum. It is essential for students to achieve mastery of the subject matter before moving on to ensure learning is coded in long-term memory. To do this, it is better to organise a curriculum that is less crowded so that more time can be spent on deliberate practice. This requires making difficult choices, and it is essential that the conversation should focus on what the core objectives are in each subject.

MODE A PRACTICES

THE FORMATIVE ACTION MODEL

A 5 STEP PROCESS TO DEVELOP INDEPENDENCE

WHAT IS IT AND WHY IS IT IMPORTANT?

To clarify the practical aspects of formative action, the Formative Action School developed a comprehensive model that is built on five foundational steps that are integral to any effective execution of formative action. These steps can be performed by the teacher, the student, or collaboratively as a class, ensuring a cohesive and responsive learning process. The model is based on the following guiding questions. **GOALS**: Get a clear picture of what you want to achieve. When will you be satisfied? **FOCUS**: What do you want your students to think about? **PROBLEMS**: Which problems can I expect my students to face?

VALENTINA DEVID

Formative action is all about eliciting evidence of your students but doing it in a very goal orientated way... Focus on data from the learning process to make informed low-stakes decisions and take effective action. (2024)

HOW DO I IMPLEMENT IT?

1. ORIENT AND PREDICT: Design an internal road map to guide students from their current state of learning to the desired outcomes. This initial step is a mental exercise for the teacher. Consider what aspects of the learning process you are curious about. Identify the common misconceptions and make a prediction about what the students already know.

2. THINK AND GENERATE: Encourage students to think and generate answers to gain a clear understanding of their thought processes. It is important for students to generate independently without their books and notes, or without talking to their peers. Focus on the quality of your questions to gain insights into your students' thinking and determine the quality of their answers.

READ MORE: *Formative Action: From Instrument to Design* by the Formative Action School

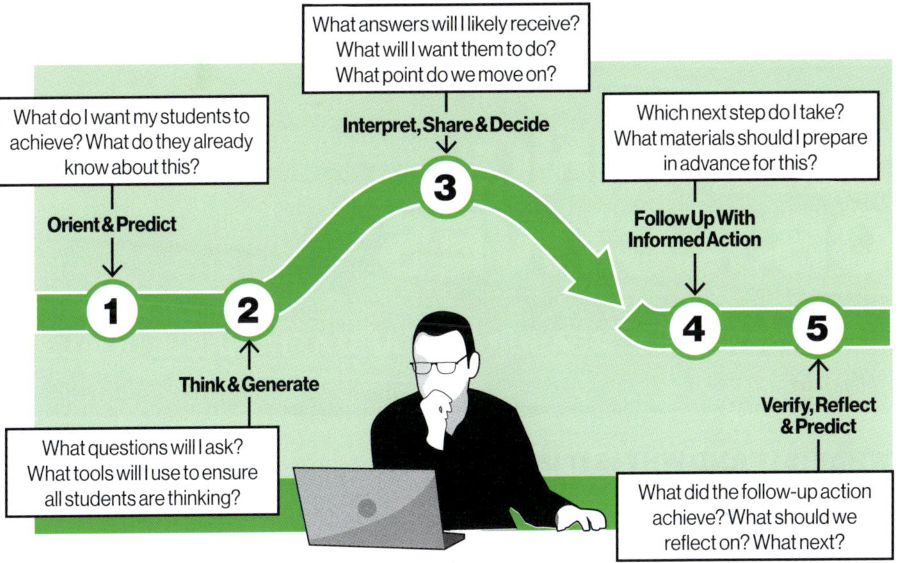

3. INTERPRET, SHARE AND DECIDE: Interpret students' answers before deciding the next steps in the process. Reflect on students' answers to check their thinking and determine if it aligns with your initial predictions. Encourage students to communicate about their answers and decide how best to proceed to the next step. The aim is to achieve at least an 80% success rate.

4. FOLLOW UP WITH INFORMED ACTION: Utilise the information elicited from students to implement the necessary follow-up action. Make an informed and logical step grounded in actionable activities that helps students make adjustments and improvements. For example, reteaching a topic or step, encouraging students to do more practice, or making problems more challenging.

5. VERIFY, REFLECT AND PREDICT: Check the effectiveness of the informed action and that the intended goals have now been met. This is crucial because when your students experience success, their motivation increases significantly. Depending on the level of success achieved, students can either move forward or engage in further improvement cycles of formative action.

RENÉ KNEYBER

Formative action is a teaching method that emphasises ongoing feedback and responsiveness in the learning process. It helps teachers make informed decisions about instructional adjustments and encourages students to actively engage in their learning journey.

MODE A PRACTICES

LEARNING OBJECTIVES

SET OBSERVABLE, MEASURABLE AND ATTAINABLE GOALS

WHAT IS IT AND WHY IS IT IMPORTANT?

Learning objectives (LOs) are clear, concise statements that define what students should know and be able to do after completing a lesson. Learning objectives and success criteria form key parts of Mode A teaching and formative assessment practices, as they help teachers and students establish a clear and shared understanding of learning goals (EEF, 2021c). Effective LOs uses plain language and explicitly make links to prior knowledge. By setting specific, measurable goals, LOs help students understand the purpose of their learning activities and improve their performance. Additionally, transparent and well-aligned LOs enhance student confidence and retention as students can see their progress and understand the relevance of their learning. This clarity not only motivates students but also enables teachers to provide targeted feedback.

DYLAN WILIAM

Brief, clear and measurable learning objectives are most useful for student learning. (1998)

HOW DO I IMPLEMENT IT?

BEHAVIOURAL, MEASURABLE, ATTAINABLE: LOs should use action verbs to describe the expected performance and the conditions under which learning should occur. Clear LOs avoid vague terms like 'understand' or 'know' and instead use specific verbs such as 'compare', 'predict' or 'describe', which better indicate what students will do (Bangerter et al, 2020). Instead of an ineffective LO: 'Students will understand the process of photosynthesis', a more effective LO is: 'By the end of this lesson, students will be able to describe the process of photosynthesis, including the roles of chlorophyll and sunlight, and explain how it contributes to plant growth.'

READ MORE: *Assessment and Classroom Learning* by Paul Black and Dylan Wiliam

COMPONENTS OF EFFECTIVE LEARNING OBJECTIVES

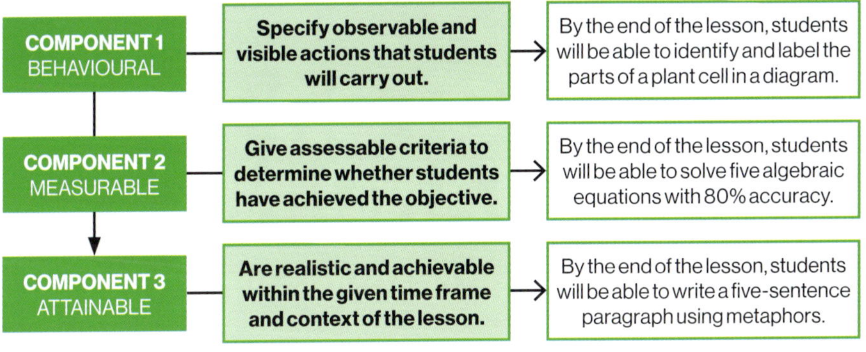

INTRODUCE PRE-QUESTIONS: Pre-questions are questions posed to students at the beginning of a lesson about material they have not yet learned. Research shows that while learning objectives capture students' attention, making them more engaged, converting these objectives into pre-questions can significantly add value to learning. Pre-questions are effective because they allow students to preview the material they will learn and help reduce overconfidence by revealing gaps in their knowledge. The multiple-choice format is an effective method to use. It is important to not reveal the answer straight away!

LEARNING OBJECTIVE: By the end of this lesson, students will be able to analyse Macbeth's character development by examining his soliloquy in Act 2, Scene 1 and explain how this reveals his inner conflict.

USE SUCCESS CRITERIA: Success criteria are specific, measurable indicators used to determine whether students have achieved a learning objective. They provide clear expectations for students and help teachers assess whether the learning goals have been met. An example is: 'Students can accurately highlight and cite key lines from the soliloquy that illustrate Macbeth's inner conflict.'

LINK TO PRIOR KNOWLEDGE: When explaining the learning objectives, it is crucial to connect the material to students' prior knowledge. For example, in a history lesson on the Industrial Revolution, a teacher might begin by asking questions or discussing the technological advancements that students have previously studied in earlier historical periods, such as the Agricultural Revolution.

MODE A PRACTICES

CHECKING FOR UNDERSTANDING

VERIFY STUDENTS ARE LEARNING WITH 'TAPPLE'

WHAT IS IT AND WHY IS IT IMPORTANT?

Checking for understanding (CFU) is a critical instructional strategy where the teacher continually verifies that students are grasping the material as it is being taught. This ongoing assessment helps determine the pace of the lesson, making it more interactive. By uncovering misunderstandings in real-time, CFU allows the teacher to adjust instruction to better meet students' needs. The EDI acronym 'TAPPLE' can be used to remember the steps of CFU. Utilising this approach for CFU throughout a lesson ensures that the instruction is engaging and responsive, increasing the likelihood of student success.

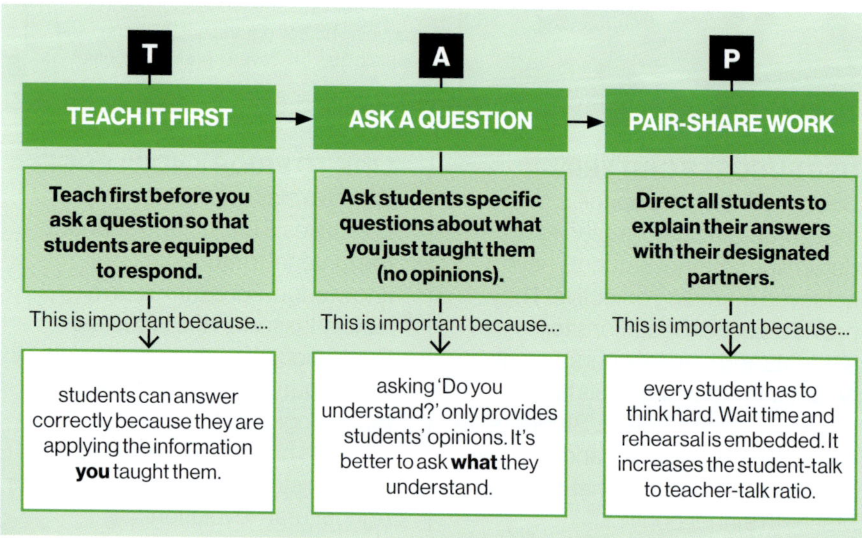

READ MORE: *Explicit Direct Instruction (EDI)* by John R. Hollingsworth and Silvia E. Ybarra

HOW DO I IMPLEMENT IT?

CHECK IN REAL-TIME: Checking for understanding (CFU) should be employed in every lesson each time you introduce a new chunk of information. Aim to check two or three students per CFU to uncover common misunderstandings or errors. This approach keeps lessons lively and interactive, ensuring that students are actively engaged. Additionally, it helps to address the misconception that Mode A instructional teaching is passive and lecture-like, highlighting its dynamic and responsive nature. For example, you could introduce CFU after modelling a concept or process and then ask students to turn and talk to their partner about the method used. Cold calling individuals will then determine if your modelled example was successful. A powerful approach is to plan CFU questions in advance of your lesson.

SILVIA E. YBARRA

Checking for Understanding (CFU) is when the teacher continually verifies that students are learning what is being taught while it is being taught.... CFU determines the pace of the lesson, makes the lesson interactive and helps to uncover misunderstandings to inform the direction of instruction. (2017)

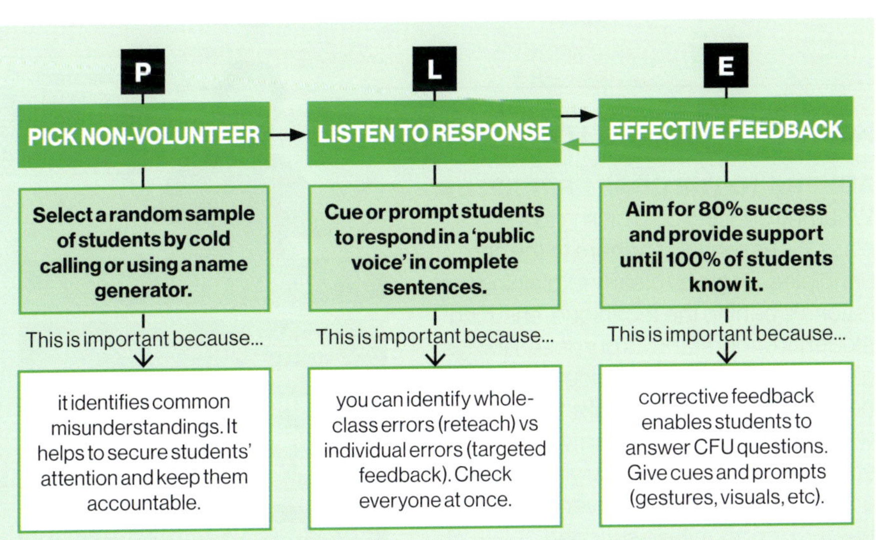

MODE A PRACTICES

COLD CALLING

VARIATIONS TO ENGAGE EVERYONE IN THINKING HARD

TOM SHERRINGTON

It's really important to keep the core idea tightly defined ... these variations help to adapt the core strategy to work effectively in a particular context.

WHAT IS IT AND WHY IS IT IMPORTANT?

Cold calling is a foundational strategy in Mode A teaching, highlighted in the first *Teaching One-Pagers* for its effectiveness in promoting cognitive engagement. By ensuring that every student is actively thinking and ready to participate, cold calling drives hard thinking and deeper learning. Sherrington (2021b) emphasises that adapting cold calling with variations allows the strategy to be tailored to different learning contexts, ensuring it remains effective. The following cold calling adaptations help keep students engaged, thus building their confidence and understanding over time. What's more, cold calling, when used artfully, becomes a tool for fostering high expectations and inclusivity in the classroom.

HOW DO I IMPLEMENT IT?

ADHERE TO THE CORE PRINCIPLES:
When introducing cold calling to a class, it's essential to adhere to the core principles. Begin by clearly explaining the rationale behind the technique, ensuring students understand its purpose. Always give ample wait time for students to think before responding and make the process warm, inclusive and supportive. Scaffold your questions to match varying levels of understanding, ensuring every student has the opportunity to succeed.

1. CLEARLY EXPLAIN RATIONALE
2. CONSISTENTLY USE WAIT TIME
3. KEEP COLD CALLING WARM
4. ASK THE SAME STUDENT AGAIN
5. SCAFFOLD YOUR QUESTIONING

READ MORE: 'Cold Call Variations' blog by Tom Sherrington

STRATEGICALLY DECIDE VARIATION: Choose the cold calling variation that best suits your class or content. Consider the needs of your students, the complexity of the material and the classroom dynamics.

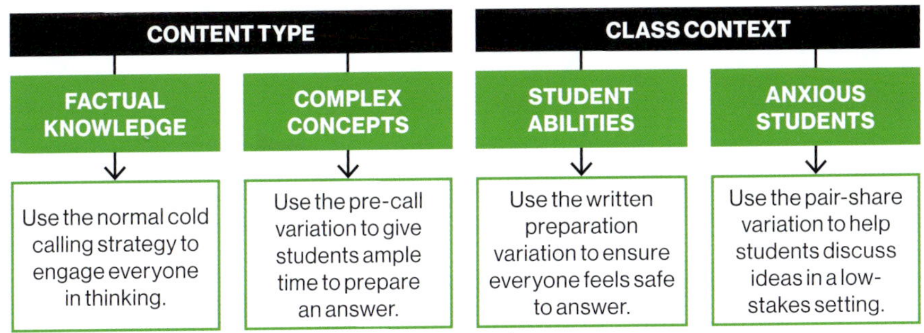

ACTIVATE PAIRED TALK: Pair-share is a highly productive strategy before cold calling. As Sherrington (2021b) explains, it gives students time to talk through their ideas, rehearsing explanations and the use of key terminology, airing any doubts or uncertainties.

PEER REVIEW CALL: After a student answers a question, cold call another student to provide feedback or to elaborate on the first student's response. This encourages active listening and hard thinking, as students must evaluate their peer's answer before giving their own.

Amir, I'd love to hear what you've written...

WRITTEN PREPARATION: This involves having students write down their answers before sharing them verbally. This can boost confidence, especially for students who may be hesitant to speak up. By giving them time to organise their thoughts and jot down responses, you keep the stakes low so students feel more safe. This method ensures that all students, including those who might need extra time, can participate in the lesson.

PRE-CALL A STUDENT: This involves notifying a student in advance that they will be invited to answer a question. This gives the them time to prepare mentally before sharing. By reducing the element of surprise, pre-call helps build confidence, especially for students who might be anxious about being put on the spot. This approach also encourages deeper thinking, as the selected student is more likely to pay close attention to their answer.

MODE A PRACTICES

TURN AND TALK

LOW-STAKES REHEARSAL & GENERATIVE LEARNING

WHAT IS IT AND WHY IS IT IMPORTANT?

'Turn and talk' is an instructional practice where students pair up to discuss a specific question or topic. This strategy promotes active participation, helping students to process ideas and articulate their thoughts in a low-stakes setting. It also serves as an effective rehearsal to boost confidence levels before sharing ideas publicly with the whole class. As Pritesh Raichura (2023) explains, turn and talk is also powerful when used for generating ideas and testing out suggestions with a partner. What's more, turn and talk can be used by students as a safe space to share with their partners where they went wrong or what they learned from the teacher's feedback.

HOW DO I IMPLEMENT IT?

MODEL AND EMBED THE ROUTINE: Research shows that having multiple opportunities to respond and actively engage in content learning improves student learning (MacSuga-Gage et al, 2015). Use turn and talk when you want students to rehearse answers or new vocabulary. Introduce the routine by modelling it so students know what successful discussion looks like. The following principles can help introduce turn and talk effectively.

1. **MAKE CRITERIA EXPLICIT**
   Face partner, eye contact, full sentences.
2. **ESTABLISH FAMILIAR CUES**
   Cue in: 'Go!' Cue out: '1, 2, 3, Eyes on me!'
3. **DIRECT WHO SPEAKS FIRST**
   State who starts to avoid dominance.
4. **GIVE CLEAR TIME LIMITS**
   Insist on tight time frames for paired talk.
5. **CIRCULATE AND MONITOR**
   Listen for misconceptions and errors.

READ MORE: *Turn and Talk* blog by Pritesh Raichura

USE A TIMER: Typically, turn and talk lasts about 20 to 30 seconds, providing just enough time for students to articulate initial thoughts without letting conversations drift off-topic. Setting a visible timer establishes a sense of urgency and motivates students to stay on task. It also signals a clear end to the discussion, which helps streamline transitions to the next part of the lesson.

THOUGHTFULLY PAIR STUDENTS: Consider which students are likely to stay on task during turn and talk. Pairing should be based on pre-established pairs in your seating plan. To create productive discussion, label each person in each pair Person A and Person B. Always direct who talks first. For example, 'Explain how you came to your answer. Person A starts. Go!'

PRITESH RAICHURA

Turn and talk is one of the techniques I use most in my classroom – perhaps 20 or more times in any given 50-minute lesson.

THE TYPICAL TURN AND TALK PROCESS INSPIRED BY PRITESH RAICHURA

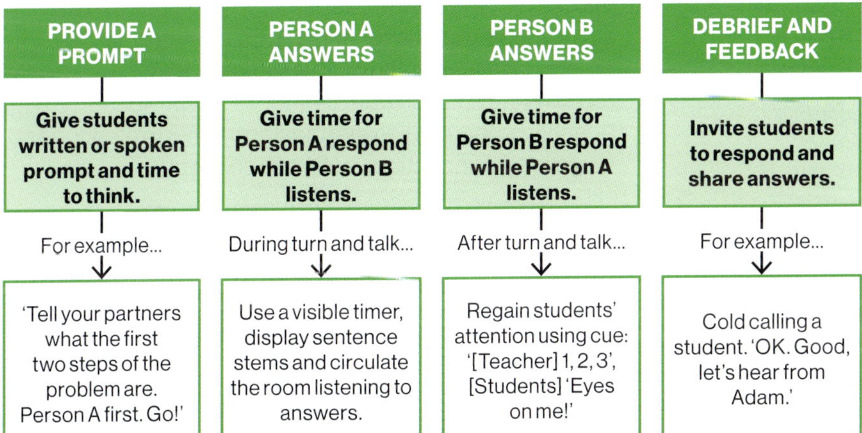

PROVIDE SENTENCE STEMS: Display sentence starters on a slide deck or verbally instruct students to 'include the following words in your answer...'. Scaffolding talk and giving extra time is important for supporting all learners in structured talk.

WAIT TIME: When asking a question or providing a prompt to the class, it's essential to allow students think time before they begin turn and talk. This pause gives them the opportunity to activate their prior knowledge and form their ideas.

MODE A PRACTICES

DO NOW

INITIATE LEARNING BEFORE TEACHING BEGINS

DOUG LEMOV

A Do Now allows the learning to start before the teaching has begun, 'maximising instructional time by getting students on task right away. (2010)

WHAT IS IT AND WHY IS IT IMPORTANT?

A 'Do Now' is a short 3–5 minute focused written activity that students begin immediately upon entering the classroom, setting a purposeful and engaging start to the lesson. According to Lemov, an effective Do Now 'allows the learning to start before the teaching has begun', maximising instructional time by getting students on task right away. When done effectively, the Do Now serves as a valuable method for engaging students in retrieval practice. Research shows that retrieval practice – actively recalling information from memory – has profound benefits on learning, strengthening memory retention and reinforcing connections between concepts.

HOW DO I IMPLEMENT IT?

EMBED DO NOW AS A ROUTINE: The Do Now routine should be completed independently and without teacher support, ideally in a dedicated section of students' books. This allows students to track their progress over time, helping them build metacognitive awareness. Research by the Education Endowment Foundation (EEF, 2018) suggests self-regulated learners are aware of their strengths and weaknesses and can motivate themselves to engage in and improve their learning.

1 Prerequisite Knowledge
2 Last Lesson Knowledge
3 Last Term Knowledge

1. **VISIBLE AND READY** Display activity in a designated area.
2. **CHALLENGING AND MEANINGFUL** Choose questions that promote recall.
3. **CONSISTENT ROUTINE** Make the routine predictable.
4. **TEACHER AUTONOMY** Tailor to department /curriculum needs.

LISTEN: *The Do Now Decider* by Adam Boxer (Carousel Learning ebook)

IMPLEMENTING DO NOW: The Do Now approach will take time to develop into a routine. Ensure expectations are high and move through the following three steps:

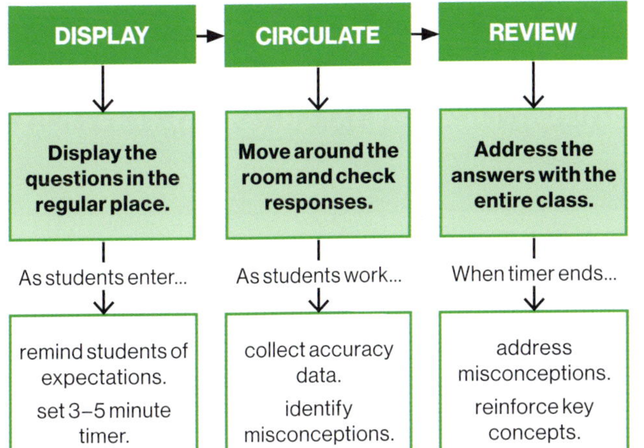

ADAM BOXER

Retrieving things from memory has profound benefits. Doing so makes things easier to recall in the future, but also connects those things more strongly to other items in memory, thus deepening the quality of the learning. (2024)

SELECT QUESTION TYPES FOR RETRIEVAL PRACTICE: Bjork (2014) emphasises that forgetting does not erase learning; instead it allows for greater gains in long-term retention when information is revisited. Thoughtfully select questions that challenge students to retrieve information from memory, especially those targeting key concepts and previously covered material.

KNOWLEDGE OVER TIME	RECENT LESSON KNOWLEDGE	PREREQUISITE KNOWLEDGE	MIX OF RECENT AND OVER TIME
Guarantees a good spread of retrieval practice over time.	Gives information about student knowledge of the topic.	Guaranteed to help students during the current lesson.	Aids retrieval over time and helps students in current lesson.

PARTICIPATION AND REVIEW: Determine where students will complete their Do Now, such as in exercise books or on mini-whiteboards. Select a review method that provides meaningful data, such as circulating to observe responses or guiding students through self-assessment. Self-assessment enables students to internalise the correct approach and develop metacognitive skills for future tasks. When reviewing as a class, focus on addressing common misconceptions and areas of difficulty, ensuring students gain clarity on challenging concepts.

MODE A PRACTICES

OPTIMISE FOCUS

SIMPLIFY CLASSROOM DESIGN TO GUIDE ATTENTION

WHAT IS IT AND WHY IS IT IMPORTANT?

Classroom focus requires the intentional design and arrangement of the learning space to help create the conditions for optimal learning. This setup is important because it directly impacts students' ability to focus, engage and interact with both the teacher and their peers. Annes et al (2023) found 85% of the students found the disorganised environment stressful and 89% felt more focused in the organised workspace.This means an effective classroom layout is not just about aesthetics; it's about creating a predictable and organised environment that runs like clockwork. Routines, flexible seating arrangements and the careful organisation of visuals are all imperative factors in optimising focus.

BLAKE HARVARD

The classroom's predictability, consistency, organisation and tidiness, allows both the teacher and students to simply focus on what is important for learning. (2024)

HOW DO I IMPLEMENT IT?

MAKE IT PREDICTABLE AND CONSISTENT: In a simple classroom, predictability and consistency are foundational to learning. Predictability means students know the behaviour rules, expectations and routines, creating a stable environment where they understand what to expect and how to engage in daily activities. Research shows students who have learned the behaviours and routines that are expected of them to the point they become unconscious and automatic won't have to think about these things while focused on learning. With their focus on learning, this aids effective transfer and retention in long-term memory (Simonsen et al, 2008).

READ MORE: *Do I Have Your Attention?* by Blake Harvard

GUIDE ATTENTION: To optimise focus, design a classroom that is engaging but not overstimulating. Avoid clutter in teaching areas and keep students' attention by using arrows and underlining and culling distracting graphics from slideshows. Research shows that signalling important or relevant learning parts to focus students' attention can increase the working memory resources available for learning (Castro-Alonso et al, 2024). An overstimulating environment can increase extraneous cognitive load, making it harder for students to concentrate. Simple classrooms and guiding students' attention reduce unnecessary cognitive demands.

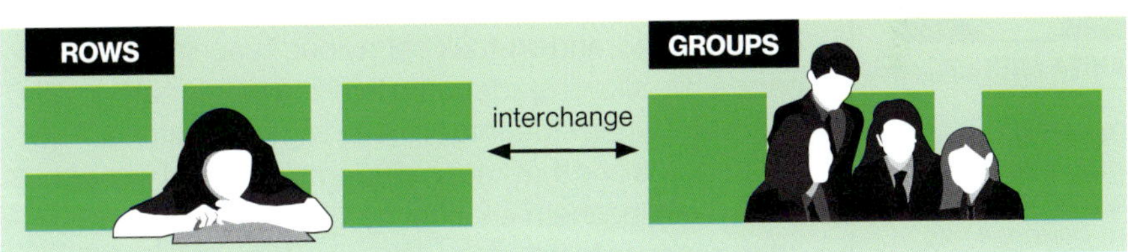

USE FLEXIBLE SEATING PLANS: Design seating plans to support different activities and classroom interactions – individual work, pairs, small groups and whole-class discussions. Regularly observe how your seating plan impacts student behaviour and learning, and be prepared to make adjustments as needed to improve the classroom environment. Busch (2024) said that 'a good seating plan resulted in many positive benefits for students, including staying more on track, being more focused on the task, and having more positive academic behaviours'.

MANAGE THE VISUALS: Designing classrooms with fewer visual distractions can help maintain attention on learning. Godwin et al (2022) showed that students remain more distracted in classrooms filled with posters compared to minimalist settings. Peps Mccrea recommends:

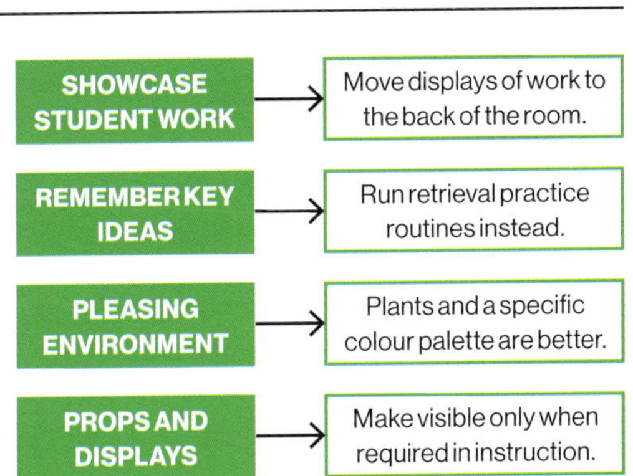

MODE A PRACTICES

LESSON PACE

OPTIMISE INSTRUCTIONAL TIME, CONTENT & FOCUS

ANITA ARCHER

Delivering instruction at an appropriate pace is crucial to optimise instructional time, the amount of content that can be presented, and on-task behavior. (2011)

WHAT IS IT AND WHY IS IT IMPORTANT?

Delivering instruction at an appropriate pace is crucial to optimise instructional time, the amount of content that can be presented, and on-task behaviour. Teaching at a brisk pace while allowing adequate thinking time is particularly important when students are learning new material. The ideal pace is one that keeps students engaged without overwhelming them – neither so slow that they lose interest nor so fast that they struggle to keep up. As Tom Needham (2020) asserts, a 'pacey' lesson is an effective lesson, where classroom time is used productively, with minimal wasted moments. The following strategies help sustain a strong pace while keeping lessons engaging through eliciting responses.

HOW DO I IMPLEMENT IT?

USE ESSENTIAL DELIVERY SKILLS: During explicit or direct instruction (DI), maintaining a fast overall pace is conducive to keeping students' attention (Engelmann, 2024). This can be achieved using the five essential delivery skills sequenced opposite (input, question, response, monitor and feedback). Plan and script explanations during the input phase to ensure conciseness and clarity, keeping lessons focused and preventing unnecessary tangents.

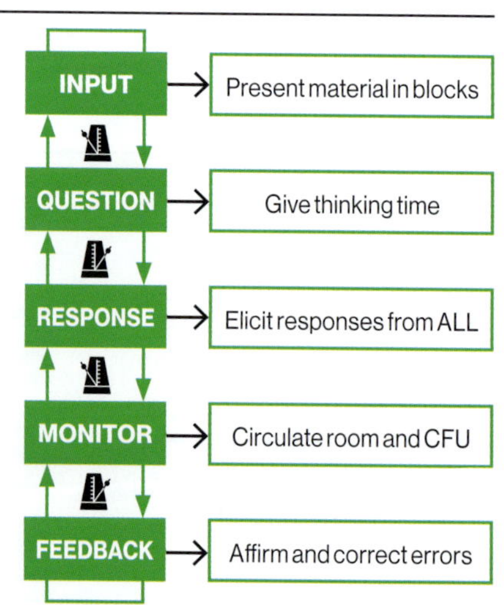

READ MORE: 'Strategies to Increase Pace' blog by Tom Needham

OPTIMISE LESSON FLOW: Maintaining a strong lesson pace helps to minimise downtime and keep students actively engaged. This can be achieved by:

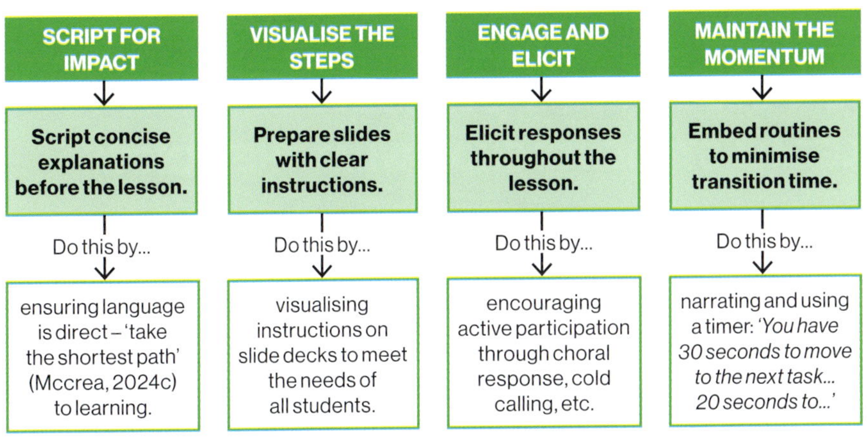

STREAMLINE RESOURCES: Prepare booklets, handouts and digital materials well in advance, ensuring they are clearly labelled and easy to access. Use consistent formats for worksheets and lesson materials to reduce confusion and conserve students' cognitive energy. Organise resources logically, whether on desks or online platforms, allowing students to get them independently.

SIGNAL TRANSITIONS: Distinctly mark the beginnings and endings of activities to help students recognise shifts in the lesson. Use clear verbal cues, pauses, or changes in tone of voice to signal transitions, creating a sense of anticipation and urgency. For example, 'OK, students. You have three minutes to write a response. Ready? Go!' Such cues signal the start of a new task and encourage prompt and active participation.

PRESENT CLEAR INSTRUCTIONS: Visualising instructions, tasks or steps helps maintain an uninterrupted flow. For each set of instructions, write them ahead of time on the board or have a slide in your PowerPoint with directions that accommodate all learners. If you are relying on giving oral directions only, think of those students that have poor listening skills: 'Tom, can you explain what are we doing?' and 'What do we do after this task?'

MODE A PRACTICES

THINKING TIME

LET ALL STUDENTS SHOW WHAT THEY KNOW

JON TAIT

When a teacher increases the wait time they give their students up to even just three seconds, students provide better answers, and teachers report a more positive classroom atmosphere. (2023)

WHAT IS IT AND WHY IS IT IMPORTANT?

Giving adequate thinking time after posing a question is crucial to ensure students can engage in active retrieval and respond effectively. Stahl (1994) found that allowing students 3 to 5 seconds to think before responding significantly enhances the quality of their answers. However, there is no magic number, as the optimal wait time depends on the complexity of the task and the students' background knowledge. Research on retrieval practice explains the act of generating an answer to a question, helps improve memory retention. If we rush the amount of time students have to retrieve information, we effectively shorten this learning opportunity. Thinking time is also inclusive as it encourages everyone to participate.

HOW DO I IMPLEMENT IT?

POSE THE QUESTION AND WAIT:
Pose a clear question or prompt, then wait in silence, making sure students don't put their hands up or speak. Depending on the complexity of the question, allow sufficient think time. Encourage students to jot down their thoughts during this quiet period to scribe their thinking. Afterward, have them discuss their ideas with a partner before sharing with the class. This ensures students have the chance to process the question in a safe space before sharing their response with the entire class.

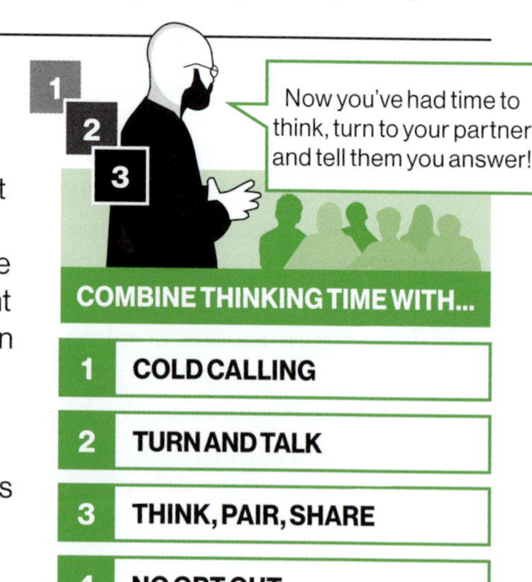

COMBINE THINKING TIME WITH...

1. COLD CALLING
2. TURN AND TALK
3. THINK, PAIR, SHARE
4. NO OPT OUT

READ MORE: 'Thinking Time: Maximising Depth and Duration of Attention' by Peps Mccrea

GIVE ADEQUATE TIME: Rowe (1974) suggested that allowing students 3 to 5 seconds of thinking time after posing a question significantly enhances the quality of their responses. For more complex questions, extended wait time is necessary. As represented in the diagram below, when discussing abstract concepts, providing up to 10 seconds or more enables students to process the information and formulate more thoughtful answers.

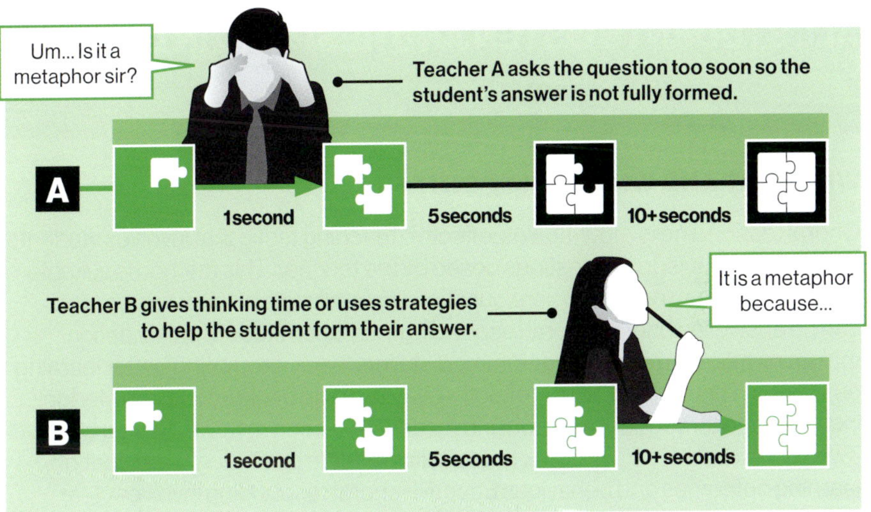

MAKE IT A CLASSROOM HABIT: Making students aware of the benefits of taking time to think before responding can make a huge difference. Practising and reminding students of the process is essential. Tell students that quality thinking and responding is required. Say things like, 'Take a moment to think about your answer'; or 'It's OK to take your time; I want to hear your best thoughts.'

PLAN BETTER QUESTIONS: Couple thinking time with pre-prepared questions to promote hard thinking. For example, instead of asking straightforward factual questions like, 'What are the main stages of photosynthesis?' ask: 'How might changes in the environment impact the different stages of photosynthesis?'

SILENCE IS GOLDEN: Do not feel the need to fill the void with your instructions. Silence is golden in that it allows students to concentrate without noise or distraction. This also means not rushing to jump in and give support or provide the answers too quickly. In practice, learning can often appear slow, uncomfortable and filled with awkward silences.

MODE A PRACTICES

CHORAL RESPONSES

ALL STUDENTS LISTEN AND RESPOND IN UNISON

WHAT IS IT AND WHY IS IT IMPORTANT?

Choral responding is a low-stakes, effective teaching tactic that involves students responding in unison to questions posed by the teacher. This method is suitable for any curriculum content where questions have a single correct answer and can be answered briefly. Choral responding increases student participation, maintains attention and provides immediate feedback, promoting better learning outcomes. This technique is an effective way to prime background knowledge, interspersed throughout a lesson and for end-of-lesson reviews. Research by Twyman et al (2018) also supports its positive effects on student participation, learning outcomes and behaviour. Effective choral responding involves clear guidelines and a lively pace to keep students engaged. Additionally, it can be adapted for various student groups, including general and special education students, from primary to secondary school levels.

HOW DO I IMPLEMENT IT?

CLEAR DIRECTION AND MODELLING: Teachers should clearly explain the types of questions that will be asked and model the expected responses.

THINKING PAUSE: A brief pause before signalling students to respond helps them process the question. The duration of the pause depends on the question and the level of mastery.

CONSISTENT SIGNALLING: Use clear and consistent signals (auditory or visual) to prompt students' responses, such as 'Class', 'How many?', or a hand movement.

READ MORE: 'Choral Response' Evidence Snacks by Peps Mccrea

PROVIDE CONSTANT FEEDBACK: Heward et al (2015) support the use of immediate verbal feedback during the choral response process.

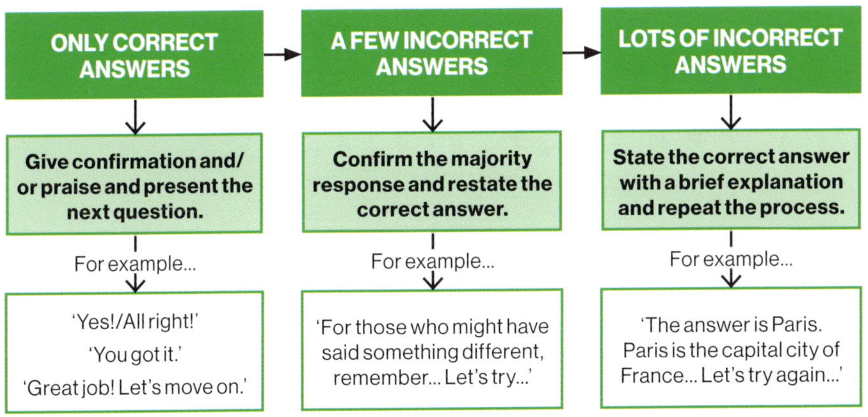

COMBINE IT WITH ACCOUNTABILITY STRATEGIES: Zach Groshell (2024) explains, 'When choral response is used in conjunction with cold calling, pair share, and other whole class engagement techniques, choral response is a powerful tool to get a pulse on attention and understanding.' Integrating choral response with accountability strategies creates a classroom environment where students are attentive and thinking hard. Choral responding provides 'good noise': the sound of students' voices engaged in active learning' (Heward et al, 2015).

USE 'CHECKS FOR LISTENING': This technique, popularisd by Pritesh Raichura, involves asking high-frequency questions that all students can answer in unison, keeping them attentive and reinforcing their understanding. By creating a culture of active participation, where all hands go up for every question, students feel encouraged to engage and contribute. This approach not only maintains the energy in the classroom but also allows teachers to quickly assess understanding and address any misconceptions. Positive reinforcement through praise helps to motivate students. To use this strategy effectively, clearly explain the expectations for participation defined by your department or school, model the type of responses you want, and use consistent and familiar signals to prompt choral responses.

ZACH GROSHELL

Choral response is a part of a culture of high expectations in which all students listen, all students respond to questions, and all students make an effort towards mastering the material.

MODE A PRACTICES

THINK-WRITE, PAIR-WRITE-SHARE

PROMOTE HARD THINKING AND ACTIVE LISTENING

POOJA K. AGARWAL

Almost all effect sizes... indicated a positive benefit from retrieval practice under wide-ranging conditions, and retrieval practice improved student learning to a greater extent than time spent on other classroom activities.

WHAT IS IT AND WHY IS IT IMPORTANT?

Think-write, pair-write and share is an adaptation of the traditional think, pair, share strategy. It promotes low-stakes engagement and accountability by providing more time for students to brainstorm and connect learning. Unlike the traditional method, where students only discuss their thoughts, this approach begins with students individually writing down their ideas, ensuring everyone has prepared contributions. Agarwal et al (2021) highlight this act of recalling previously learned information with no notes – improves long-term learning and memory. In the pairing phase, students exchange ideas and record their partner's best ideas, encouraging active listening and reflection. Finally, rather than sharing one by one, the teacher gathers ideas while circulating, displaying them to invite class discussion and feedback.

HOW DO I IMPLEMENT IT?

STEP 1: THINK AND WRITE INDEPENDENTLY Giving adequate thinking time is essential for students to perform retrieval practice properly. During this time, ensure the room is silent so that students can concentrate. The act of writing down their ideas acts as a free-recall opportunity, challenging students to actively pull out information from long-term memory. Encourage students to use mini-whiteboards where possible to reinforce a low-stakes approach where students can easily erase or edit their answers.

READ MORE: 'Retrieval Practice Consistently Benefits Student Learning' by Pooja Agarwal et al

STEP 2: PAIR AND WRITE After generating their own ideas, students pair up to discuss what they have written, sharing their thoughts with a partner. In this variation, each student not only listens but also actively records their partner's best idea. This encourages attentive listening and fosters a sense of accountability, as students know they may later share their partner's ideas with the class.

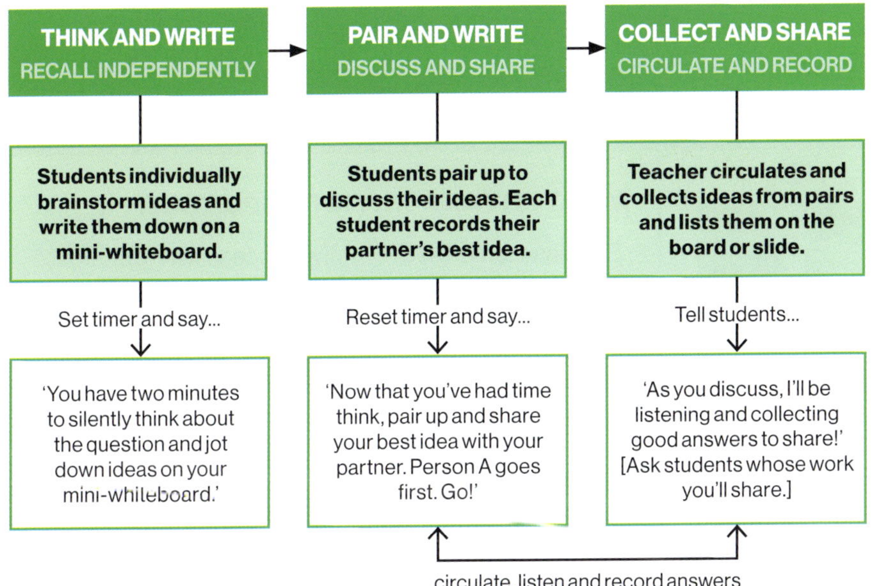

STEP 3: COLLECT AND SHARE For the final step, share insights gathered from the paired activity. Rather than cold calling, use a prepared list of ideas gathered from observing the pairs during the previous steps. This streamlines the sharing process, allowing for a broader range of ideas to be presented efficiently. Pre-call (ask privately) students during the pair-write stage to make sharing low stakes and comfortable for students. Recording a range of ideas not only values each student's input but also reinforces a sense of accountability ensuring all learners are thinking.

MODE A PRACTICES

SELF-ASSESSMENT

BUILDING AN INTERNAL METACOGNITIVE VOICE

JOHN HATTIE

Expert teachers engage students in learning and develop in their students' self-regulation, involvement in mastery learning, enhanced self-efficacy, and self-esteem as learners. (2003)

WHAT IS IT AND WHY IS IT IMPORTANT?

Self-assessment is a reflective process where students evaluate their own work using specific criteria. Wiliam (2018) asserts that this process improves students' ability to monitor and regulate their own learning processes, which significantly improves their learning outcomes by activating students as owners of their own learning. Ross (2006) also supports this view, showing that self-assessment contributes to higher student achievement by helping students set higher standards and persist in their efforts. In other words, it helps students become active participants in their learning journey and develop skills such as self-regulation and metacognitive talk.

HOW DO I IMPLEMENT IT?

EXPLAIN RUBRICS AND EXAMPLES OF MASTERY: To implement effective self-assessment, first simplify your rubric by breaking down criteria into basic elements, such as sections or paragraphs, to build understanding step by step. Guide students through the rubric by walking them through each step, providing clear examples and asking probing questions to encourage their input and reflections. To create great work, students need clear examples of excellence based on the rubric. Demonstrating mastery can involve showcasing model examples, student work or even through videos or images. Generating discussion and producing checklists on the main features of excellent work is also powerful.

READ MORE: 'Metacognition and self-regulation guidance' report by the EEF

UTILISE EXAM WRAPPERS: Exam wrappers are student self-evaluation feedback tools that offer teachers and students a way to evaluate and analyse errors, and revision patterns, for a given exam. Education Endowment Foundation (2021d) explain this can help improve students' accuracy of judgement.

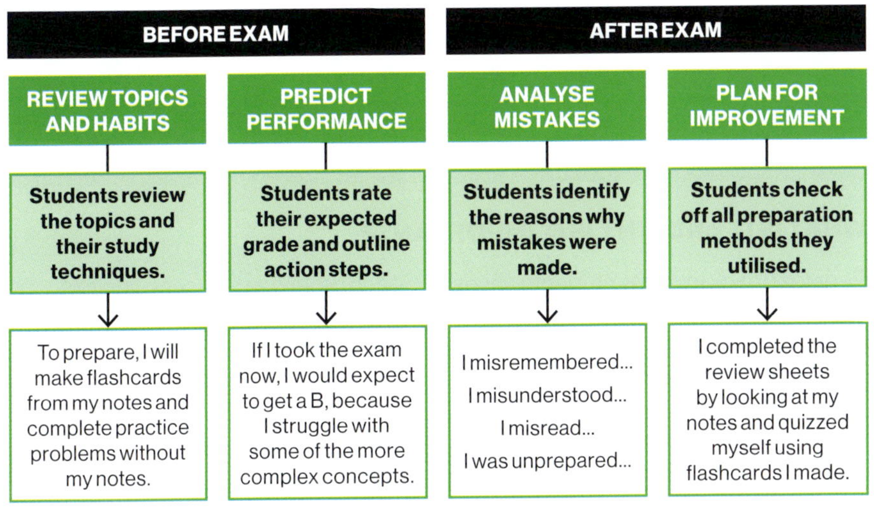

INTRODUCE STUDENT PORTFOLIOS: Create portfolios with work samples from the beginning, middle and end of a unit to help students track their learning progression. This process allows students to compare and assess their initial understanding with their current knowledge, visualising their growth over time. This method enables students to identify areas for improvement, recognise changes in their skill levels, and plan next steps for their learning journey.

CREATE LEARNING LOGS: Learning logs allow students to document their learning activities, reflecting on what they did, what they learned, and any questions they have. This promotes metacognitive thinking by prompting students to think critically about their learning strategies and outcomes. For example, after a lesson, students write down the key points they understood, identify aspects they found challenging and note what they need to review for future learning.

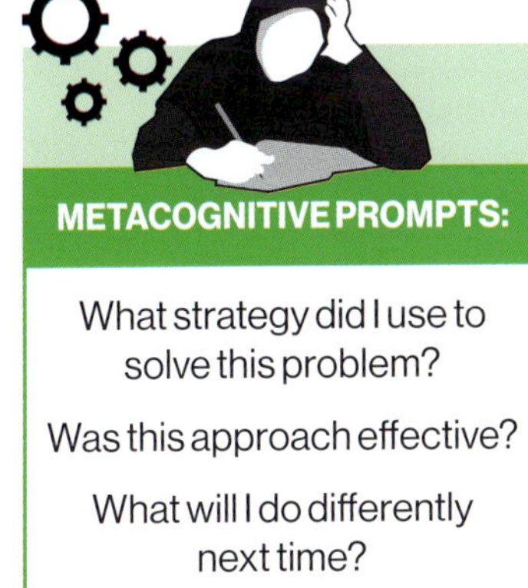

METACOGNITIVE PROMPTS:

What strategy did I use to solve this problem?

Was this approach effective?

What will I do differently next time?

MODE A PRACTICES

PEER FEEDBACK

MODEL AND SCAFFOLD CONSTRUCTIVE TALK

WHAT IS IT AND WHY IS IT IMPORTANT?

Peer feedback involves students assessing each other's work according to a set of criteria and providing specific feedback for improvement. This not only improves the quality of the work but also improves the learners themselves by strengthening their metacognitive skills and self-regulation, making them more aware of their own learning processes. Black et al (2004) show peer work is valuable because the interchange will be in language that students naturally use and because students learn by taking the roles of teachers and examiners. It is important to model and scaffold this process to make it work effectively.

PAUL BLACK

Peer assessment turns out to be an important complement to self-assessment. Peer assessment is uniquely valuable because students may accept criticisms of their work from one another that they would not take seriously if the remarks were offered by a teacher.

HOW DO I IMPLEMENT IT?

MODEL USING ANONYMOUS EXAMPLES: With your class, model and discuss how to give structured, specific and actionable feedback to an anonymous piece of work. Co-construct sentence starters that are both supportive and constructive. For example: 'In the second paragraph, your description of the setting is very vivid. One area you could expand on is...', 'Work on your thesis statement...'.

REQUIRE A CONVERSATION: As Wiliam (2011) explains, 'Feedback should cause thinking. It should be focused; it should relate to the learning goals that have been shared with the students; and it should be more work for the recipient than the donor.' After providing written comments, ask students to have a conversation to explain their feedback and action steps with their partner. This will help clarify any misunderstandings and consolidate ideas.

READ MORE: *Why Learning Fails (And What To Do About It)* by Alex Quigley

TEACH THE 'SPARK' METHOD TO IMPROVE WRITING: Mark Gardner (2019) has a useful acronym to remember what constitutes quality feedback: SPARK (specific, prescriptive, actionable, referenced and kind). Structured peer talk is beneficial because it negates some of the problems usually associated with peer feedback, such as depth, accuracy and credibility (Gielen et al, 2010).

S	P	A	R	K
SPECIFIC	**PRESCRIPTIVE**	**ACTIONABLE**	**REFERENCED**	**KIND**
Comments are linked to a discrete word, phrase or sentence.	**Offers a solution or strategy to improve the work.**	**Leaves the peer knowing what steps to take for improvement.**	**Directly references the task criteria, requirements or target skills.**	**All comments are framed in a kind and supportive way.**
For example...	For example...	For example...	For example...	For example...
In the second paragraph, your use of 'illustrates' is powerful. It clearly shows how the character feels.	To strengthen your argument in the third paragraph, consider using a quote from the text. You can find quotes on page 45.	Try breaking down the long sentence in the fourth paragraph into two shorter sentences. This will make it clearer.	Your introduction meets the criteria well by clearly stating your thesis. However, you need to expand on...	Your story is engaging! The imagery you use brings the scenes to life. One small suggestion: add more dialogue to show...

CONDUCT GALLERY CRITIQUE: Students display their work around the room and engage in a 'walkthrough' where they provide and receive feedback from their peers using sticky notes. This encourages students to view each other's work from different perspectives. By rotating through the displays, students can offer kind, helpful and specific feedback. This not only improves the depth of feedback but also promotes critical reflective learning, as students learn to articulate constructive criticism and appreciate varied approaches to the same task.

MODE A PRACTICES

FOUR QUARTERS MARKING

INCREASE LEARNING AND REDUCE WORKLOAD

WHAT IS IT AND WHY IS IT IMPORTANT?

The book *What Does This Look Like in the Classroom?* by Carl Hendrick and Robin Macpherson (2017) includes a fascinating interview with Dylan Wiliam about implementing feedback in the classroom. Wiliam proposes what he calls, 'four quarters marking' where only 25% of student work is marked in detail, 25% is skimmed, 25% undergoes student self-assessment, and the remaining 25% is peer-assessed. The four quarters marking approach aims to shift the feedback burden on to students, fostering greater ownership of their learning and addressing both the effectiveness of feedback and teacher workload.

CARL HENDRICK

As a profession, we are to some extent, our own worst enemy. Using marking policies that have little impact on student achievement and a negative impact on teacher workload and morale makes little sense.

HOW DO I IMPLEMENT IT?

MANAGE EXPECTATIONS WITH CAREGIVERS:
Wiliam suggests that school leaders should manage expectations with parents, clarifying that limiting detailed feedback to 25% of student work is a strategic choice backed by research aimed at improving teaching quality and student learning outcomes.

25% MARK IN DETAIL AND MAKE IT ACTIONABLE:
According to Wiliam (2018b), the main purpose of feedback is 'to improve the student and not the work'. He stresses that feedback must help students improve by providing steps that prompt a specific action. Get students to do something concrete like redrafting, or to act as detectives to find and fix errors in their own work.

READ MORE: *What Does This Look Like in the Classroom?* by Carl Hendrick and Robin Macpherson

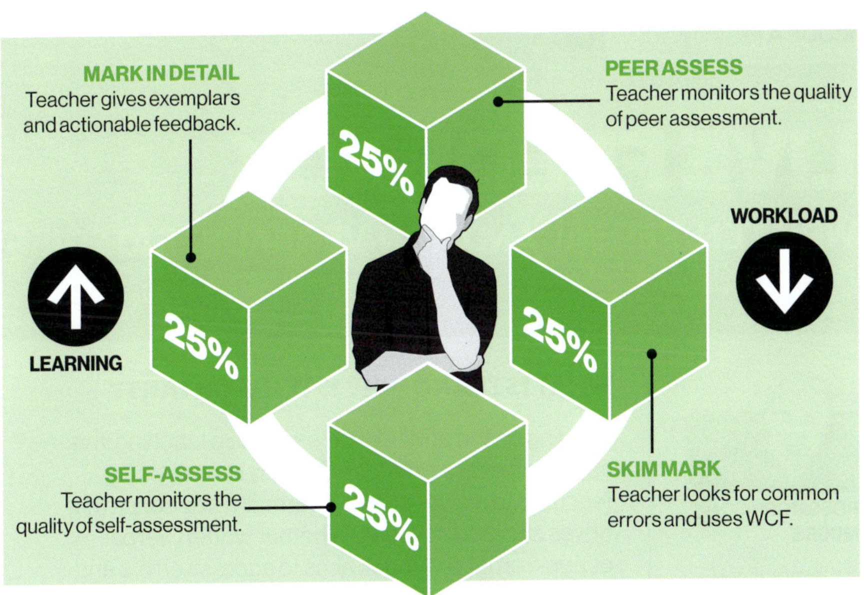

25% USE EXEMPLARS FOR SELF-ASSESSMENT: Dylan Wiliam advocates for using exemplar essays and problems to encourage students to self-assess and benchmark their work against concrete examples of success. This is a better approach than giving detailed marking which, if not actionable, can be overlooked.

25% SKIM AND USE WHOLE-CLASS FEEDBACK: Whole-class feedback shifts the focus from individual comments to addressing the progress across the class. This involves summarising and giving feedback on the key points of strength and areas for improvement for the class rather than marking each student's work in detail.

25% PEER ASSESS WITH 2 STARS AND A WISH: In his book *Embedded Formative Assessment*, Wiliam explains students can be taught how to provide effective peer feedback by identifying two things they find good about the work and a 'wish' – a suggestion for improvement based on clear success criteria.

DYLAN WILIAM

I recommend what I call 'four quarters marking'. I think that teachers should mark in detail 25% of what students do, should skim another 25%, students should then self-assess about 25% with teachers monitoring the quality of that and finally, peer assessment should be the other 25%.

MODE A PRACTICES

LIVE FEEDBACK

WRITTEN, VERBAL AND NON-VERBAL STRATEGIES

ROSS MORRISON MCGILL

To better support our teachers... we must move towards a deeper understanding of formative assessment. (2024)

WHAT IS IT AND WHY IS IT IMPORTANT?

Building on the principle of responsive teaching, this approach offers workload-friendly strategies for teachers to deliver effective formative feedback that drives student progress. Whether written, verbal, or non-verbal, feedback aims to address errors and misconceptions responsively, ensuring it is actionable and allowing students to improve while it still remains relevant. Interactive feedback fosters meaningful teacher-student engagement, transforming improvement into a two-way process. As Brown et al (2014) explain, 'Mastery requires both the possession of ready knowledge and the conceptual understanding of how to use it.'

HOW DO I IMPLEMENT IT?

FORMATIVE ASSESSMENT TYPES:
In *Guide to Feedback*, Ross Morrison McGill delves into evidence-informed feedback strategies vital to effective formative assessment. Drawing inspiration from Hattie and Timperley's seminal work *The Power of Feedback*, McGill highlights the importance of written, verbal and non-verbal feedback to enhance student learning while minimising teacher workload. He identifies three pivotal types of formative assessment:

WRITTEN | **VERBAL** | **NON-VERBAL**

FEEDBACK HOW AM I GOING?
Reflect on student progress in comparison with their previous efforts.

FEED-UP WHERE AM I GOING?
Compare student progress with the learning objective and set clear goals.

FEED-FORWARD WHERE TO NEXT?
Guide students on how to apply learning to future activities or problems.

READ MORE: *Guide to Feedback* by Ross Morrison McGill

WRITTEN THE ORANGE BOX: The orange box strategy helps to reduce workload and move learners forward in small steps. During a lesson, choose one area of a student's work and draw an orange (or green!) box around it. This targeted approach focuses attention on one aspect for improvement, supported by verbal feedback. Ask the student to respond by editing their work in a different coloured pen so that you can easily see the improvements.

VERBAL THE PPIPL STRATEGY: Verbal dialogue is an engaging and targeted method to help students improve and move forward. McGill (2022) calls his approach the 'praise, probe, identify, plan, lock' (PPIPL) strategy, which helps discourage teachers from providing students with the answers or correcting every single error in a piece of work. Instead, this five-step process helps teachers direct students by engaging in dialogue and giving them concrete steps to put into action right away.

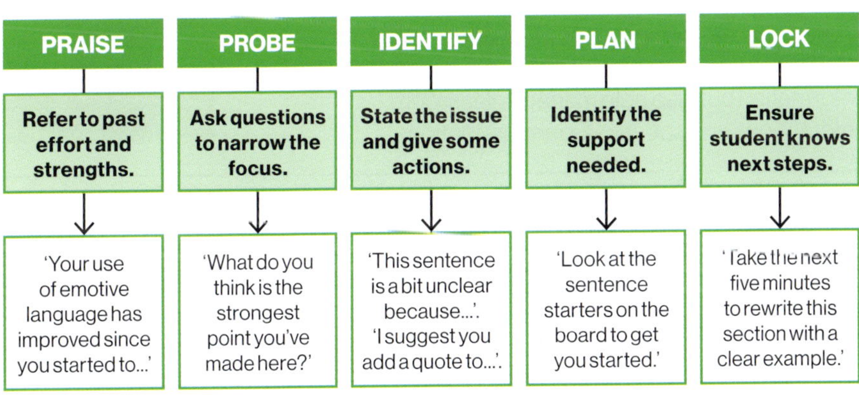

NON-VERBAL GESTURES AND CUES: Non-verbal strategies can subtly guide student improvement. Techniques like pointing, nodding or raising an eyebrow can draw attention to specific areas of work without interrupting the flow of the lesson. Hand signals can be used to indicate common errors, such as circling a finger to signify rechecking a sentence or tapping on a section to focus attention. Physical demonstrations, like miming punctuation use or showing fractions with hand gestures, can make abstract concepts more concrete.

MODE A PRACTICES

GESTURES

GIVE VISUAL AND PHYSICAL REPRESENTATIONS

WHAT IS IT AND WHY IS IT IMPORTANT?

Gestures are body movements that play a critical role in communication and Mode A teaching in the classroom. Research shows that gestures help bridge the gap between abstract concepts and students' understanding by providing visual and kinaesthetic representations of ideas. They support verbal explanations, reduce ambiguity and enhance the clarity of complex topics (Maldini et al, 2017). By incorporating gestures, teachers can make learning more concrete to improve student understanding and retention. Gestures not only aid in conveying information but also help manage classroom interactions and secure students' attention.

SUSAN GOLDIN-MEADOW

Gesture is often better suited to conveying certain types of information than speech. Gesture can therefore work with speech to convey a richer message. (2023)

HOW DO I IMPLEMENT IT?

INTEGRATE GESTURES IN LESSON PLANNING: Plan specific gestures that align with key concepts your are teaching. Use hand movements to illustrate complex ideas or abstract concepts such as the orbit of planets in the solar system. Incorporate iconic gestures that represent the meaning of words. For example, moving your hands in an upward motion to illustrate 'rise'. Goldin-Meadow (2023) suggests gesture can work with speech to convey a richer message than the message conveyed in speech alone . This ties into ideas on embodied cognition that posits our cognitive processes are not just situated in the brain but are distributed across the entire body.

READ MORE: *Thinking with Your Hands* by Susan Goldin-Meadow

TYPES OF GESTURES: The primary types of gestures relevant to most educators include iconic, deictic, and regulator gestures, each serving a unique function in the learning process (Novack et al, 2015).

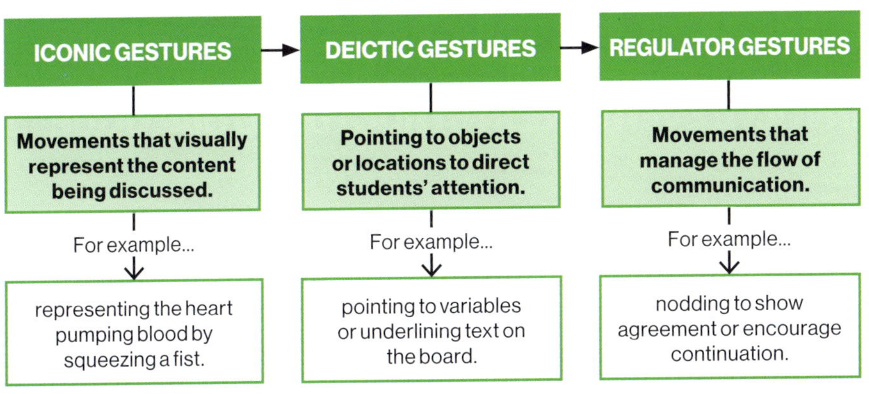

USE NON-VERBAL CUES FOR CLASSROOM MANAGEMENT: Incorporate specific gestures as non-verbal cues to manage classroom behaviour and transitions. For example, develop a set of standard hand signals to indicate when students should stop talking, line up or pay attention. This not only reduces the need for verbal interruptions but also helps maintain attention. Using gestures to signal transitions between activities can help students understand and anticipate the next steps, which helps to improve the overall flow of the lesson.

ENCOURAGE STUDENTS TO GESTURE: Encourage students to use gestures when explaining their thoughts or solving problems. Research shows that just telling students to move their hands as they explain can bring out new ways of thinking about the problem and increase learning. Provide opportunities for students to externalise their understanding through gestures in group discussions and presentations. For instance, have students use their hands to illustrate concepts like two plates colliding and rising in geography to show plate convergence. Asking students to explain their thinking to the class with gestures deepens their shared understanding and helps solidify fledgling ideas.

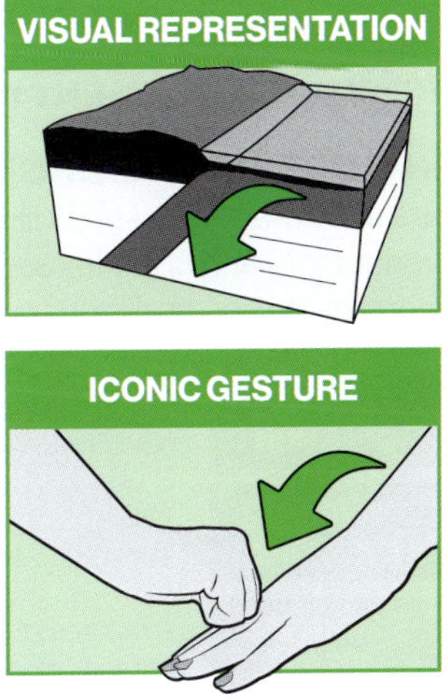

MODE A PRACTICES

DISCUSSIONS

INVOLVE EVERYONE IN STRUCTURED DIALOGUE

WHAT IS IT AND WHY IS IT IMPORTANT?

Discussion is an effective Mode A strategy that promotes active listening and hard thinking. When thoughtfully structured, class discussions encourage participation, balance students' perspectives and engage them in meaningful oracy. The teacher's role is like a conductor in an orchestra, bringing in diverse voices, guiding the flow and ensuring harmony in the exchange of ideas. Implementing purposeful questioning, pair-sharing and whole-class reflection helps to ensure that every student has a voice, while summarising key points reinforces learning and provides clarity. A safe and inclusive space for dialogue is key for building knowledge and developing communication skills.

HOW DO I IMPLEMENT IT?

INCLUDE THE MAIN INGREDIENTS: In structured discussions, students are encouraged to 'speak like an essay', using formal language, subject-specific vocabulary and complex sentence structures (Didau, 2018). Model the language from the get-go and focus on the main ingredients for success:

PLAN THE QUESTION	Plan an open-ended question before the lesson aligned with the learning objective: *'What do you think: should historical monuments ever be removed?'*
INVOLVE EVERYONE	Active participation from everyone is key. Utilise turn and talk or think, pair, share first if students require a safe space to think and field their ideas.
SUMMARISE IDEAS	To address transience, record information at the end of the discussion in collaboration with the class: *'In summary, we started with* [write]... *then...'*

READ MORE: *Class Discussion Forensics* blog by Tom Sherrington

USE ABC – 'ADD, BUILD OR CHALLENGE': This method encourages meaningful and fluent discussions by ensuring follow-up contributions improve dialogue. Students must respond by either adding new information, building on a peer's idea, or challenging a viewpoint with a respectful counterargument.

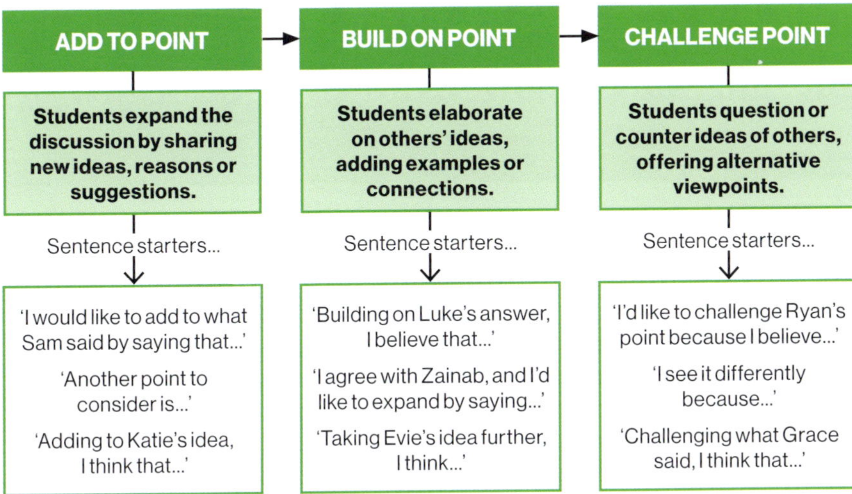

CONTROL THE FLOW: Use follow-up questions such as: 'What do you mean by alliances causing the war?' Acknowledge differences: 'What makes your interpretation of the character's actions opposite to Ben's?' And ask questions to help students connect to their prior knowledge: 'What did we study about erosion that helps us explain how valleys are shaped?'

CLICKS AND SEAT SIGNALS: Effective classroom discussions require strategies to ensure smooth flow and active participation. Harry Fletcher-Wood (2014) suggests using non-verbal 'seat signals' to minimise interruptions while keeping students engaged. For example, students can click to show agreement, cross fingers to indicate inaudibility or point to reference a peer's comment. These signals ensure everyone is included, encourage active listening, and create a more focused discussion environment, allowing ideas to flow without constant verbal interruptions.

DAVID DIDAU

Talk is a powerful lever for cognitive change... Talk can be used not to see what pupils think, but to change it. By asking them to express their ideas in academic language we can have a surprising impact on pupils'... academic language, and therefore to be academically successful.

MODE A PRACTICES

NOTE-TAKING

ORGANISE INFORMATION AND BOOST RETENTION

ROBERT MARZANO

To effectively delete, substitute and keep information, students must analyse the information at a fairly deep level.

WHAT IS IT AND WHY IS IT IMPORTANT?

Focused note-taking is a structured strategy designed to improve knowledge retention by actively engaging students in processing information. Unlike passively copying down notes, this approach encourages students to filter, prioritise and synthesise key information into concise summaries. Fiorella et al (2015) on generative learning explain that summarising encourages learners to make sense of new information by integrating it with prior knowledge. Teaching students how to take focused notes not only helps to consolidate knowledge but also engages students in deeper cognitive processing.

HOW DO I IMPLEMENT IT?

EXPLICITLY TEACH NOTE-TAKING: When students copy information word-for-word, they leave no capacity in their working memory for analytical thinking. Rosenshine et al (1996) concluded that strategies that develop the analytical element of summarising, produce the most powerful effects. By explicitly teaching students effective note-taking strategies, teachers can help them identify the underlying structure of information. This helps them to process, organise and condense content effectively, promoting deeper understanding and long-term retention.

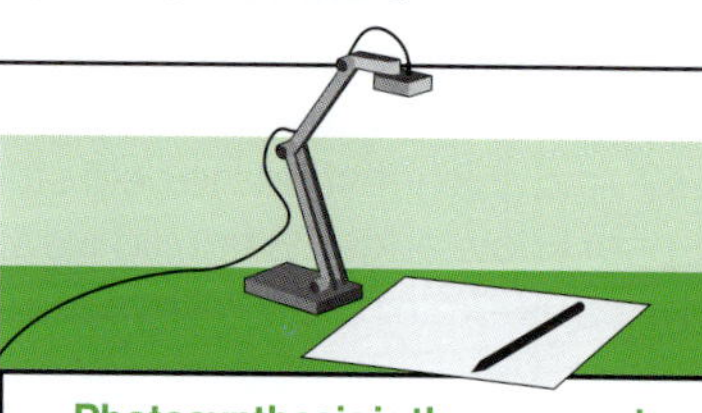

Photosynthesis is the process by which green plants use sunlight to create food. ~~*During this process,*~~ **plants take in carbon dioxide** ~~*from the air and water from the soil. Using the energy from sunlight,*~~ **they convert these substances into glucose,** ~~*which serves as food for the plant.*~~ **Oxygen is released as a byproduct** ~~*of this process.*~~

↓

Photosynthesis is how green plants use sunlight to turn carbon dioxide and water into glucose (food) while releasing oxygen as a byproduct.

READ MORE: *Classroom Instruction that Works* by Robert Marzano, Debra Pickering and Jane Pollock

DELETE, SUBSTITUTE, KEEP FRAMEWORK:

Summarising and note-taking are essential yet challenging skills. David Goodwin (2021) explains that 'the process of summarising is not about simply reducing the length of a text, but about identifying and retaining the most important information'. He recommends Robert Marzano's (2001) framework, rooted in cognitive psychology, which simplifies the process into three key actions: delete, substitute and keep. Students learn to delete unnecessary information, substitute complex terms with simpler ones and keep the essential elements. This helps students moving beyond surface-level copying and think deeply about the material taught.

DAVID GOODWIN

Summarising is difficult for students because they often struggle to distinguish between what is noteworthy and what is less important.

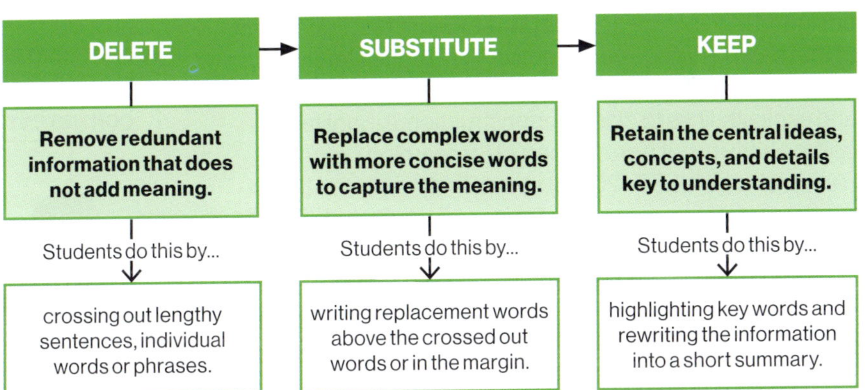

CORNELL NOTES: Developed by Walter Pauk (1974), the Cornell Notes System is a structured method that can improve retention. In the main notes section, students record key points during a lesson. The left-hand column is used for writing questions, keywords or prompts that help clarify and review the material. Writing questions helps clarify meanings, reveal relationships, establish continuity and strengthen memory. Finally, the summary section at the bottom provides a concise recap space for students.

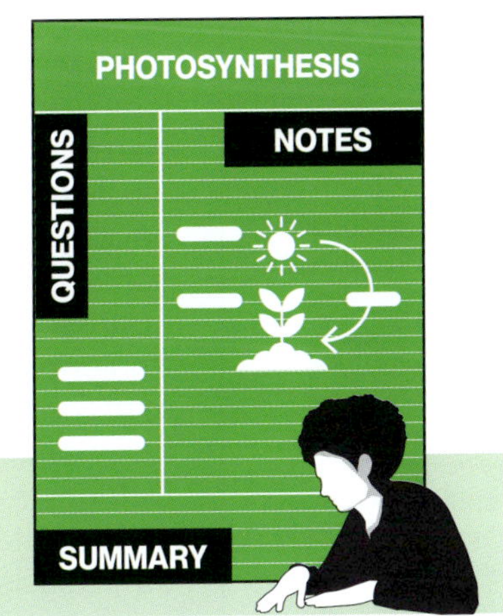

MODE A PRACTICES 

HOMEWORK

NURTURE A HOMEWORK CULTURE THAT WORKS

WHAT IS IT AND WHY IS IT IMPORTANT?

Homework is an important extension of classroom learning designed to reinforce and deepen students' understanding of the material. Integrated effectively and consistently, homework builds schemas, supports rehearsal of content and explicitly links to classroom instruction. It is not just a bolt-on activity but a crucial part of the learning process. Research by the EEF (2021e) shows that homework has a positive impact on average (+ 5 months), particularly with students in secondary schools. It is everyone's responsibility to properly embed homework into a school. This nurtures a culture of high expectations and builds independent learning habits that prepare learners for future academic challenges.

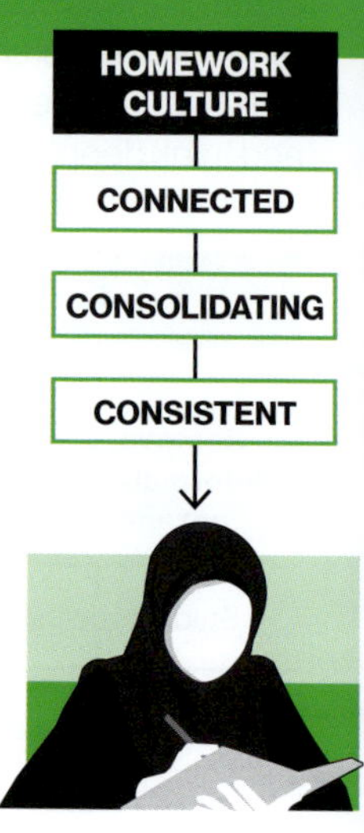

JO CASTELINO

Homework is not one of those things that needs to take hours and hours. It's about building those small habits and independence, getting students to see that they can sit there, do something, and succeed at it.

HOW DO WE IMPLEMENT IT?

LINK IT TO CLASSROOM LEARNING: Homework is most effective when it is an integral part of classroom learning, not just an additional task. This means it must be tied to the core knowledge that students need to know in any given curriculum. Consider how homework will augment these skills in the classroom. Furthermore, utilise the data from homework tasks to inform the direction of teaching and to make responsive adjustments. The quality of homework tasks is more important than the amount of time spent. Determine when students are ready to practice or consolidate already learned information, and use this as the basis to design and implement effective tasks.

READ MORE: *The Homework Conundrum* by Jo Castelino

SET HOMEWORK CONSISTENTLY: Teacher and author of *The Homework Conundrum*, Jo Castelino recommends to set homework once per week or fortnight on a specific day. Consistency helps students build a routine and manage their time effectively. It is also important to ensure teachers have the autonomy to follow up on the learning in the classroom, allowing them to tailor homework to their students' needs. Schedules or homework timetables are also helpful because they provide a clear structure for students, helping them to prioritise tasks and balance their workload. Collaborate with departments to ensure an equal spread across subjects.

BUILD SELF-EFFICACY AND INTRINSIC MOTIVATION: Bempechat (2019) found that regular high-quality homework plays a crucial role fostering self-efficacy and motivation in students. By setting tasks that students can accomplish independently and providing clear instructions, homework improves students' perceptions of their competence and motivates them 'to confront ever-more-complex tasks and develop resilience in the face of difficulty, and learn to embrace rather than shy away from challenge'.

BALANCE WORKLOAD:
Assign homework in short and manageable bursts. For example, a teacher might set a 20 minute retrieval practice exercise to consolidate learning from the lesson. While research indicates that more homework can be effective, it's crucial to maintain a balance with the context of the school and students' other commitments. Use whole-class feedback to streamline the process and provide high-quality, actionable insights.

MAKE STUDENTS THINK:
Harnessing research from cognitive science, such as Bjork's concept of desirable difficulties, helps to create learning experiences that improve retention. The goal is to foster deep learning and critical thinking skills in students. Homework is an integral part of this process. By setting spaced retrieval practice for homework, students can regularly review and reinforce what they have learned, leading to better long-term retention.

MODE A PRACTICES

INSTRUCTIONAL PLAYS

ACTIONS TO GUIDE LEARNING DURING INSTRUCTION

NANCY FREY

Teachers who are truly talented at offering guided instruction seem to have internalised instructional moves that foster learning.

DOUG FISHER

Guided instruction is ultimately about the instructional moves that the teacher makes... Getting started can seem overwhelming unless you break it down into manageable phases.

WHAT IS IT AND WHY IS IT IMPORTANT?

Instructional plays refers to the actions taken by teachers to support students during instruction. These moves provide scaffolding to help bridge the gap between students' current understanding and their learning goals. According to research, these instructional actions include questioning to check for understanding, prompting cognitive and metacognitive work, and providing cues to shift students' attention when needed. Building these skills promotes active participation and encourages students to take small steps towards mastering content.

HOW DO I IMPLEMENT IT?

CHECK WITH DIFFERENT QUESTION TYPES:

1. **ELICITATION QUESTIONS**
   'Who?', 'What?', 'Where?', 'When?', 'How?'
2. **ELABORATION QUESTIONS**
   'What other information do I need to know?'
3. **CLARIFICATION QUESTIONS**
   'Can you show me where you found that information?'
4. **DIVERGENT QUESTIONS**
   'Do butterflies and moths have anything in common?'
5. **HEURISTIC QUESTIONS**
   'What clues in the diagram might help you learn the process?'

READ MORE: 'Identifying Instructional Moves During Guided Learning' by Doug Fisher and Nancy Frey

INSTRUCTIONAL DECISION MAKING TREE BY NANCY FREY AND DOUG FISHER (2013)

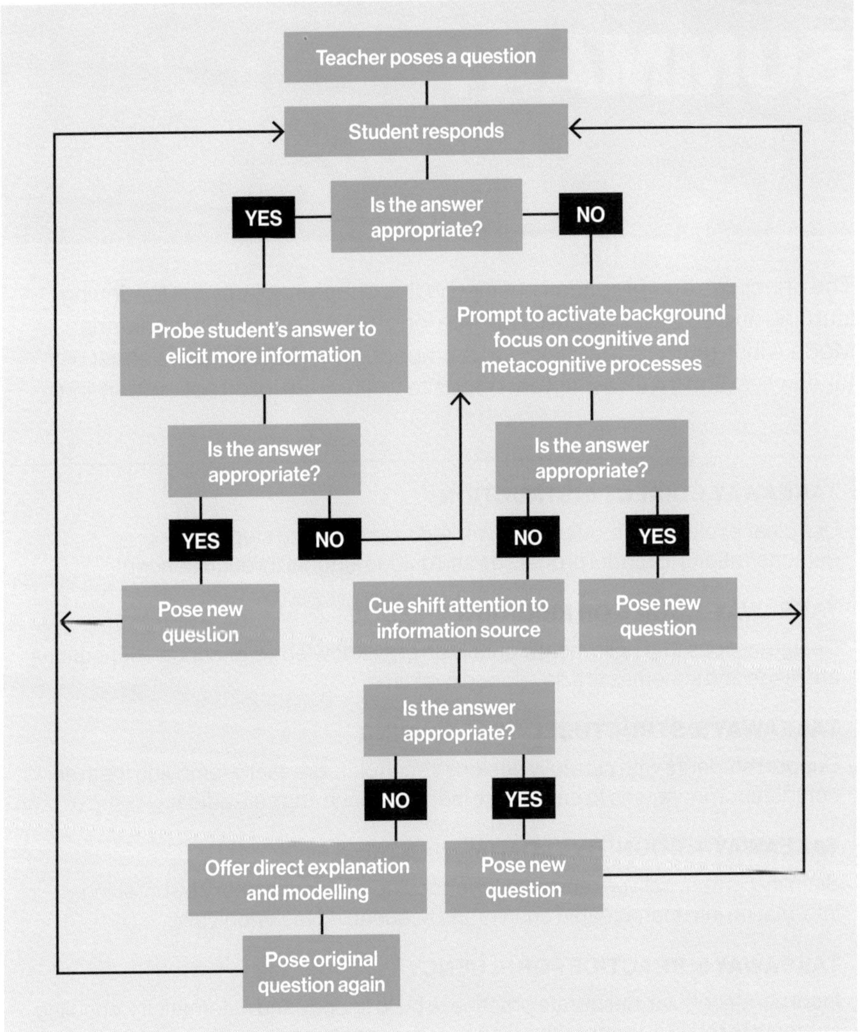

UTILISE A RANGE OF CUES AND PROMPTS: Prompts and cues are essential tools for guiding student thinking and attention. Use prompts like, 'What can you do to help yourself?' to stimulate problem-solving or 'Remember how we approached this type of problem last time?' to activate background knowledge. Visual cues such as 'Look at the diagram again [points]. What does it tell you?' can help redirect focus, while verbal cues like 'This word is tricky, so pay attention to all the letters' draw attention to critical points.

SUMMARY

The principles and practices outlined in this chapter are crucial for driving learning and encoding knowledge into long-term memory. To summarise Mode A instructional teaching and its impact, I've created a concise list of takeaways along with a diagram opposite to illustrate its effect on learning.

TAKEAWAY 1: DIRECT INSTRUCTION

Use clear explanations, questions, worked examples and step-by-step demonstrations to model processes and guide students through concepts.

TAKEAWAY 2: BUILD ON PRIOR KNOWLEDGE

Design lessons that build incrementally on prior knowledge, ensuring connections are made and schemas are developed over time.

TAKEAWAY 3: STRUCTURED SCAFFOLDING

Support students with carefully designed scaffolds, gradually removing them as competence increases to encourage independence and self-efficacy.

TAKEAWAY 4: COGNITIVE LOAD MANAGEMENT

Simplify content delivery and avoid overloading working memory by breaking information into manageable chunks and sequencing tasks logically.

TAKEAWAY 5: PRACTICE FOR FLUENCY

Incorporate regular, deliberate practice to build fluency and automaticity, enabling students to retain and apply knowledge with confidence.

TAKEAWAY 6: EFFORTFUL LEARNING

Incorporate challenges like retrieval practice, interleaving and spaced repetition to strengthen memory and promote long-term retention.

TAKEAWAY 7: FORMATIVE ASSESSMENT

Embed frequent, low-stakes assessments to monitor understanding, provide immediate feedback and inform teaching adjustments for optimal progress.

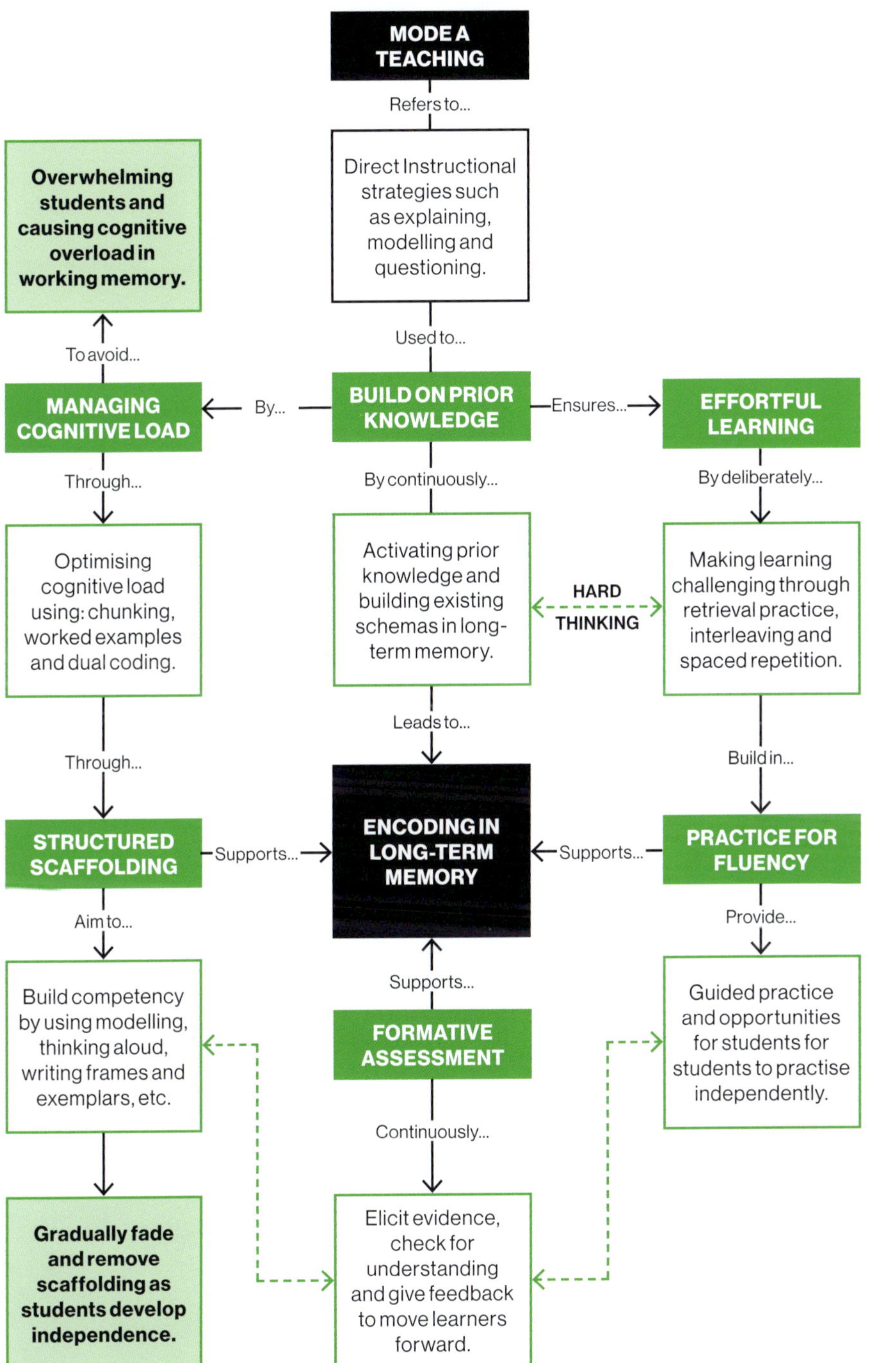
MODE A TEACHING
Refers to...
Direct Instructional strategies such as explaining, modelling and questioning.
Used to...
BUILD ON PRIOR KNOWLEDGE
By...
MANAGING COGNITIVE LOAD
To avoid...
Overwhelming students and causing cognitive overload in working memory.
Ensures...
EFFORTFUL LEARNING
By continuously...
Activating prior knowledge and building existing schemas in long-term memory.
HARD THINKING
By deliberately...
Making learning challenging through retrieval practice, interleaving and spaced repetition.
Through...
Optimising cognitive load using: chunking, worked examples and dual coding.
Through...
STRUCTURED SCAFFOLDING
Supports...
Leads to...
ENCODING IN LONG-TERM MEMORY
Supports...
Build in...
PRACTICE FOR FLUENCY
Aim to...
Build competency by using modelling, thinking aloud, writing frames and exemplars, etc.
Gradually fade and remove scaffolding as students develop independence.
Supports...
FORMATIVE ASSESSMENT
Continuously...
Elicit evidence, check for understanding and give feedback to move learners forward.
Provide...
Guided practice and opportunities for students for students to practise independently.

SCHOOL CULTURE
A series of strategic principles and practical strategies to help establish the conditions for growth

MODE A TEACHING
A focused collection of evidence-based principles and practices designed to enhance classroom instruction

MODE B TEACHING
A set of practices that foster agency, collaboration and open-ended exploration to deepen and extend knowledge

READ MORE
Studies, books and blogs that are referenced throughout the one-pagers and inspired the collections

Teaching
one
Pagers
2
VOLUME

MODE B TEACHING

STUDENT AGENCY AND EXPLORING THE POSSIBILITIES

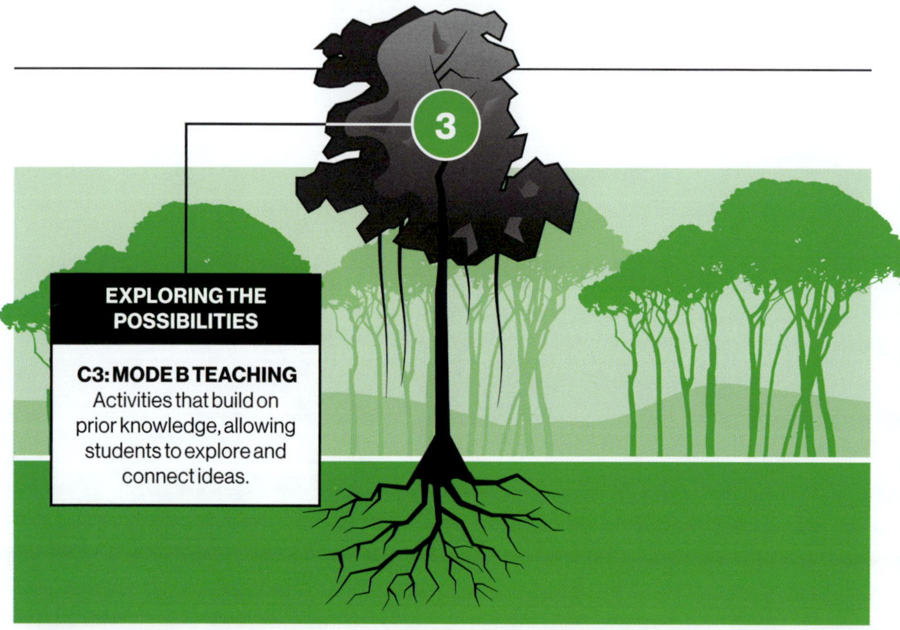

Does your curriculum balance Mode A practices with enriching activities that are valued for their own sake, supporting student agency and construction of richer schemas?

The final element of *The Learning Rainforest* metaphor is the tree's vibrant, expansive canopy, symbolising the opportunities for growth and exploration: *Exploring the Possibilities*. As educators, it is our task to ensure we intertwine solid instructional practices with activities that allow students to express, extend and build knowledge in different ways.

Mode B teaching often includes activities that we value for their own sake, rather than because of some specific evidence for their efficacy. For example, students might learn poetry by heart, give a speech in front of their peers or take part in a dramatic performance. These activities have inherent value. However, they work best when supported by secure knowledge typically acquired through instructional Mode A teaching. At the same time, Mode B activities are not about 'discovery learning' or constructivism as a teaching approach. Rather, they involve providing students with greater agency, choice and open-ended exploration to help them develop richer schemas.

Mode B strategies might occupy less time in the curriculum but they are absolutely necessary for helping students grow. As Sherrington (2017) explains: 'Sometimes we don't do something because it necessarily is the most effective – "because it works"; we do it because we give it value for its own sake – we think it should form part of a student's learning experience.' This aligns with Sherrington's description of classroom learning within a *rainforest system*. As you can see, he stresses that sometimes this environment nurtures student freedom and agency while maintaining quality and rigour:

> Classroom learning is sometimes characterised by an experimental approach. Teachers try out new ideas all the time, do not expect standard responses and create a culture in which students can select from a wide range of possible options – for example, in the pace of their learning, the sequence of tasks or the mode of response. Importantly, despite the rich variety and openness of the rainforest, it isn't a case of 'anything goes'. Only learning and teaching that are effective survive... there has to be quality and rigour in whatever shape or form the learning takes. There is nothing soft or safe about it.

A strong foundation of secure knowledge is essential before Mode B experiences can be implemented. Educator Clare Sealy explains that without a strong core of semantic memory (organised schemas), students lack the essential knowledge and connections needed to fully benefit from more open-ended learning experiences. Sealy (2019) explains that the deliberate building of knowledge creates the groundwork for deeper, more flexible learning. In other words, Mode B activities, such as debates, presentations or creative projects, rely on this well-developed knowledge base in order to deepen and extend learning.

The idea that creativity and knowledge are in opposition is a false dichotomy. In reality, *creativity is a process for developing and deepening knowledge*. Mode B fosters creativity by offering students opportunities to make choices, experiment and explore imaginative lines of

CLARE SEALY

The deliberate building of semantic memory is much more likely to result in long-lasting, flexible, and transferable memory than putting most of your energies into the episodic basket, so the former should form the bulk of what we spend our time on.

inquiry. These processes are not separate from knowledge development; they actively contribute to building more interconnected and flexible schemas in long-term memory. By providing agency and encouraging creative exploration, Mode B experiences enable students to refine and expand their understanding in ways that go beyond what Mode A alone can achieve.

This process of developing deep and meaningful knowledge is explored thoroughly in Martin Robinson's outstanding book *Trivium 21c*, where he illustrates the relationship between grammar, dialectic, and rhetoric – three pillars that form the foundation of an empowering educational model. The diagram below demonstrates how these elements work together to support a balanced curriculum:

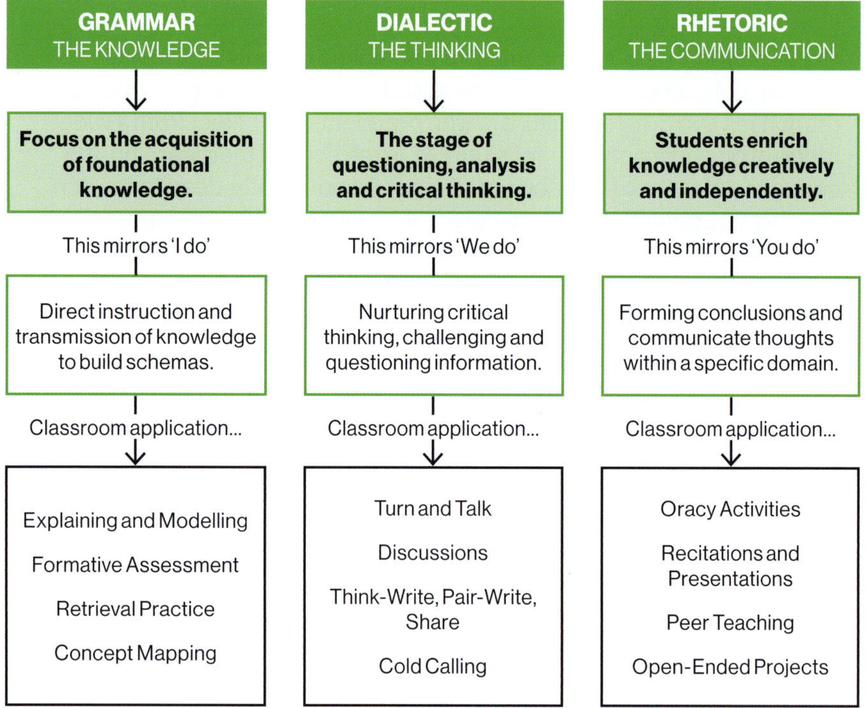

The relationship between these three pillars – grammar, dialectic, and rhetoric – is not strictly sequential but interchanging, varying by subject and context. In fact, they work together in harmony. For instance, direct instruction (grammar) might introduce a topic, while dialectic questioning probes students to dig deeper, encouraging them to analyse and challenge ideas. Together, these approaches help construct more robust and interconnected schemas that ensures knowledge is not only acquired but also explored.

For me, Robinson's definition of rhetoric, represents the communication element of Mode B. Essentially, it is the art of expressing learning through various mediums – whether through an essay, speech, artwork or performance. This aspect of 'Trivium thinking' promotes freedom of expression within structured boundaries, allowing creativity to flourish but at the same time, empowering students to enrich their understanding and communicate meaning. Robinson explains, this balance in the Trivium is like a three-legged stool: all parts are essential for it to function.

To embed this approach into the curriculum, schools should consider three guiding questions: *What knowledge do students need to learn? What critical thinking skills do they need to develop? How will they communicate their understanding?* For example, in an English literature unit on George Orwell's *Animal Farm*, students need foundational knowledge (grammar) to understand the context of the Russian Revolution and the allegorical nature of the text, and dialectic skills to present a key argument about themes like power, corruption or inequality. Rhetoric comes into play when students communicate their thoughts and conclusions effectively, whether through a written essay, a presentation, a debate, or even a creative project that demonstrates and adds to their understanding.

For schools, this means the curriculum must be carefully designed to integrate these important elements. Schools should ask: *Which topics offer rich, foundational knowledge that can challenge students and encourage dialectic thinking, ultimately opening the door to creative expression*? We want to guide students towards confident, purposeful expression rather than achieving the best exam results and simply chasing data. Unfortunately, *plantation schools* – focused heavily on outcomes and compliance – often neglect the dialectic stage. These schools fail to provide the necessary space for students to engage deeply with what they are learning, limiting opportunities for critical thinking. This can leave students ill-prepared to question, analyse and connect ideas, reducing learning

MARTIN ROBINSON

The goal of education is freedom – empowering students to think for themselves and make their own choices… Teaching isn't just about filling students with facts; it's about teaching them to connect ideas and see the bigger picture. (Lovell, 2020)

TOM SHERRINGTON

We simply want students to experience that kind of learning for its own sake… These things might not, in themselves, yield superior measurable learning outcomes in terms of long-term memory – they might simply create valuable experiential memories of their own. (2017)

to memorisation rather than cultivating curiosity and an independent thirst to learn more.

When discussing the role of shaping education, Sherrington (2017) explains, 'The great responsibility we have as teachers – as well as the joy and privilege – is to find the balance; to synthesise our values, our experience, and our research-informed wisdom into a coherent set of ideas that put our philosophy into action.' He emphasises that our curriculum and teaching should strive to be as evidence-informed as possible, while also 'allowing ourselves to be surprised by alternative forms of excellence that we didn't expect or control'. This balance between structure and openness is at the heart of creating a rich, dynamic rainforest. As educators, our end goal is to nurture well-rounded individuals who are prepared to make meaningful contributions to the world. By providing a balanced educational diet, we can guide students on a journey towards wisdom – grounded in the pursuit of knowledge, fueled by curiosity, and inspired by a sense of wonder. As Martin Robinson (2013) explains, 'This should be a journey that builds enthusiasm and a hunger to know more, and which develops the habits of mind, adaptability and creativity that have enabled educated people to make real contributions to the great conversations of their time.'

At this stage of our rainforest journey, it is important to clarify that Mode A:Mode B ratios are often misrepresented and misunderstood. In *The Learning Rainforest*, Tom Sherrington stresses that his suggested 80:20 split is merely a rough estimate – his own hunch based on what he observed in his teaching. It is not a recommendation or a fixed guideline. The balance between Mode A and Mode B will naturally vary depending on the subject, context and teacher preferences. For example, in a subject like mathematics, the ratio might lean more towards 95:5, whereas in music it could be closer to 50:50. The key point is that Mode A (structured, knowledge-building teaching) typically forms the majority, while Mode B (open-ended, exploration) plays a smaller but essential role. Ultimately, the balance is fluid, reflecting the needs of the curriculum and the students in your context.

For Mode B strategies to be introduced effectively, they require thought and rigour. On a practical level, upstream thinking – anticipating and planning for potential challenges – is crucial to ensure their success. From my own experience, Mode B can be notoriously difficult to map out because of its inherently unpredictable nature. Creative, open-ended activities often evolve in unexpected directions, requiring flexibility and adaptability from both teachers and students. However, with careful planning, embedded routines and a clear structure (rooted in grammar), these strategies can lead to some of the most rewarding and transformative learning experiences. Trust me!

Below is a list of recommended prerequisites needed to assist with the successful implementation of Mode B strategies. Prerequisites matter because they lay the groundwork for these experiences to have real impact. Without them, Mode B activities risk feeling superficial or overly-chaotic, leaving students without the necessary tools for success. Personally, I've seen how poorly planned learning experiences can quickly unravel and lead to apathy and shallow learning outcomes. Obviously not all prerequisites are needed for every Mode B strategy – however, when required, getting these elements in place helps ensure the process is purposeful, challenging, and rewarding.

As you don your explorer's hat for the final time and venture into the vibrant rainforest canopy, the culmination of *The Learning Rainforest* metaphor, take a moment to consider which prerequisites apply and how they might be addressed in your context. Furthermore, consider how the summaries in **Collection 3: Mode B Teaching** can be tailored and embedded meaningfully into your school's curriculum.

JAMIE CLARK

Creativity is not separate from knowledge development – it is a process for refining, deepening and expanding knowledge, enabling students to construct richer, more interconnected schemas through meaningful exploration and expression.

PREREQUISITE 1: EMBEDDED ROUTINES

Necessary routines to ensure the activity runs efficiently, maximising learning time and minimising disruptions (for example, assigning roles, time limits, etc).

PREREQUISITE 2: DEDICATED CURRICULUM TIME

Planned time set aside in a learning sequence dedicated to fostering deep engagement and exploration of the key knowledge from the topic.

PREREQUISITE 3: PHYSICAL SPACE

Appropriate learning spaces to facilitate group work, discussions or hands-on activities in a safe and focused setting (for example, a break-out space).

PREREQUISITE 4: ACCESS TO TECHNOLOGY

Equitable access to technology to support research, collaboration or creative work as required by the task.

PREREQUISITE 5: ACCOUNTABILITY MECHANISMS

Established tools like rubrics, group roles or self-assessment checklists to help ensure students stay on track and maintain high-quality work.

PART 3/3

MYTHS AND TRUTHS

WHY ARE THESE MYTHS AND TRUTHS IMPORTANT?

Exploring the possibilities is vital to a healthy educational diet. As outlined earlier, Mode B helps to provide memorable and holistic learning experiences. Clare Sealy (2019) notes that while memorable experiences have their place, particularly for broadening horizons or fostering social and moral development, they should supplement, not replace, structured teaching aimed at building knowledge. The myths and truths on this one-pager are useful for teachers to reflect on their instructional choices and strike a balance between engaging experiences and the deliberate development of long-term knowledge.

TEACHER-LED INSTRUCTION & STUDENT-CENTRED LEARNING ARE OPPOSITES

TOM SHERRINGTON

In a school curriculum that is rich and broad, leading to deep learning, both teacher-led learning and student-centredness will be woven together; blended and sequenced; integrated in a proportionate manner. (2019)

MYTH: Teacher-led instruction and student-centred learning are often seen as opposites, with one approach framed as rigid and controlling, while the other is considered empowering and engaging. This belief creates a false dichotomy, suggesting that educators must *choose* between being directive or fostering independence, with no middle ground.

TRUTH: In reality, teacher-led instruction and student-centred learning complement each other. As highlighted in *The Learning Rainforest*, effective teaching combines structured guidance to build knowledge with student-centred strategies that promote discovery, collaboration and self-regulation. While teacher-led instruction should take precedence, opportunities for independent engagement (Mode B) should sit alongside expert guidance (Mode A).

STUDENTS CAN BUILD KNOWLEDGE THROUGH DISCOVERY

DAVID AUSUBEL

The most important single factor influencing learning is what the learner already knows. Ascertain this and teach him accordingly. (1968)

MYTH: Discovery learning, where students explore topics on their own to uncover concepts and ideas, is often believed to lead to deeper understanding and retention. This approach assumes that students are best served by finding answers themselves, encouraging creativity and critical thinking without the constraints of structured, background knowledge.

TRUTH: In reality, effective learning depends on a foundation of solid background knowledge. Research shows that students need a robust base of prior knowledge to connect new ideas. David Ausubel explains 'the most important single factor influencing learning is what the learner already knows'. Without this foundation, discovery learning can be overwhelming and overload working memory as students lack the context to make sense of complex ideas.

MULTIMEDIA PRODUCES MORE LEARNING THAN LIVE INSTRUCTION

RICHARD E. CLARK

Media are mere vehicles that deliver instruction but do not influence student achievement any more than the truck that delivers our groceries causes changes in our nutrition. (1983)

MYTH: Multimedia (blending text, video images, etc) produces more learning than traditional media or live instruction. This belief suggests that using multimedia improves learning outcomes more than conventional methods, such as direct teacher instruction. However, research by Clark et al (2005) shows no significant evidence that multimedia alone leads to better results. Instead, what impacts learning are the instructional strategies employed, not the media format itself.

TRUTH: The truth is that instructional methods, not the medium, drive effective learning. While multimedia can produce valuable learning experiences, its effectiveness depends on how it's used. Using clear explanations, prompts to promote hard thinking, and opportunities for practice enhances learning, whether the material is presented digitally or in a traditional classroom setting.

PART 3/3

THE LEARNING RAINFOREST

MODE B: EXPLORING THE POSSIBILITIES

TOM SHERRINGTON

In The Learning Rainforest, Mode B teaching strategies will happen alongside and interwoven with the more direct instructional Mode A teaching. Although they might occupy less time, they are still vital.

WHAT IS IT AND WHY IS IT IMPORTANT?

In *The Learning Rainforest*, Sherrington discusses *exploring the possibilities* through Mode B strategies, which build on acquired knowledge and allow students to express understanding in different ways. Essentially, Mode B strategies are opportunities for students to explore, experiment and apply what they have learned. Central to this is a rich, enacted curriculum that blends direct instructional Mode A teaching with sprinklings of Mode B. Sherrington (2017) notes, 'Sometimes we don't do something because it is necessarily the most effective... we do it because we give a value for its own sake.' **Collection 3: Mode B Teaching** embodies this philosophy, providing summaries that not only deepen understanding but also nurture curiosity and inspire awe.

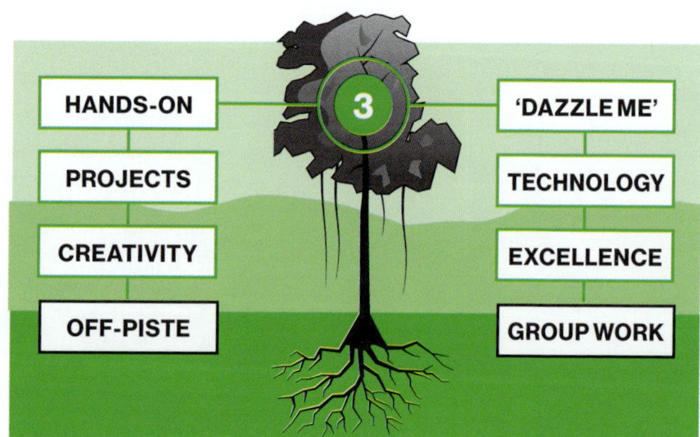

READ MORE: *Trivium 21c* by Martin Robinson

PROJECTS AND HANDS-ON LEARNING: Hands-on opportunities refer to 'concrete resources' that make learning more tangible. Sherrington mentions examining artefacts, making maps and experiments. Extended projects enable students with the freedom to pursue their interests and explore their knowledge in creative ways. A well-designed curriculum is key to accommodating these opportunities. They involve dedicating time and balancing support with independence. Rigour is key: It is important to ask 'What has the student learned?' rather than 'What has the student made?'

MODE B STRATEGIES AND IDEAS: Weave in a variety of opportunities for students to build on their prior knowledge. Sherrington's suggestions are taken from his years of experience in the classroom and observing great teachers:

HANDS ON	PLAY DETECTIVE	DEEP END	AUTHENTIC EXPERIENCES
Physical, tangible experiences to represent subject concepts.	Problem-solving, code-breaking, applying rules independently.	Design a challenge to put students in the struggle zone.	Real-world experiences: history walks, field trips.

GET CREATIVE	DAZZLE ME	OFF-PISTE	CLASS FORUM
Capture learning in a chosen format: booklet, video, slideshow.	Creative, open-ended response with clear parameters.	Stop and connect learning to student interests, real-world events.	Online space to collate learning through various digital modes.

FURTHER POSSIBILITIES: Make learning something that students can engage in both inside and outside the classroom. Online spaces for sharing learning through various digital modes (videos, images, text) can empower students to take ownership of their learning. Once students have a solid grounding of foundational knowledge, strategies like flipping the classroom or challenging students to 'teach it back' through reciprocal teaching can deepen their understanding. Mode B requires teachers to scaffold effectively and provide students with tools that foster independence, creativity and confidence.

MODE B PRACTICES

ORACY

GIVE STRUCTURED OPPORTUNITIES FOR TALK

WHAT IS IT AND WHY IS IT IMPORTANT?

Oracy, a term coined by Andrew Wilkinson in the 1960s, refers to the ability to express oneself fluently and grammatically in speech. It encompasses a set of competencies related to spoken language, similar to how literacy pertains to reading and writing skills. Oracy is important because it promotes reasoning and enables students to articulate their thoughts and engage in meaningful discussion with others. Maurice Galton (Millard et al, 2016) explains that 'talk allows you to construct and then reconstruct ideas, which is the major way in which we learn'. As a Mode B approach, teachers should aim to embed oracy into regular classroom teaching rather than treating it as an add-on. We can do this by integrating oracy tasks across different subjects and activities.

HOW DO I IMPLEMENT IT?

CREATE ORACY GUIDELINES: All teachers at School 21 in London are oracy teachers. To help students develop their oral communication skills, the school have developed a framework for oracy that enables teachers to teach using oracy strategies across the school, creating opportunities for every child (aged 4–18) to talk and listen in every lesson. To support their framework, the school have developed the following discussion guidelines for their students and teachers.

DISCUSSION GUIDELINES (2022)	
1	We give proof of listening
2	We respect others' ideas
3	We follow the discussion roles
4	We are prepared to change our mind
5	We invite others into our discussion
6	We try to reach a shared agreement

READ MORE: 'Talking in Class' blog post by Emelina Minero for Edutopia

INSTIGATOR
The starter who begins conversations: 'What do you think...'
BUILDER
Building on and developing others' answers: 'That was a good point... it could also...'
CHALLENGER
Arguing against, provoking like a competitor: 'You said X, but...'
CLARIFIER
Making things clearer like a commentator: 'What do you mean when you say...'
PROBER
Asks questions to go deeper into responses: 'Can you tell us a little more...'
SUMMARISER
Summarises and makes judgements : 'Am I right in thinking...'

CREATE DISCUSSION ROLES:

To aid their framework, School 21 developed these discussion roles for their students to teach them how to talk. To introduce discussion roles to your students, it is important to model them first. School 21 teachers play recorded videos of themselves having conversations, and have their students analyse, identify and discuss the roles they played (Minero, 2016). Designate these roles for more controversial or challenging talking points. For example: 'Technological advancements are more important than environmental conservation.'

TEACH PAIRED TALK AND ACTIVE LISTENING:

Utilising strategies such as 'turn and talk' can help to teach quality probing questions and how to have an effective disagreement. Explicitly model active listening by demonstrating how to focus on the speaker, maintain eye contact, and provide appropriate verbal and non-verbal feedback, such as nodding or summarising ideas.

PLAN QUALITY TALK TASKS: Setting structured 'talk tasks' where students reflect on their learning or discuss a visual prompt can help to promote classroom talk. For example, asking students to discuss the possible reasons behind a character's actions: Partner A: 'I think Character A was motivated by [fear/ambition/love/etc.] because...'. Partner B: 'I agree/disagree with you because...'.

USE SENTENCE STEMS TO SCAFFOLD TALK:

Using sentence stems in discussions helps students articulate their thoughts and build on each other's ideas. For example, a student might say, 'Linking to [student's name]'s point, I think that...'. Sentence stems also guide students in explaining their learning, such as starting with, 'I began solving this problem by...'.

ROBIN ALEXANDER

We have known for a long time that talk is essential to children's thinking and learning, and to their productive engagement in classroom life... We now have additional evidence, from over 20 major international studies, that high quality classroom talk raises standards in the core subjects. (2012)

MODE B PRACTICES

OPEN-ENDED PROJECTS

PROVIDE CHOICE IN HOW TO SHOWCASE LEARNING

WHAT IS IT AND WHY IS IT IMPORTANT?

Providing students with choice in how they demonstrate their understanding sparks creativity, builds agency and boosts engagement. After teaching a topic, allow students to select a format that resonates with their interests and strengths. This builds student agency and enables them to explore mediums they find personally intriguing. For example, students might choose to work independently or collaboratively to create a presentation, write a poem, design an infographic, construct a model, or produce a short video to present to a real-world audience.

RON BERGER

When students know that their finished work will be displayed, presented, appreciated and judged – whether by the whole class, other classes, families or the community – work takes on a different meaning! (2003)

PROJECT: Based on your knowledge of Macbeth after his encounter with the witches, explain his mindset and how it reflects his ambition and inner conflict. Demonstrate your understanding in a format of your choice.

HOW DO I IMPLEMENT IT?

ESTABLISH THE EXPECTATIONS: Strike the right balance between guidance and freedom. Provide enough structure to give students clarity and direction without stifling their creativity. At the same time, ensure the task isn't so open-ended that students struggle to produce anything meaningful. Furthermore, be very clear about the content of the project – it should be focused entirely on the concept or skill that has just been taught.

READ MORE: *An Ethic of Excellence: Building a Culture of Craftsmanship with Students* by Ron Berger

UTILISE DIGITAL MODES: When getting creative, provide students with suggestions of different digital modes with which they can showcase their understanding of a topic, piece of research or ideas discussed in class. Providing they have access to the digital tools, consider the modes below. It is important that students select a format that they are familiar with otherwise they will spend too much time thinking about the tool not the learning itself!

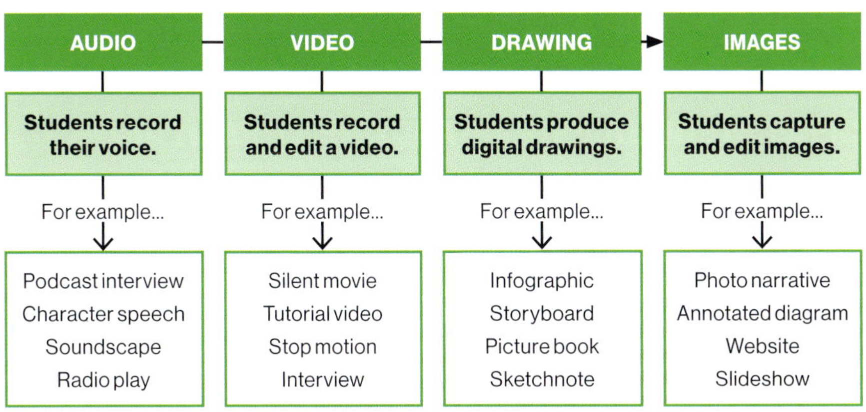

SHOW EXEMPLAR PROJECTS: Showing and discussing example projects helps students to see gold standard outcomes. As Ron Berger (2003) points out: 'No amount of words can convey what one good model tells me... I want my students to carry around pictures in their head of quality work.' Make a habit of saving models of the final projects and also models of any earlier drafts so that students can see both the creative and refinement process.

CREATE FOR AN AUDIENCE: For larger-scale, open-ended projects, making students' work public promotes a sense of value and validation for their efforts. According to research by Ryan et al (2000), this approach builds intrinsic motivation by allowing individuals to feel competent and autonomous while engaging in meaningful activities. Here are some ways schools can share excellence:

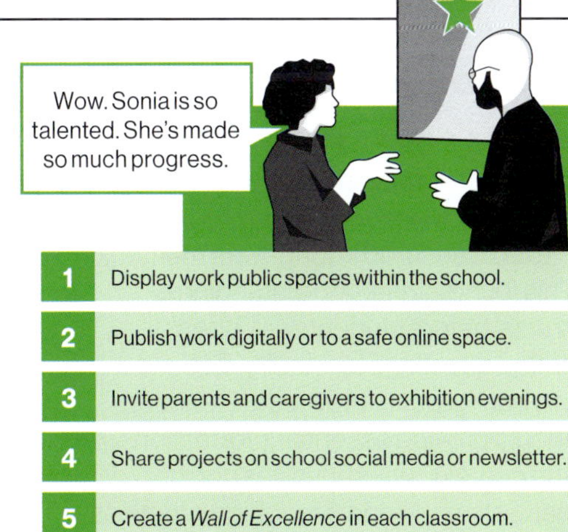

1. Display work public spaces within the school.
2. Publish work digitally or to a safe online space.
3. Invite parents and caregivers to exhibition evenings.
4. Share projects on school social media or newsletter.
5. Create a *Wall of Excellence* in each classroom.

MODE B PRACTICES

INQUIRY LEARNING CYCLES

GENERATE BIG QUESTIONS AND GIVE STUDENT AGENCY

TREVOR MACKENZIE

Having students follow their passions, curiosities and wonderings are unique benefits afforded by the inquiry model.

WHAT IS IT AND WHY IS IT IMPORTANT?

Inquiry-based learning (IBL) aligns neatly with the principles of Mode B teaching due to its values-driven and student-centred approach. An inquiry cycle focuses on a specific topic and actively engages students by encouraging them to ask 'big questions', conduct research, and create meaningful real-world outcomes. It is about the process, not the product, which means teachers must carefully scaffold the inquiry cycle so that it progressively builds students' agency and provides artefacts, provocations (thought-provoking items) and resources to support their learning.

HOW DO I IMPLEMENT IT?

MODE A COMES FIRST: It is important that before engaging students' IBL cycles, they need solid knowledge on the topic secured in long-term memory. This foundational understanding is crucial before students ask open-ended questions for inquiry. To build this background knowledge, teachers should provide essential information and context, which involves core instructional Mode A teaching practices.

1. **ACTIVATE PRIOR KNOWLEDGE**
2. **TEACH REQUIRED KNOWLEDGE**
3. **GENERATE 'BIG QUESTIONS'**
4. **SCAFFOLD THE RESEARCH**
5. **FEEDBACK AND SHARE**

READ MORE: *Inquiry Mindset* by Trevor MacKenzie

SCAFFOLD THE INQUIRY PROCESS: Trevor MacKenzie (2018) explains that scaffolding is critical to the inquiry process. Diving straight into 'free inquiry' can cognitively overload students. MacKenzie outlines 'four types of inquiry' that gradually build students' skills and confidence by gradually increasing the level of independence and releasing responsibility from the teacher.

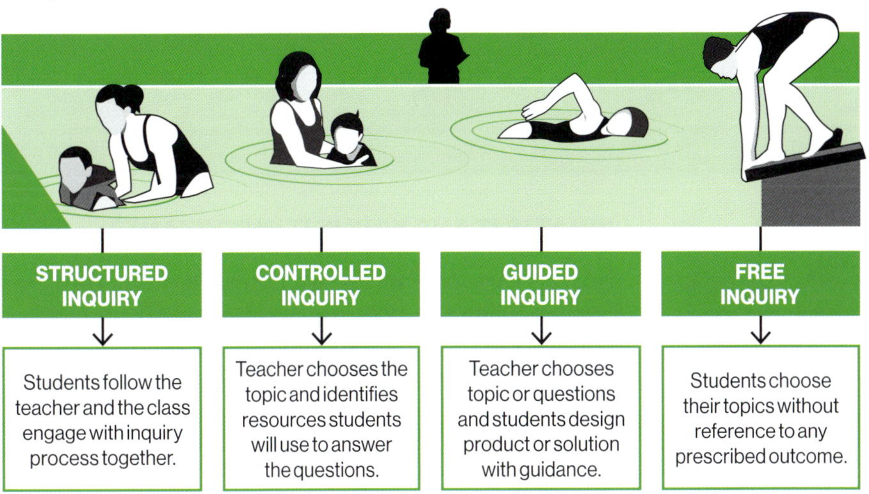

GENERATE 'BIG QUESTIONS': During inquiry, it is the teacher's role to guide exploration rather than deliver the information. Co-construct rich questions with students and make them visible in the classroom. Work with colleagues to craft provocations, resources and guiding (scaffolded) questions to support students in the inquiry process.

ENGAGE IN RESEARCH: Get students to work together to access prior knowledge and brainstorm what they already know. Prompt them to review their ideas and scaffold the research phase by providing research booklets with links or helpful sources. Weave in real-life artefacts and work through the research phase collectively.

ASSESSMENT IN INQUIRY: Use formative assessment to guide students throughout their inquiry, ask questions to check their understanding and provide individual or group feedback. Give students agency by challenging them to show their learning in any way but be sure to show models of exemplar work to open their minds to the possibilities. Leverage the power of talk by facilitating and scaffolding oracy – whoever is doing the talking is likely doing the learning (MacKenzie, 2021). When switching from the learning to performance zone (see page 57), guide students to select curated evidence they are most proud of to assess.

MODE B PRACTICES

PEER TEACHING

EMPOWER STUDENTS TO LEARN BY TEACHING

JOHN HATTIE

Cooperative learning is most powerful after the students have acquired sufficient surface knowledge to then be involved in discussion and learning with their peers – usually in some structured manner.

WHAT IS IT AND WHY IS IT IMPORTANT?

Research by John Hattie (2012) highlights the act of teaching others as a high-impact strategy. This is often referred to as the Protégé Effect. Nestojko et al (2014) show that teaching others compels students to clarify their own thinking, deepen understanding and recall key points more effectively than studying alone. By organising and connecting material, students strengthen long-term memory retention. Peer teaching also enables teachers to identify and address misconceptions early, preventing them from becoming entrenched in students' long-term memory. Like any Mode B strategy, peer teaching requires students to have a solid grasp of the material before they attempt to teach it to peers or the class.

HOW DO I IMPLEMENT IT?

FOCUS ON SPECIFIC CONCEPTS: Narrow down the focus of the peer teaching activity to a specific concept or idea just taught. This will ensure students' are not overwhelmed by the information they are expected to include.

ENGLISH	**Year 9s** peer teach how the theme of loneliness is represented in chapter four of *Of Mice and Men*, explaining how Steinbeck uses symbolism.
MATHS	**Year 8s** peer teach how to solve simultaneous equations by demonstrating and guiding partners step-by-step through the method.
SCIENCE	**Year 5s** peer teach the water cycle, using a diagram to teach their partner how evaporation happens.
HISTORY	**Year 11s** peer teach the causes of World War I, teaching their partners about key factors like alliances, militarism and nationalism.

READ MORE: *Visible Learning* by John Hattie

MAP THE PROCESS: Peer teaching can be done in one lesson (for example through think, pair, share) or mapped across lessons following this process:

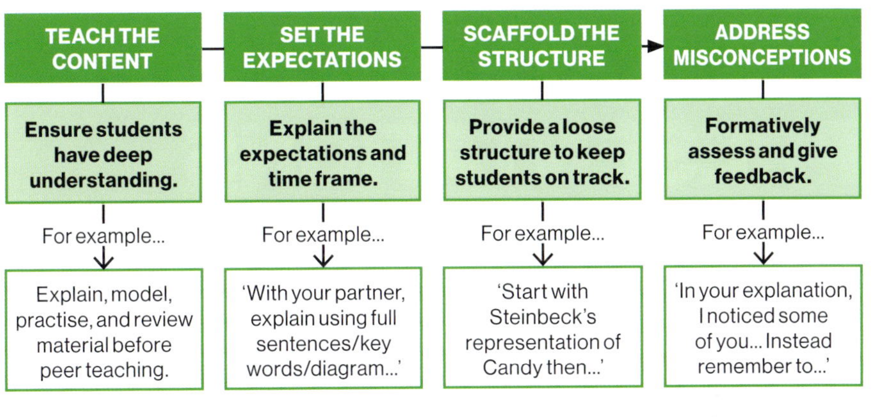

USE THE RECIPROCAL METHOD: After explaining a concept or process – such as the parts of a plant – students work in pairs and alternate between the role of the teacher and learner. One student explains the material to their partner, repeating key information, such as naming each part, describing its function, and explaining its relationship to the whole. This reinforces the 'teacher' student's understanding as they explain their knowledge and ensures the 'learner' student gains clarity by asking questions and engaging in 'why' and 'how' questioning.

PRIME STUDENTS: Inform students at the start of the lesson that one of them will teach at the end, without revealing who. Fiorella et al (2013) show that the act of teaching, rather than just preparing to teach, leads to deeper and more lasting understanding through the use of metacognitive strategies.

ADD RIGOUR: For peer teaching tasks spanning several lessons, challenge students to use diagrams and academic vocabulary to explain with greater rigour. Technology can also enhance the process. For example, students could record and rehearse their explanations before presenting their videos to the class.

MODE B PRACTICES

RECITATIONS AND PRESENTATIONS

MEMORISE, REHEARSE AND PERFORM TO AN AUDIENCE

DANIEL PINK

Intrinsic motivation – the drive to do something because it is interesting, challenging and absorbing – is essential for high levels of creativity.

WHAT IS IT AND WHY IS IT IMPORTANT?

Recitations involve students memorising and performing poems, speeches or passages aloud, while presentations require them to share research, ideas or creative work with their peers. Both of these Mode B strategies, often found in arts-based subjects, emphasise clarity of communication, build confidence and support schema development to consolidate knowledge. As Daniel Pink (2019) highlights, these activities foster students' engagement and intrinsic interest, making learning both meaningful and impactful.

HOW DO I IMPLEMENT IT?

LINK TO LEARNING AND EXTEND KNOWLEDGE: Ensure topics and texts are carefully selected so that they link to and extend the learning done in class. Be mindful of the ability of students and setting anything too challenging or lengthy:

ENGLISH	**Recitation:** After studying language in sonnets, students memorise and recite a Shakespearean sonnet, focusing on delivery techniques such as tone and pace.
MATHS	**Presentation:** After studying and solving geometry problems, students create and present a real-world scenario where geometry is applied (e.g. designing a park).
HISTORY	**Recitation:** After studying the events of WWI, students recite Churchill's *We Shall Fight on the Beaches* speech, and explain its significance in the context of WWII.
SCIENCE	**Presentation:** After conducting an experiment investigating the effect of light on plant growth students present findings including graphs, images and conclusions.

READ MORE: *Drive: The Surprising Truth About What Motivates Us* by Daniel Pink

RECITATIONS

SHOW MODELS OF EXCELLENCE: Share examples of strong recitations to inspire students. Show sample student responses and discuss strengths and challenges. Watch professionals at work too; for example, Dame Judi Dench reciting a Shakespearean sonnet.

UTILISE RETRIEVAL PRACTICE: Teach students essential retrieval practice strategies to support them with memorising the material. Encourage active recall by using flashcards and practising recitations in chunks before combining them. Regular low-stakes practice lessons can strengthen memory, build confidence and motivation.

USE FEEDBACK LOOPS: Dylan Wiliam (2024) says, 'The best formative assessment processes often leave no written evidence; just a smarter decision by the teacher about what to do next. During rehearsal lessons, provide verbal feedback to guide students in refining their recitations focusing on tone, clarity or content.

PRESENTATIONS

SLIDE SET UP: Working memory can only hold a small amount of information at once, so it is crucial that students reduce cognitive load and keep slides simple. This means limiting text to key points, using visuals to support understanding, and ensuring a clear, logical flow of information. According to Kirschner et al (2006), 'Working memory load is determined by the complexity of the material being learned and the manner in which it is presented.' Provide students with a slideshow scaffold including student-friendly steps on how to reduce cognitive load.

TELL A STORY: Daniel Willingham (2021) explains that the human mind is well-suited to understanding and remembering stories, as they have a familiar structure and include the four Cs: causality, conflict, complications and character. Teach students to structure learning around a similar framework to make their presentations more memorable.

MODE B PRACTICES

VIDEO TUTORIALS

PROJECTS TO EXPLAIN AND VISUALISE IDEAS

RICHARD E. MAYER

People learn more deeply from words and pictures than from words alone.

WHAT IS IT AND WHY IS IT IMPORTANT?

Video tutorials are a powerful Mode B strategy that engage students in retrieving prior knowledge and explaining their ideas through supporting visuals. By creating their own tutorials, students also practise summarising concepts, reinforcing and deepening their understanding. To help students produce effective tutorials, teachers can draw on multimedia learning principles, guiding them in combining words and visuals to communicate ideas clearly. Key techniques include keeping visuals simple, using cues to highlight main points, and breaking information into manageable steps – all essential for delivering clear and impactful explanations.

HOW DO I IMPLEMENT IT?

TEACH MULTIMEDIA LEARNING PRINCIPLES: For students creating tutorial videos, here are the top five relevant principles from Mayer's (2002) work:

MULTIMEDIA	Use visuals alongside spoken narration. Visuals should support the explanation directly, making complex ideas more accessible.
COHERENCE	Keep the tutorial focused by including only essential information. Avoid extra images, sounds or details that don't directly support the main topic.
MODALITY	Pair visuals with spoken narration rather than on-screen text. This allows viewers to process information without overloading their visual channel.
SEGMENTING	Break the tutorial into clear, logical steps or sections, allowing viewers to follow at their own pace. This makes it easier for viewers to process.
SIGNALLING	Use cues like highlights, arrows or bold text to emphasise key points, helping guide viewers' attention to the most important information in each section.

 READ MORE: *Multimedia Learning* by Richard E. Mayer

SCAFFOLD THE PROCESS: Like any project, it is important to scaffold the process. Provide a structure for the project and resources with helpful sentence starters or prompts. Break down the project into three key phases:

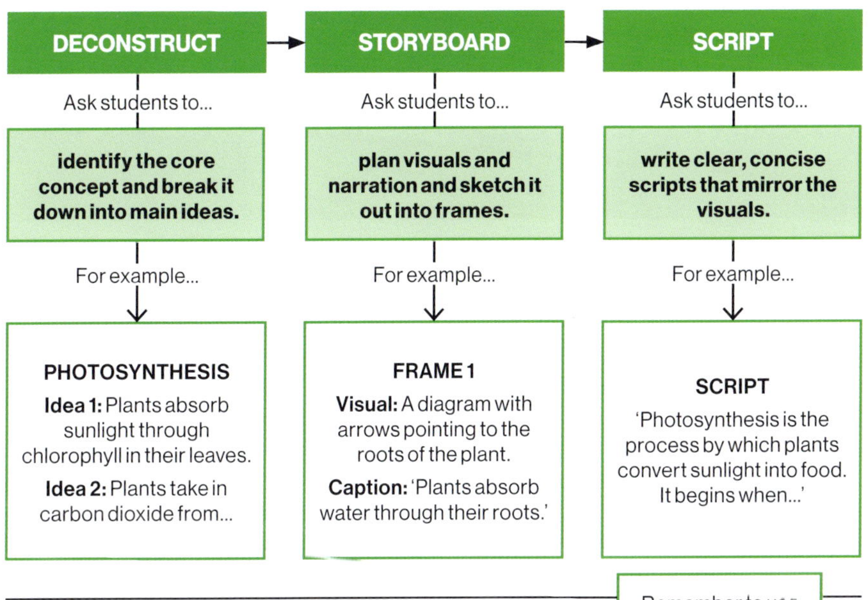

MODEL QUALITY TUTORIAL: Show students examples of effective tutorial videos that successfully incorporate multimedia principles, such as clear visuals paired with narration. Discuss why these videos work well, pointing out specific techniques used to simplify complex information and guide attention.

USE ADVANCED ORGANISERS: Research shows that 'people learn more deeply from a multimedia message when they know the names and characteristics of the main concepts' (Mayer, 2009). Encourage students to introduce key terms, definitions and foundational ideas related to the topic before diving into detailed explanations. This can be done through introductory handouts, brief presentations or visual guides that provide important context, helping to create a mental framework for viewers to build on as they watch the tutorial video.

MODE B PRACTICES

DEBATES

RESEARCH IDEAS AND PRESENT ARGUMENTS

WHAT IS IT AND WHY IS IT IMPORTANT?

Debates involve structured discussions where students take opposing sides on a topic, presenting arguments and counterarguments. As a Mode B teaching strategy, debates engage students in critical thinking, effective communication, and the opportunity to see multiple perspectives. Preparing for debates in class helps students deepen their knowledge on a specific topic by encouraging them to research, analyse evidence and build logical arguments. As outlined by the report by the Oracy Education Commission (2024), 'Speech and debate provide opportunities for students to develop critical thinking and reasoning skills that are of benefit across all curricular learning and to active citizenship both at school and in later life.' They also provide students with a platform to explore complex issues and build confidence in public speaking.

HOW DO I IMPLEMENT IT?

START SMALL: Begin with low-stakes debates on simpler topics to build confidence and model the process. For example, ask students to discuss a 'for' or 'against' position on a relatable topic, such as 'Should homework be compulsory?' Rotate between light, engaging topics and deeper curriculum-based ones to maintain interest throughout the year. During this process, teach, set and reinforce clear rules for constructive dialogue and active listening.

HISTORY	Should the Romans be remembered more for their achievements or their brutality?
ART	Should digital art be considered equal to traditional art?
SCIENCE	Should humans focus on exploring space or saving Earth's ecosystems?
ENGLISH	Does social media improve or damage communication skills?

READ MORE: 'We Need to Talk' report by the UK Oracy Education Commission

ORGANISE IN GROUPS OR PAIRS: In paired debate activities (using strategies such as think, pair, share), students can focus on direct exchanges, building confidence in presenting and countering arguments. Group debates, on the other hand, foster collaboration as team members brainstorm, divide responsibilities and refine their arguments together. Use roles – such as speaker, researcher, or rebuttal lead – to ensure active involvement from all participants.

PROVIDE A FRAMEWORK: Teaching students' roles and scaffolding the debate is crucial and ensures a structured, inclusive and productive discussion.

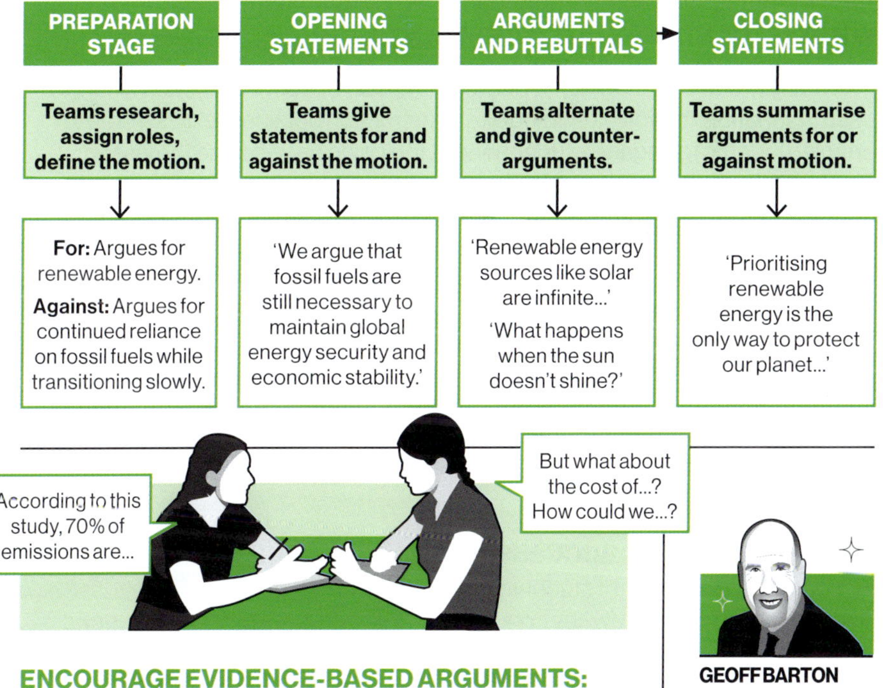

ENCOURAGE EVIDENCE-BASED ARGUMENTS: The report notes that the study of speech and debate (through the study of rhetoric) is a key aspect of oracy education. Complementing their subject-led learning, these practices help students to explore the relationship between persuasion, argumentation and evidence. They learn how arguments can be evaluated in relation to reason; knowledge or fact; and community or audience. Encourage students to support their claims with credible sources, such as research studies, historical examples, or expert opinions.

GEOFF BARTON

Now more than ever, young people must ask questions, articulate ideas, build arguments, and learn to disagree agreeably as active participants in democracy. (OEC, 2024)

MODE B PRACTICES

FLIPPED LEARNING

BUILD KNOWLEDGE BY PRE-LEARNING CONTENT

WHAT IS IT AND WHY IS IT IMPORTANT?

Like many Mode B strategies, flipped learning is an effective approach when used in variation. It involves shifting direct instruction outside the classroom to enable students to engage with learning at their own pace before the lesson. For example, students might watch a video on ecosystems and complete a concept map at home. In class, they build on this by answering deeper questions, engaging in hands-on experiences and discussing misconceptions. This approach works similarly to an advanced organiser, cognitively preparing students for what they are about to learn (Ausubel, 1968). By organising information (verbal, written or graphical) before the lesson, students are better equipped to make meaningful connections and fully engage during class time.

HOW DO I IMPLEMENT IT?

SET THE STAGE FOR SUCCESS:
Research has found that if students have the opportunity to preview key concepts ahead of class time, the face-to-face session can be more effectively used for active learning where concepts are analysed and applied (McLaughlin et al, 2014). This can be done effectively if the following mechanisms are in place first. For flipped learning to work, students must be taught how to study independently and how to engage with pre-class material. This ensures they are prepared for in-depth discussions and active learning in the classroom.

1. **COMMUNICATE EXPECTATIONS** Outline rationale and what to expect.
2. **MAKE EXPLICIT LINKS** Connect in and out of class learning.
3. **SCAFFOLD THE PROCESS** Provide structure and resources.
4. **KEEP IT SIMPLE** Use familiar technology or resources.
5. **PLAN IN-CLASS CONSOLIDATION** Provide subsequent deep learning tasks.

READ MORE: *Mode A and Mode B Teaching: A Key Concept in the Learning Forest* video by Seneca CPD

A SUGGESTED FLIPPED LEARNING PROCESS

AT HOME	IN CLASS	FOLLOW-UP
Introduce foundational knowledge before the classroom session.	**Use class time for active, deeper learning on the topic.**	**Consolidate learning and assess next steps – reteach or move on.**
For example...	For example...	For example...
Videos or screencasts explaining key concepts. Readings or curated articles summarising main ideas. Self-paced interactive modules or quizzes.	**COLLABORATIVE WORK:** Think, pair, share, class discussions, or peer teaching. **HANDS-ON:** Experiments, role-playing, or design challenges.	Make links to prior learning. Extended problem sets or projects integrating new concepts. Self-assessment or peer feedback on collaborative work.
Students record learning by...	The teacher's role is to ...	The teacher's role is to ...
completing a concept map or answering focus questions. summarising or drawing the main ideas and listing questions for clarification in class time.	act as a facilitator, guiding and scaffolding students as they engage. use formative assessments, like quizzes or verbal check-ins, to check for understanding.	provide additional resources, reteach in small groups or provide targeted support for students needing further clarification.

BLEND MODE A AND MODE B: The in-class part of flipped learning is where knowledge comes alive. Building on the foundation of pre-learned material, class shifts focus to discussion, exploration and applying concepts in meaningful ways. Tom Sherrington (2020) highlights this stage as a powerful blend of Mode A and Mode B. The teacher's role is to provide guidance to clarify misconceptions and deepen understanding while empowering students to take ownership of their learning through collaborative problem-solving, hands-on tasks and reflective discussions. This balance of structure and autonomy maximises engagement and fosters critical independent thinking, making class time highly impactful.

TOM SHERRINGTON

Learning requires discipline in building knowledge and also space for creativity and exploration. Both modes work best when they complement each other.

MODE B PRACTICES

HANDS-ON EXPERIENCES

ADD DEPTH AND JOY TO THE CURRICULUM

WHAT IS IT AND WHY IS IT IMPORTANT?

The hallmark of a well-designed curriculum lies in its ability to provide students with opportunities to step outside classroom norms and engage in hands-on experiences. These active, out-of-the-seat moments not only help consolidate knowledge but also make abstract ideas tangible and memorable. Research by Graham Nuthall (2007) highlights that for information to be encoded in long-term memory, students need to encounter it in varied ways and contexts, revisiting concepts from multiple angles. For example, using blocks in maths to grasp abstract concepts or designing and testing parachutes to understand air resistance in science. These Mode B moments are about experiencing the joy of learning not just about ticking off curriculum requirements. Create opportunities for students to connect with the world around them and spark their curiosity.

HOW DO I IMPLEMENT IT?

CONCRETE TO ABSTRACT: Hands-on experiences act as a vital bridge between concrete understanding and abstract thinking. Start with tangible materials, like using blocks to teach fractions, and gradually move to abstract representations to help deepen understanding, improve retention and enhance students' ability to apply learning in different contexts.

1. **BUILD CURIOSITY AND ENGAGEMENT**
   Show replicas of artefacts (Roman coins).
2. **CLARIFY ABSTRACT CONCEPTS**
   Use blocks to model fractions.
3. **REINFORCE KEY CONCEPTS**
   Make simple circuits with batteries and light bulbs.
4. **PROMOTE COLLABORATION**
   Groups build a model bridge and test its strength.
5. **EXPLORE REAL-WORLD APPLICATIONS**
   Test the aerodynamics of paper plane designs.

READ MORE: *The Hidden Lives of Learners* by Graham Nuthall

A SUGGESTED PROCESS FOR IMPLEMENTING HANDS-ON TASKS

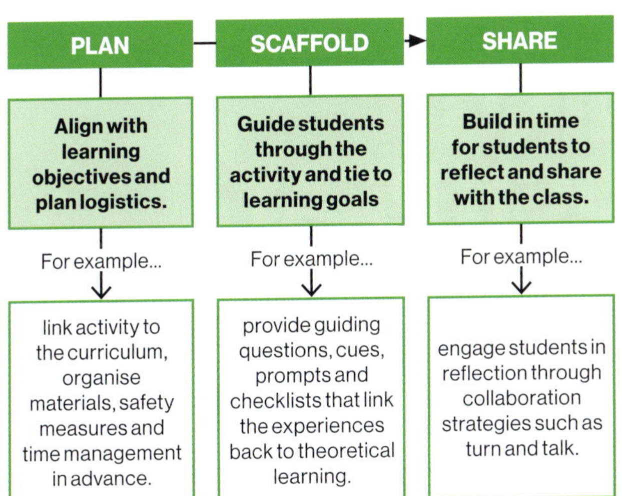

NEIL MERCER

It is perhaps too often forgotten in the analysis of teaching and learning that one legitimate goal for a teacher is to make information memorable. (1995)

BUILD IN COMPETITION: Competition can improve student motivation when done thoughtfully. Research suggests that competitive elements can boost achievement and motivation, particularly when tasks are straightforward and the competition is framed as constructive and playful (Fülöp, 2000, 2004; Lam et al, 2001). For example, designing a bridge-building challenge or a timed maths problem-solving activity can encourage students to push their limits and develop a sense of accomplishment.

PROVIDE STRUCTURE: Hands-on experiences thrive when supported by clear, purposeful structure. For instance, when conducting a group experiment in science, provide step-by-step instructions on the board and set clearly defined roles so that all students contribute meaningfully. Using tools like checklists, time limits and checkpoints reduces ambiguity, builds psychological safety and helps students stay focused.

MODE B PRACTICES

LEARNING THROUGH PLAY

NURTURE CHILDREN'S CURIOSITY, GROWTH AND CREATIVITY

WHAT IS IT AND WHY IS IT IMPORTANT?

Learning through play connects child-led exploration with instructional teaching, making it an effective Mode B approach for younger students. In primary classrooms, play-based learning is important for fostering young students' cognitive, social, and emotional development. It aligns closely with play-based inquiry learning, a pedagogy that nurtures curiosity, agency, and holistic growth by immersing children in open-ended, meaningful experiences. This approach positions children as active participants in their learning journey while emphasising the teacher's role in scaffolding and guiding their exploration. As Bass et al (2015) explain, 'Play-based inquiry learning classrooms promote open-ended provocations and learner choice while addressing intentional teaching objectives.'

GARDEN EXPLORERS
Find a plant that has...

HOW DO I IMPLEMENT IT?

SET THE STAGE: Ask any teacher of younger students and they will tell you that play builds critical thinking, collaboration, communication and creativity – key competencies for learning. To maximise its chance of success, it's important to set the stage and ensure the following principles are understood.

1. **CHILD-CENTRED EXPLORATION**
Students' ideas, interests and curiosities guide play experiences which fosters agency.

2. **INTENTIONAL TEACHING**
Tune in to students' play, offering guidance to extend and scaffold their thinking.

3. **HOLISTIC DEVELOPMENT**
Provide opportunities for students to interact and share experiences through talk, turn-taking, etc.

 READ MORE: Play-Based Learning and Intentionality Practice Resource by AERO

GUIDE STUDENT PLAY: Guided play allows teachers to scaffold learning by asking thought-provoking questions that help students connect their experiences to new knowledge. Use open-ended prompts, introduce challenges and subtly steer activities to align with curriculum goals. For example, during a pretend shop activity, a teacher might ask, 'How many coins do you need to buy this?' or 'What else might a customer ask for?' These interactions spark curiosity, deepen engagement and foster critical skills, ensuring play remains purposeful and joyfully enriching.

KATH MURDOCH

Play is inquiry. It is what we do when we are trying to figure something out. It is driven by curiosity and joy. (2024)

CREATE PLAY-BASED PROVOCATIONS: Create environments with open-ended sensory materials. For example, dramatic play areas, sensory bins or construction blocks that invite exploration and discovery. This allows students to engage in hands-on, physical experiences that spark their imagination. Ensure all learning is linked back to overarching questions and learning intentions. For example, a campfire scene could be set up to teach storytelling and story structure. Students might be prompted to role-play campers, tell stories around the fire and collaborate to build narratives, blending creativity with learning.

REFLECT AFTER PLAY: After play activities, create opportunities for students to discuss and share their experiences. Prompt them with questions like 'What did you notice while building your tower?' These reflective discussions help children consolidate their learning, build metacognitive skills, and make connections to prior knowledge. Additionally, teachers can use this feedback to plan future play-based provocations that extend the learning journey.

SUMMARY

One of the key takeaways from *The Learning Rainforest* is the importance for schools to find a healthy balance – particularly between instructional teaching and creative opportunities for students to extend knowledge. Although Mode B only plays a minor role in the rainforest, it is a key component that helps to shape independence, build confidence and consolidate ideas. As Martin Robinson explains in *Trivium 21c*, 'Schools should ensure that opportunities to perform and communicate are at the heart of what they do.'

To make these concepts tangible and actionable, I have outlined five practical takeaways (also visualised in the diagram opposite). These takeaways reflect the symbiotic relationship between Mode A and B in a healthy curriculum.

TAKEAWAY 1: STRONG FOUNDATIONS

Ensure students have secure, well-structured knowledge (grammar) through Mode A teaching before engaging in more open-ended, student-centred tasks.

TAKEAWAY 2: CHALLENGE THROUGH DIALOGUE

Encourage students to think critically and engage in deep questioning (dialectic) to challenge material, evaluate and refine their ideas.

TAKEAWAY 3: CREATIVE EXPRESSION

Provide opportunities for students to communicate learning through purposeful activities (rhetoric), such as oracy, performance or creative experiences.

TAKEAWAY 4: FLEXIBILITY AND ADAPTATION

Recognise that Mode B activities can be unpredictable. Plan carefully but remain flexible, adapting as needed to meet the challenges and opportunities.

TAKEAWAY 5: MODE A AND MODE B CURRICULUM

Design a rich curriculum that prioritises Mode A instructional teaching and knowledge-building while weaving in enriching Mode B learning experiences.

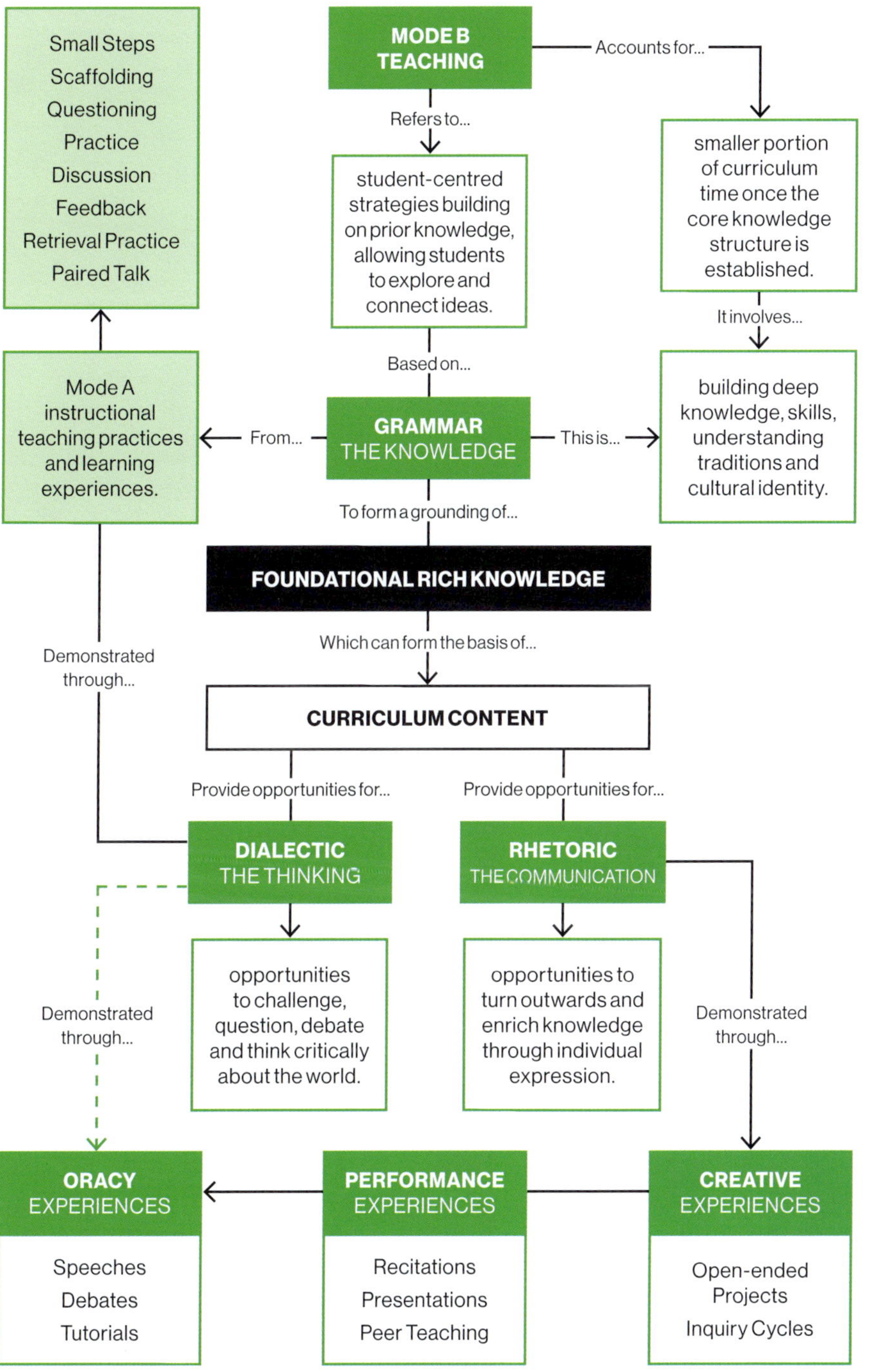

MODE B TEACHING
Accounts for...
smaller portion of curriculum time once the core knowledge structure is established.
It involves...
building deep knowledge, skills, understanding traditions and cultural identity.
Refers to...
student-centred strategies building on prior knowledge, allowing students to explore and connect ideas.
Based on...
GRAMMAR THE KNOWLEDGE
This is...
From...
Mode A instructional teaching practices and learning experiences.
Small Steps
Scaffolding
Questioning
Practice
Discussion
Feedback
Retrieval Practice
Paired Talk
To form a grounding of...
FOUNDATIONAL RICH KNOWLEDGE
Which can form the basis of...
CURRICULUM CONTENT
Provide opportunities for...
Provide opportunities for...
Demonstrated through...
DIALECTIC THE THINKING
opportunities to challenge, question, debate and think critically about the world.
RHETORIC THE COMMUNICATION
opportunities to turn outwards and enrich knowledge through individual expression.
Demonstrated through...
Demonstrated through...
ORACY EXPERIENCES
Speeches
Debates
Tutorials
PERFORMANCE EXPERIENCES
Recitations
Presentations
Peer Teaching
CREATIVE EXPERIENCES
Open-ended Projects
Inquiry Cycles

SCHOOL CULTURE

A series of strategic principles and practical strategies to help establish the conditions for growth

MODE A TEACHING

A focused collection of evidence-based principles and practices designed to enhance classroom instruction

MODE B TEACHING

A set of practices that foster agency, collaboration and open-ended exploration to deepen and extend knowledge

READ MORE

Studies, books and blogs that are referenced throughout the one-pagers and inspired the collections

READ MORE

Agarwal, P. K., Nunes, L. D. and Blunt, J. R. (2021). 'Retrieval practice consistently benefits student learning: A systematic review of applied research in schools and classrooms', *Educational Psychology Review*, 33(4), 1409–1453.

Alexander, R. (2012). 'Improving Oracy and Classroom Talk in English Schools: Achievements and Challenges', *Primary First*, 10, 22–29.

Allen, B. (2017). 'Making Teaching a Job Worth Doing (again)'. https://rebeccaallen.co.uk/wp-content/uploads/2010/07/2017-11-becky-allen-on-workload.pdf.

Allen, K. A., Kern, M. L., Rozek, C. S., McInerney, D. M. and Slavich, G. M. (2021). 'Belonging: A review of conceptual issues, an integrative framework, and directions for future research', *Australian Journal of Psychology*, 73(1), 87–102.

Allison, S. and Tharby, A. (2015). *Making Every Lesson Count: Six Principles to Support Great Teaching and Learning*. Crown House Publishing Limited.

Annes, C. K., Taylor, J. A. and Hallock, R. M. (2023). 'The Effect of Workspace Tidiness on Schoolwork Performance of High School Students', *Journal of Emerging Investigators*, 6.

Archer, A. L. and Hughes, C. A. (2011). *Explicit Instruction: Effective and efficient teaching*. Guildford Press.

Ashbee, R. (2024). *School Staff Culture: Knowledge Building, Reflection and Action*. David Fulton.

Ashman, G. (2016). 'Example-problem pairs', Filling the Pail [blog] 9 February. www.gregashman.wordpress.com/2016/02/09/example-problem-pairs/.

Atkins, R. (2023). *The Art of Explanation: How to Communicate with Clarity and Confidence*. Wilfire.

Australian Education Research Organisation (AERO). (2023a). Acknowledgement and praise: Practice resource for primary and secondary schools. Australian Education Research Organisation.

Australian Education Research Organisation. (2023b). How students learn best. www.edresearch.edu.au/research/research-reports/how-students-learn-best-overview-evidence.

Ausubel, D. P. (1968). *Educational Psychology: A Cognitive View*. Holt, Rinehart & Winston.

Bangerter, M. and Trebilco, J. (2020). Three ingredients for better learning outcomes. Monash University Learning and Teaching [blog] 15 January. www.monash.edu/learning-teaching/news/blog/ingredients-for-better-learning-outcomes.

Bass, S. and Walker, K. (2015). *Early Childhood Play Matters*. ACER Press.

Bempechat, J. (2019). 'The Case for (Quality) Homework: Why It Improves Learning, and How Parents Can Help', *Education Next*, Winter.

Bennett, T. (2017). *Creating a culture: How school leaders can optimise behaviour. Independent review of behaviour in schools*. Department for Education.

Berger, R. (2003). *An Ethic Excellence Grade 3-8: Building A Culture of Craftsmanship With Students*. Pearson.

Berninger, V. W., Abbott, R. D., Abbott, S. P., Graham S. and Richards, T. (2002). 'Writing and Reading: Connections Between Language by Hand and Language by Eye', *Journal of Learning Disabilities*, 35(1), 39–56.

Bjork, R. (gocognitive) (2014). The Theory of Disuse and the Role of Forgetting in Human Memory. YouTube, 8 October. https://youtu.be/Hv6Vye1JCjo?si=Elr4deWCbhYuilgo.

Bjork, E. and Bjork, R. (2011). 'Making things hard on yourself, but in a good way: Creating desirable difficulties to enhance learning', *Psychology and the Real World: Essays illustrating fundamental contributions to society*, 56–64.

Black, P., Harrison, C., Lee, C., Marshall, B. and Wiliam, D. (2004). 'Working Inside the Black Box: Assessment for Learning in the Classroom', *Phi Delta Kappan*, 86(1), 14.

Black, P. and Wiliam, D. (1998). 'Assessment and classroom learning', *Assessment in Education: Principles, Policy & Practice*, 5(1), 7–74.

Boxer, A. (2024). Retrieving Better Guide: A Guide to Retrieval Practice. https://www.carousel-learning.com/teaching-and-learning/resources

Brown, P. C., Roediger, H. L. and McDaniel, M. A. (2014). *Make It Stick: The science of successful learning*. Harvard University Press.

Busch, B. (2024). 'The psychology behind a great seating plan', InnerDrive Blog [blog] 19 August. www.innerdrive.co.uk/blog/psychology-of-seating-plans/

Busch, B. and Watson, E. (2023). *Teaching & Learning Illuminated: The Big Ideas, Illustrated*. Routledge.

Castelino, J. (2024). *The Homework Conundrum*. David Fulton.

Castro-Alonso, J. C., Ayres, P., Zhang, S. and de Koning, B. (2024). 'Research Avenues Supporting Embodied Cognition in Learning and Instruction', *Educational Psychology Review*, 36(1).

Centre for Education Statistics and Evaluation (CESE). (2020). Supporting high academic expectations: Every student is known, valued and cared for in our schools. NSW Department of Education.

Cepeda, N. J., Vul, E., Rohrer, D., Wixted, J. T. and Pashler, H. (2008). 'Spacing Effects in Learning: A Temporal Ridgeline of Optimal Retention', *Psychological Science*, 19(11), 1095–1102.

Chi, M. T. H., Feltovich, P. J. and Glaser, R. (1981). 'Categorization and representation of physics problems by experts and novices', *Cognitive Science*, 5(2), 121–152.

Chiles, M. (2023). *Powerful Questioning Strategies for Improving Learning and Retention in the Classroom*. Crown House Publishing.

Chiles, M. (@m_chiles). (2024). 'The first step is to establish what are the core principles to assessment. We define each principle...', 6 October [Tweet/X], https://x.com/mchiles/status/1842835636421525677.

Christodoulou, D. (2014). *Seven Myths about Education*. Routledge.

Clark, R. E. (1983). 'Reconsidering research on learning from media', *Review of Educational Research*, 53(4), 445–459.

Clark, R. E. and Feldon, D. F. (2005). Five Common but Questionable Principles of Multimedia Learning. In R. Mayer (ed), *The Cambridge Handbook of Multimedia Learning* (pp. 97-115). Cambridge University Press.

Clear, J. (The Paula Faris Show). (2023). 'How to build atomic habits in our kids with James Clear', 5 September [YouTube], https://www.youtube.com/watch?v=I3CbGffoRBw.

Coe, R., Aloisi, C., Higgins, S. and Major, L. E. (2014). *What Makes Great Teaching? Review of the Underpinning Research.* Sutton Trust.

Corno, L. (2008). 'On Teaching Adaptively', *Educational Psychologist*, 43(3), 161–173.

Cottingham, S. (2022a). 'No more teaching tips and tricks', Evidence for Teachers [blog] 5 February. www.overpractised.wordpress.com/2022/02/05/no-more-teaching-tips-and-tricks.

Cottingham, S. (2022b, May 22). Schemas and learning discussion. [Interview by C. Barton]. Tips for Teachers podcast.

Crome, S. (2023). *The Power of Teams: How to create and lead thriving school teams.* John Catt Educational.

Devid, V. (2024). 'What is Formative Assessment? Or as we call it, Formative Action...', [LinkedIn], https://www.linkedin.com/posts/valentina-devid-99192529_education-formativeassessment-teaching-activity-7272607859312414722-YBW1/.

Didau, D. (2014). Listen Up: Improving the Quality of Classroom Discussion, The Learning Spy [blog] 12 March. www.learningspy.co.uk/learning/listen-improving-quality-classroom-discussion/.

Didau, D. (2018). 'How to explain... structured discussion', The Learning Spy [blog] 9 November. www.learningspy.co.uk/literacy/how-to-explain-structured-discussion/.

Dowley, M. and Lovell, O. (2024). *The Classroom Management Handbook: A Practical Blueprint for Engagement and Behaviour in Your Classroom and Beyond.* John Catt Educational.

Drok, H. and van de Graaf, F. (2024). 'Five core principles for formative action', The Formative Action School [online] 11 January. www.formative-action.com/five-core-principles-for-formative-action.

Dunlosky, J. (2013). 'Strengthening the Student Toolbox: Study strategies to boost learning', *American Educator*, Fall.

Dweck, C. (2007). *Mindset: The New Psychology of Success.* Random House.

Eastwood, O. (2021). *Belonging: The Ancient Code of Togetherness.* Quercus.

Education Endowment Foundation. (2018). Metacognition and self-regulated learning. https://educationendowmentfoundation.org.uk/education-evidence/guidance-reports/metacognition.

Education Endowment Foundation. (2019). Putting Evidence to Work: A School's Guide to Implementation. https://educationendowmentfoundation.org.uk/education-evidence/guidance-reports/implementation.

Education Endowment Foundation. (2020). Special Educational Needs in Mainstream Schools: Guidance Report. https://.educationendowmentfoundation.org.uk/tools/guidance-reports/special-educational-needs-disabilities.

Education Endowment Foundation. (2021a). Effective Professional Development: Guidance Report. https://educationendowmentfoundation.org.uk/education-evidence/guidance-reports/effective-professional-development.

Education Endowment Foundation. (2021b). Mastery Learning. https://educationendowmentfoundation.org.uk/education-evidence/ teaching-learning-toolkit/mastery-learning.

Education Endowment Foundation. (2021c). Teacher feedback to improve pupil learning. https://educationendowmentfoundation.org.uk/education-evidence/guidance-reports/feedback.

Education Endowment Foundation. (2021d). Metacognition and Self-Regulated Learning. Guidance report. https://educationendowmentfoundation.org.uk/education-evidence/guidance-reports/metacognition.

Education Endowment Foundation. (2021e). Homework. https://educationendowment foundation.org.uk/education-evidence/teaching-learning-toolkit/homework.

Education Endowment Foundation (2023). Supporting self-knowledge through modelling. https://educationendowmentfoundation.org.uk/news/supporting-self-knowledge-through-modelling.

Engelmann, K. (2024). *Direct Instruction: A Practitioner's Handbook*. John Catt Educational.

Facer, J. (2024). *The ResearchED Guide to Professional Development*. John Catt Educational.

Feldon, D. F. (2007). 'Cognitive load and classroom teaching: The double-edged sword of automaticity', *Educational Psychologist*, 42(3), 123–137.

Fiorella, L. and Mayer, R. E. (2013). 'The relative benefits of learning by teaching and teaching expectancy', *Contemporary Educational Psychology*, 38(4), 281–288.

Fiorella, L. and Mayer, R. E. (2015). *Learning as a Generative Activity: Eight Learning Strategies that Promote Understanding*. Cambridge University Press.

Fisher, D. and Frey, N. (2013). *Gradual release of responsibility instructional framework*. International Reading Association.

Fletcher-Wood, H. (2014). 'How can I make classroom discussion flow? Clicks & seat signals to keep Abdullahi focused', Improving Teaching [blog] 14 September. www.improvingteaching.co.uk/2014/09/14/how-can-i-ensure-classroom-discussions-flow-clicks-seat-signals-keeping-abdullahi-focused/.

Francis, B. (2020). Foreword. In: Education Endowment Foundation [EEF]. Special educational needs in mainstream schools: Guidance report. https://educationendowmentfoundation.org.uk/education-evidence/guidance-reports/send.

Frauenhofer, S.-M. (TED at Work.) (2023). Unlocking your learners' potential: How to embrace both learning and performing at work, Ted@Work [online] 6 June. https://tedatwork.ted. com/blog/embrace-learning-and-performing-at-work/.

Freire, P. (1996). *Pedagogy of the Oppressed*. Penguin.

Frey, N. and Fisher, D. (2010). 'Identifying Instructional Moves During Guided Learning', *The Reading Teacher*, 64(2), 84–95.

Fülöp, M. (2000). 'The effects of competition on achievement motivation in students, *Educational Studies'*, 26(2), 115–124.

Fülöp, M. (2024). 'Competiton as a Culturally Constructed Concept'. In C. Baillie, E. Dunn, & Y. Zheng (eds), *Travelling Facts. The Social Construction, Distribution, and Accumulation of Knowledge* (pp. 124-148). Campus Verlag.

Gardner, M. (2019). Teaching Students to Give Peer Feedback. www.edutopia.org/article/teaching-students-give-peer-feedback.

Gardner, B., Lally, P. and Wardle, J. (2012). 'Making health habitual: The psychology of 'habit-formation' and general practice', *British Journal of General Practice*, 62, 664–666.

Gielen, S., Peeters, E., Dochy, F., Onghena, P. and Struyven, K. (2010). 'Improving the effectiveness of peer feedback for learning', *Learning and Instruction*, 20(4), 304-315.

Gill, A. S. (2024). [Interview with Jamie Clark]. The Saturday Show Live with Jamie Clark.

Teachers Talk Radio. YouTube, 10 August. https://www.youtube.com/watch?v=r6VeXvB_LoI.

Gill, B., Shoji, M., Coen, T. and Place, K. (2016). The content, predictive power, and potential bias in five widely used teacher observation instruments. U.S. Department of Education, Institute of Education Sciences, National Center for Education Evaluation and Regional Assistance. https://files.eric.ed.gov/fulltext/ED569941.pdf.

Godwin, K. E. and Fisher, A. V. (2022). 'Effect of Repeated Exposure to the Visual Environment on Young Children's Attention', *Cognitive Science*, 46.

Goldin-Meadow, S. (2023). *Thinking with Your Hands: The Surprising Science Behind How Gestures Shape Our Thoughts*. Basic Books.

Goodrich, J. (2024). *Responsive Coaching*. John Catt Educational.

Goodrich, J. and Howard, K. (2024). Responsive Coaching Interview with Josh Goodrich and Kat Howard (Part 1). Steplab [online] 11 June. https://steplab. co/resources/responsive-coaching-interview-with-josh-goodrich-and-kat-howard-part-1/66d9c8820982810001156be2.

Goodwin, D. (2021). 'Delete, substitute and keep: A practical guide for teaching summarising and note-taking', Goodwin23 [blog] 3 February. www.mrgoodwin23.wordpress.com/2021/02/03/delete-substitute-and-keep-a-practical-guide-for-teaching-summarising-and-note-taking/.

Groshell, Z. (2024, October). Effective explanations in teaching [Webinar transcript]. InnerDrive Teacher CPD Academy.

Hammond, J. and Gibbons, P. (2005). 'Putting scaffolding to work: The contribution of scaffolding in articulating ESL education', *Prospect*, 20(1),6–25.

Harvard, B. (2024). The Simple Classroom, The Effortful Educator [blog] 2 October. www.theeffortfuleducator.com/2024/10/02/the-simple-classroom/.

Hattie, J. (2003, October). Teachers make a difference: What is the research evidence? Paper presented at the Building Teacher Quality: What does the research tell us ACER Research Conference, Melbourne, Australia.

Hattie, J. (2012). *Visible Learning for Teachers: Maximizing Impact on Learning*. Routledge.

Hattie, J. and Timperley, H. (2007). 'The Power of Feedback', *Review of Educational Research*, 77(1), 81–112.

Hendrick, C. (2017). 'Four Quarters Marking – a workload solution?', Kesgrave High School [blog] 4 September. https://khsbpp.wordpress.com/2017/09/04/four-quarters-marking-a-workload-solution/

Hendrick, C. and Macpherson, R. (2017). *What Does This Look Like in the Classroom? Bridging the Gap Between Research and Practice*. John Catt Educational.

Heward, W. L. and Wood, C.L. (2015, April). Improving educational outcomes in America: Can a low-tech generic teaching practice make a difference? Wing Institute.

Hirsch, E. D. (2000). 'You can always look it up ... Or can you?', *American Educator*, Spring 2000.

Hollingsworth, J. R. and Ybarra, S. E. (2017). *Explicit Direct Instruction: The Power Of The Well-Crafted, Well-Taught Lesson*. Corwin.

Hughes, H. (2024, 27 December). 'Been reading and writing a lot about belonging for staff in schools and today I have revisited this great paper Allen et al. (2021)...', [online] LinkedIn. https://www.linkedin.com/posts/dr-haili-hughes-178479186 been-reading-and-writing-a-lot-about-belonging-activity-7272262501239508992-X-TI.

Huntington Research School. (2023). 'Adaptive Teaching: What the Core Content Framework for ITTs can help us understand about the shift from differentiation to adaptive teaching'. https://researchschool.org.uk/huntington/news/adaptive-teaching.

Jones, K. (2024a). 'The lingering learning styles myth', Evidence Based Education [blog] 5 August. https://evidencebased.education/the-lingering-learning-styles-myth/.

Jones, K. (2024b). *Feedback: Strategies to support teacher workload and improve pupil progress*. John Catt Educational.

Karpicke, J. D. and O'Day, G. M. (2024). 'Elements of effective learning', In M. J.Kahana and A. D. Wagner (eds) *The Oxford Handbook of Human Memory, Volume II: Applications*. Oxford University Press.

Katz, I. and Assor, A. (2006). 'When choice motivates and when it does not', *Educational Psychology Review*, 18(4), 429–442.

Kellogg, R. T. (2008). 'Training Writing Skills: A Cognitive Developmental Perspective', *Journal of Writing Research*, 1(1), 1–26.

Kirschner, P. A, (2009). 'Epistemology or Pedagogy, That Is the Question', *Constructivist Instruction: Success or Failure?*, May, 144–157.

Kirschner, P. A., Sweller, J. and Clark, R. E. (2006). 'Why minimal guidance during instruction does not work: An analysis of the failure of constructivist, discovery, problem-based, experiential, and inquiry-based teaching', *Educational Psychologist*, 4(2), 75–86.

Kirschner, P. A. and Neelen, M. (2018). 'No feedback, no learning', 3-star learning experiences [blog] 5 June. https://3starlearningexperiences.wordpress.com/2018/06/05/no-feedback-no-learning/.

Lam, S., Yim, P. and Law, J. (2001). The impact of competition on task performance: A study of competitive motivation in the classroom, Journal of Educational Psychology, 93(3). 490–499.

Lemov, D. (2010). *Teach Like a Champion: 49 Techniques that Put Students on the Path to College*. Jossey-Bass.

Lemov, D. (2021). *Teach Like a Champion 3.0: 63 Techniques that Put Students on the Path to College*. Jossey-Bass.

Lovell, O. (Host). (2020). The Trivium and the Purpose of Education: A Conversation with Martin Robinson. [Audio podcast episode]. In Education Research Reading Room (E Triple R). Available at: https://ollielovell.com/errr-podcast.

Lovell, O., Boguslav, A. and Goodrich, J. (2024). 'Professional Development & Cognitive Load', Steplab [online] 27 September. https://t.co/bnG4wnSaY2.

MacKenzie, T. (2018). *Inquiry Mindset: Nurtuing the Dreams, Wonders, and Curiosities of Our Youngest Learners*. Elevate Books Edu.

MacKenzie, T. (2021). *Inquiry Mindset Assessment Edition: Scaffolding a Partnership for Equity and Agency in Learning*. Elevate Books Edu.

Maldini, A., Usodo, B. and Subanti, S. (2017). Gesture analysis of students majoring in mathematics education in micro teaching process. AIP Conference Proceedings, 1868, 050006.

MacSuga-Gage, A. S. and Simonsen, B. (2015). 'Enhancing teachers' use of opportunities to respond to improve students' behavior and academic outcomes: A systematic review', *Education and Treatment of Children*, 38(2), 211–239.

Marzano, R. J., Pickering, D. J. and Pollock, J. E. (2001). *Classroom Instruction that Works: Research-Based Strategies for Increasing Student Achievement.* ASCD.

Mayer, R. E. (2001). *Multimedia Learning.* Cambridge University Press.

Mayer, R. E. (2002). 'Cognitive theory and the design of multimedia instruction: An example of the two-way street between cognition and instruction', *New Directions for Teaching and Learning*, 89.

Mayer, R. E. (2009). *Multimedia Learning* (2nd ed). Cambridge University Press.

McCormick, C. and Collins, P. (2014). 'Evaluating the effectiveness of Bite Size professional development sessions for engaging busy professionals', *Health Information and Libraries Journal*, 31(1), 66–72.

Mccrea, P. (2020). *Motivated Teaching: Leveraging the science of learning to boost attention and effort in the classroom.* Oneway Ltd.

Mccrea, P. (2023). 'Effective feedback', 28 September [online] Evidence snacks. https://snacks.pepsmccrea.com/p/effective-feedback.

Mccrea, P. (2024a). 'Stakes sweet spot', 14 December [online] Evidence Snacks. https:// snacks.pepsmccrea.com/p/stakes-sweet-spot.

Mccrea, P. (2024b). 'The power of routines', 14 March [online] Evidence Snacks. https://snacks.pepsmccrea.com/p/the-power-of-routines.

Mccrea, P. (2024c). 'Take the shortest path', 12 January [online] Evidence Snacks. https://snacks.pepsmccrea.com/p/take-the-shortest-path.

McGill, M. R. (2024). *The Teacher Toolkit Guide to Feedback: Turning Theory into Practice.* Bloomsbury.

McLaughlin, J. E., Roth, M. T., Glatt, D. M., Gharkholonarehe, N., Davidson, C. A., Griffin, L. M., Esserman, D. A. and Mumper, R. J. (2014). 'The flipped classroom: a course redesign to foster learning and engagement in a health professions school', *Academic Medicine*, 89(2), 236–243.

Mercer, N. (1995). *The Guided Construction of Knowledge: Talk Amongst Teachers and Learners.* Multilingual Matters.

@TeacherToolkit. (2022). Taking Live Marking Two Steps Forward, @TeacherToolkit[online] 1 November 1, https://www.teachertoolkit. co.uk/2022/11/01/taking-live-marking-two-steps-forward/.

Millard, W. and Menzies, L. (2016). Oracy – The State of Speaking in Our Schools. The Centre for Education and Youth. Voice 21.

Minero, E. (2016). 'Talking in Class', edutopia [online] 15 September.

Murdoch, K. (2024). 'Following a train of thought: A conversation (diablog) with Sean Walker about play, inquiry, and learning', Kate Murdoch [blog] 7 February. https://www.kathmurdoch.com.au/blog/2024/2/7/following-a-train-of-thoughtnbspanbsp-conversation-diablog-with-sean-walker-about-play-inquiry-and-learning.

Needham, T. (2020). 'Strategies to Increase Pace', tomneedhamteach [online] 8 September. www.tomneedhamteach.wordpress.com/2020/09/08/pace/.

Nestojko, J. F., Bui, D. C., Kornell, N. and Bjork, E. L. (2014). 'Expecting to teach enhances learning and organization of knowledge in free recall of text passages', *Memory & Cognition*, 42, 1038–1048.

Novack, M. and Goldin-Meadow, S. (2015). 'Learning from Gesture: How Our Hands Change Our Minds', *Educational Psychology Review*, 27(3), 405–412.

Nuthall, G. (2007). *The Hidden Lives of Learners*. NZCER Press.

OECD (2013). PISA 2012 Results: Ready to Learn (Volume III): Students' Engagement, Drive and Self-Beliefs. OECD Publishing.

Ooi, L. and Cortina, K. S. (2023). 'The interaction of competition and cooperation in educational settings', *Frontiers in Education*, 8.

Oracy Education Commission. (2024). We need to talk: The report of the Commission on the Future of Oracy Education in England. https://oracyeducationcommission.co.uk/oec-report/.

Pauk, W. (1974). *How to Study in College*. Houghton Mifflin.

Pearce, J. and Moore, I. (2024). *Bjork and Bjork's Desirable Difficulties in Action*. John Catt Educational.

Pearson, P. D. and Gallagher, M. C. (1983). 'The gradual release of responsibility model of instruction', *Contemporary Educational Psychology*, 8(3), 317–344.

Pink, D. H. (2009). *Drive: The Surprising Truth About What Motivates Us*. Riverhead Books.

Posselt, J. R. and Lipson, S. K. (2016). 'Competition and its toll on underrepresented students: Implications for belonging and mental health', *Educational Researcher*, 45(6), 360–372.

Quigley, A. (2023). 'Adaptive teaching: how to use 'microadaptations'', TES magazine [online] 30 December. https://www.tes.com/magazine/teaching-learning/general/adaptive-teaching-how-use-microadaptations.

Raichura, P. (2023, December 30). 'Turn and talk', Bunsen Blue [online] 30 December. https://bunsenblue.wordpress.com/2023/12/30/turn-and-talk/.

Robinson, M. (2013). *Trivium 21c: Preparing Young People for the Future with Lessons from the Past*. Independent Thinking Press.

Rogers, B. (2024). 'How teachers should lead for good behaviour', Tes Magazine [online] 3 January. https://www.tes.com/magazine/teaching-learning/ general/bill-rogers-teacher-good-behaviour-schools.

Rosenshine, B. (2012). 'Principles of Instruction: Research-based strategies that all teachers should know', *American Educator*, 36(1), 12–39.

Rosenshine, B., Meister, C. and Chapman, S. (1996). 'Teaching Students to Generate Questions: A Review of the Intervention Studies', *Review of Educational Research*, 66(2), 181–221.

Ross, J. A. (2006). 'The Reliability, Validity, and Utility of Self- Assessment', *Practical Assessment, Research & Evaluation*, 11(10).

Rowe, M. B. (1974). 'Wait-time and rewards as instructional variables, their influence on language, logic, and fate control: Part one—wait-time', *Journal of Research in Science Teaching*, 11(2), 81–94.

Rowe, M. B. (1986). 'Wait Time: Slowing Down May Be a Way of Speeding Up!', *Journal of Teacher Education*, 37(1), 43–50.

Ruiz Martin, H. (2024). *How Do We Learn? A Scientific Approach to Learning and Teaching (Evidence-Based Education)*. Jossey-Bass.

Ryan, R. M. and Deci, E. L. (2000). 'Self-determination theory and the facilitation of intrinsic motivation, social development, and well-being', *American Psychologist*, 55(1), 68–78.

Ryrie Jones, B. (Knowledge for Teachers podcast). (2024, 1 June). Bron Ryrie Jones on Responsive Teaching and Instruction Playbooks. https://podcasts.apple.com/au/podcast/knowledge-for-teachers/ id1668548426?i=1000657494381.

Sealy, C. (2019). *The ResearchEd Guide to Education Myths: An Evidence- Informed Guide for Teachers*. John Catt Educational Ltd.

Sharma, L. (2023). *Building Culture: A Handbook to Harnessing Human Nature to Create Strong School Teams*. John Catt Educational.

Sherrington, T. (2017). *The Learning Rainforest*. John Catt Educational.

Sherrington, T. (2018a). 'Mode A, Mode B: Effective teaching and a rich, enacted curriculum', Teacherhead [online] 22 April. https://teacherhead. com/2018/04/22/mode-a-mode-b-effective-teaching-and-a-rich-enacted-curriculum/.

Sherrington, T. (2018b). 'The Learning Rainforest: A Model for Great Teaching and Learning', Teacherhead [online] 18 March. https://teacherhead. com/2018/03/18/the-learning-rainforest-a-model-for-great-teaching-and-learning/.

Sherrington, T. (2019). *The ResearchEd Guide to Education Myths: An Evidence-Informed Guide for Teachers*. John Catt Educational.

Sherrington, T. [Seneca CPD]. (2020). 'Mode A and Mode B Teaching: A Key Concept in the Learning Forest'. [YouTube] 4 June. https://www. youtube.com/watch?v=ZU4W6mOpA1U.

Sherrington, T. (2021a). 'What is the purpose of assessment in education?', Teacherhead [online] 12 July. https://teacherhead.com/2021/07/12/what-is-the-purpose-of-assessment-in-education/.

Sherrington, T. (2021b). 'Cold call variations', Teacherhead [online] 29 August. https://teacherhead.com/2021/08/29/cold-call-variations/.

Sherrington, T. (2022). 'Five ways to secure progress through modelling', Teacherhead [online] 15 June. https://teacherhead.com/2022/06/15/five-ways-to-secure-progress-through-modelling/.

Shimamura, A. (2018). *MARGE:A Whole-Brain Learning Approach for Students and Teachers*. CreateSpace Independent Publishing.

Simonsen, B., Fairbanks, S., Briesch, A., Myers, D. and Sugai, G. (2008). 'Evidence-based practices in classroom management: Considerations for research to practice', *Education & Treatment of Children*, 31(3), 351–380.

Sinek, S. (2009). *Start with Why: How Great Leaders Inspire Everyone to Take Action*. Portfolio.

Stahl, R. J. (1994). 'Using "Think-Time" and "Wait-Time" Skillfully in the Classroom'. ERIC Digest, ERIC Clearinghouse for Social Studies/Social Science Education.

Steplab. (2022). 'A Beginner's Guide to Instructional Coaching (Version 1.1)', Steplab [online] 1 September. https://steplab.co/beginners-guide.

Surma, T., Vanhees, C., Wils, M., Nijlunsing, J., Crato, N., Hattie, J., Muijs, D., Rata, E., Wiliam, D. and Kirschner, P. A. (2025). *Developing curriculum for deep thinking: The knowledge revival*. SpringerBriefs in Education.

Swain, N. (2024). *Harnessing the Science of Learning: Success Stories to Help Kickstart Your School Improvement*. Routledge.

Sweller, J. (1988). 'Cognitive load during problem solving: Effects on learning', *Cognitive Science*, 12(2), 257–285.

Sweller, J. (1994). 'Cognitive load theory, learning difficulty, and instructional design', *Learning and Instruction*, 4(4), 295–312.

Tait, J. (2023). 'Wait a second? Let's think about giving students time to think', SecEd [online] 15 May. https://www.sec-ed.co.uk/content/best-practice/wait-a-second-let-s-think-about-giving-students-time-to-think.

TES Magazine. (2017). 'Bill Rogers on Behaviour'. [Youtube] 27 January. https://www.youtube.com/watch?v=KTxGXiuLgb4.

Tips for Teachers (2022). 'Tip #3: To reduce choppy time in lessons, use a front loaded means of participation & wait for golden silence'. [YouTube] 10 March. https://youtu.be/hpEynzRJmos.

Tse, D., Langston, R. F., Kakeyama, M., Bethus, I., Spooner, P. A., Wood, E. R., Witter, M. P. and Morris, R. G. M. (2007). 'Schemas and memory consolidation', *Science*, 316(5821), 76–82.

Twyman, J. S. and Heward, W. L. (2018). 'How to improve student learning in every classroom now', *International Journal of Educational Research*, 87, 78–90.

Urhahne, D. and Wijnia, L. (2023). 'Theories of motivation in education: An integrative framework', *Educational Psychology Review*, 35(2), article 45.

Voice 21. (2022). 'Discussion Guidelines: School 21', Voice21 [online] August. https://voice21.org/wp-content/uploads/2022/08/Voice21-ClassroomPracticeToolkit-DiscussionGuidelines.pdf.

Weinstein, Y., Sumeracki, M. and Kuepper-Tetzel, C. (n.d.). Effective Learning Strategies. The Learning Scientists. https://www.learningscientists.org/blog/2017/4/20-1.

Wigfield, A. and Eccles, J. S. (1992). 'The development of achievement task values: A theoretical analysis', *Developmental Review*, 12(3), 265–310.

Wiliam, D (2011). *Embedded Formative Assessment*. Bloomington: Solution Tree Press.

Wiliam, D. (SSAT). (2012). 'SSAT Conference Keynote 2012'. [YouTube] 5 December. https://www.youtube.com/watch?v=r1LL9NX1hUw.

Wiliam, D. (Education Scotland). (2018a). 'Self and Peer Assessment'. [YouTube] 27 July. https://www.youtube.com/watch?v=YtP4X5VIs9Y.

Wiliam, D. [@dylanwiliam]. (2018b). https://x.com/dylanwiliam/status/977265017279033344.

Wiliam, D. [@dylanwiliam]. (2024, November 6). Feedback is only formative if it changes the learner's performance. [Tweet/X]. https://x.com/dylanwiliam/status/1857576345355825464.

Wiliam, D., Fisher, D. and Frey, N. (2024). *Student Assessment: Better Evidence, Better Decisions, Better Learning*. Corwin.

Willingham, D. T. (2006). 'How Knowledge Helps', *American Educator*, Spring. https://www.aft.org/ae/spring2006/willingham.

Willingham, D. T. (2009). *Why don't students like school? A cognitive scientist answers questions about how the mind works and what it means for the classroom*. Jossey-Bass.

Willingham, D. T. (2021). *Why don't students like school?: A cognitive scientist answers questions about how the mind works and what it means for the classroom* (2nd ed). Jossey-Bass.

Kirschner, P. A. and Hendrick, C. (2020). *How learning happens: Seminal works in educational psychology and what they mean in practice*. Routledge.